LEGENDARY STAR-LORD

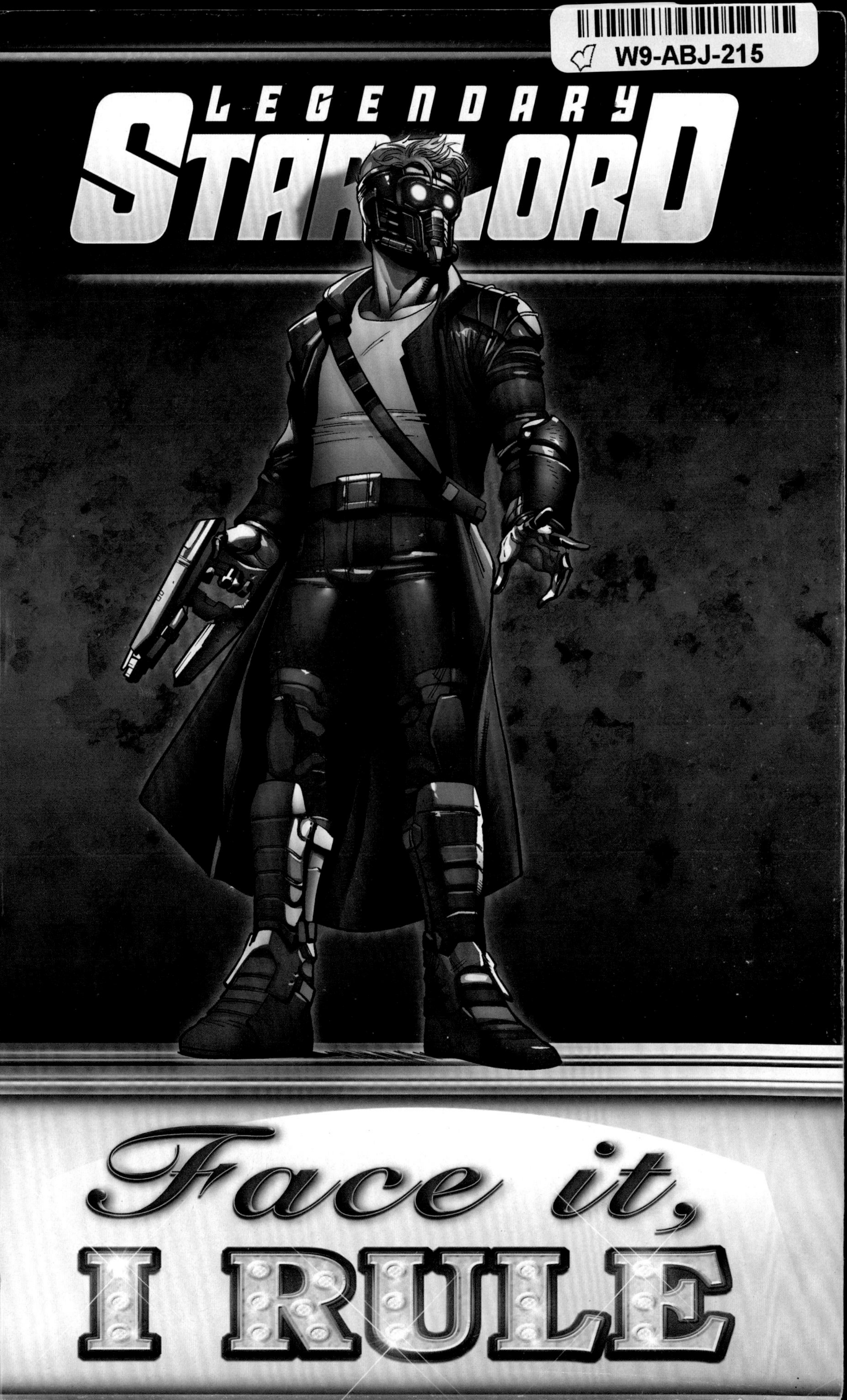

Face it, I RULE

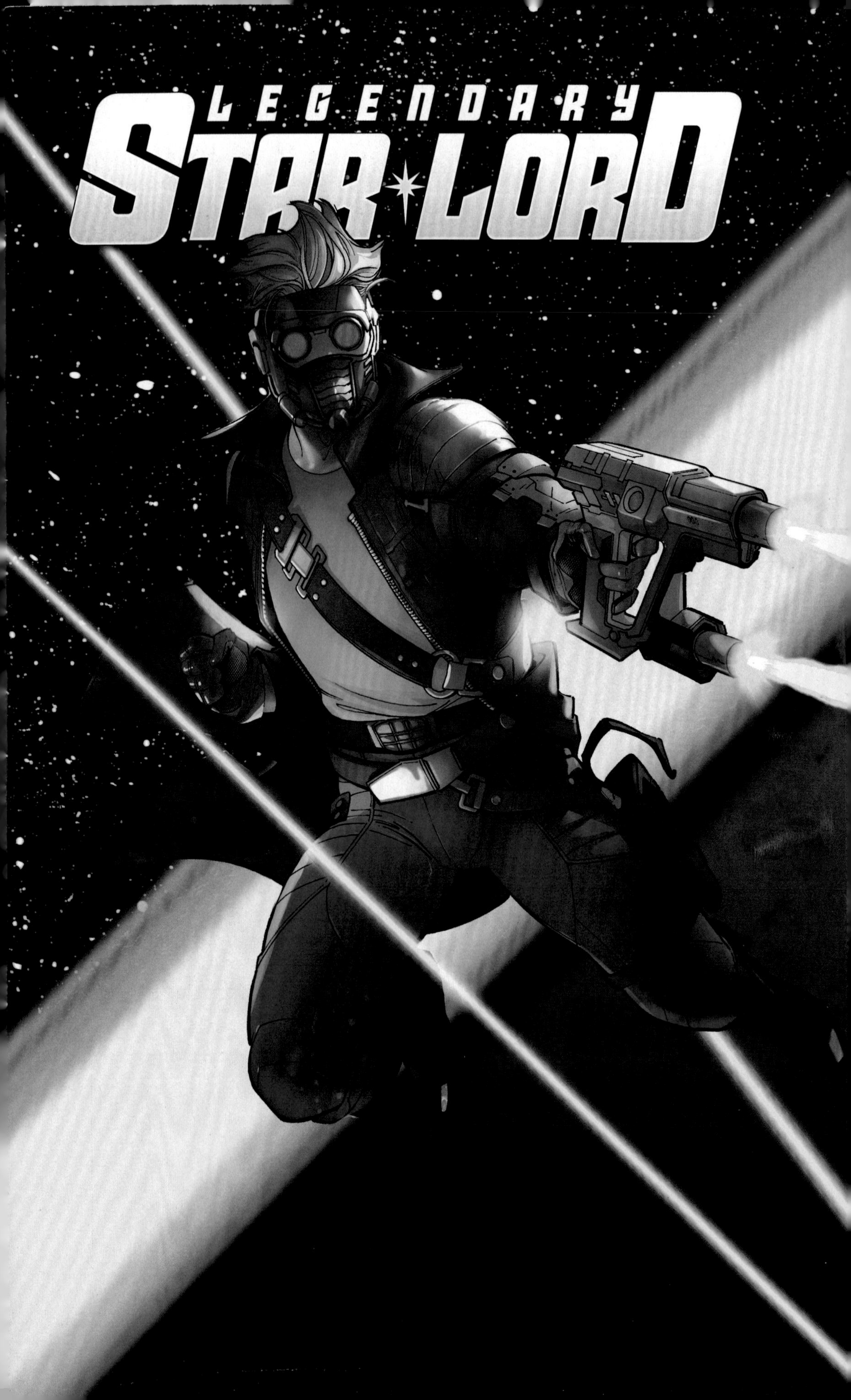
LEGENDARY
STAR-LORD

FACE IT, I RULE

WRITER: **SAM HUMPHRIES**
PENCILER: **PACO MEDINA** WITH
FREDDIE WILLIAMS II (#4)
INKER: **JUAN VLASCO** WITH
FREDDIE WILLIAMS II (#4)
COLORIST: **DAVID CURIEL**
LETTERER: **VC'S JOE CARAMAGNA**

COVER ART: **STEVE MCNIVEN** & **JUSTIN PONSOR** (#1)
AND **PACO MEDINA** (#2-5)
ASSISTANT EDITORS: **XANDER JAROWEY** &
FRANKIE JOHNSON
EDITOR: **MIKE MARTS**

COLLECTION EDITOR: **ALEX STARBUCK**
ASSISTANT EDITOR: **SARAH BRUNSTAD**
EDITORS, SPECIAL PROJECTS: **JENNIFER GRÜNWALD** & **MARK D. BEAZLEY**
SENIOR EDITOR, SPECIAL PROJECTS: **JEFF YOUNGQUIST**
SVP PRINT, SALES & MARKETING: **DAVID GABRIEL**
BOOK DESIGNER: **NELSON RIBEIRO**

EDITOR IN CHIEF: **AXEL ALONSO**
CHIEF CREATIVE OFFICER: **JOE QUESADA**
PUBLISHER: **DAN BUCKLEY**
EXECUTIVE PRODUCER: **ALAN FINE**

LEGENDARY STAR-LORD VOL. 1: FACE IT, I RULE. Contains material originally published in magazine form as LEGENDARY STAR-LORD #1-5. First printing 2015. ISBN# 978-0-7851-9159-9. Published by MARVEL WORLDWIDE, INC., a subsidiary of MARVEL ENTERTAINMENT, LLC. OFFICE OF PUBLICATION: 135 West 50th Street, New York, NY 10020. Copyright © 2015 Marvel Characters, Inc. All rights reserved. All characters featured in this issue and the distinctive names and likenesses thereof, and all related indicia are trademarks of Marvel Characters, Inc. No similarity between any of the names, characters, persons, and/or institutions in this magazine with those of any living or dead person or institution is intended, and any such similarity which may exist is purely coincidental. **Printed in Canada.** ALAN FINE, EVP - Office of the President, Marvel Worldwide, Inc. and EVP & CMO Marvel Characters B.V.; DAN BUCKLEY, Publisher & President - Print, Animation & Digital Divisions; JOE QUESADA, Chief Creative Officer; TOM BREVOORT, SVP of Publishing; DAVID BOGART, SVP of Operations & Procurement, Publishing; C.B. CEBULSKI, SVP of Creator & Content Development; DAVID GABRIEL, SVP Print, Sales & Marketing; JIM O'KEEFE, VP of Operations & Logistics; DAN CARR, Executive Director of Publishing Technology; SUSAN CRESPI, Editorial Operations Manager; ALEX MORALES, Publishing Operations Manager; STAN LEE, Chairman Emeritus. For information regarding advertising in Marvel Comics or on Marvel.com, please contact Niza Disla, Director of Marvel Partnerships, at ndisla@marvel.com. For Marvel subscription inquiries, please call 800-217-9158. **Manufactured between 11/28/2014 and 1/5/2015 by SOLISCO PRINTERS, SCOTT, QC, CANADA.**

10 9 8 7 6 5 4 3 2 1

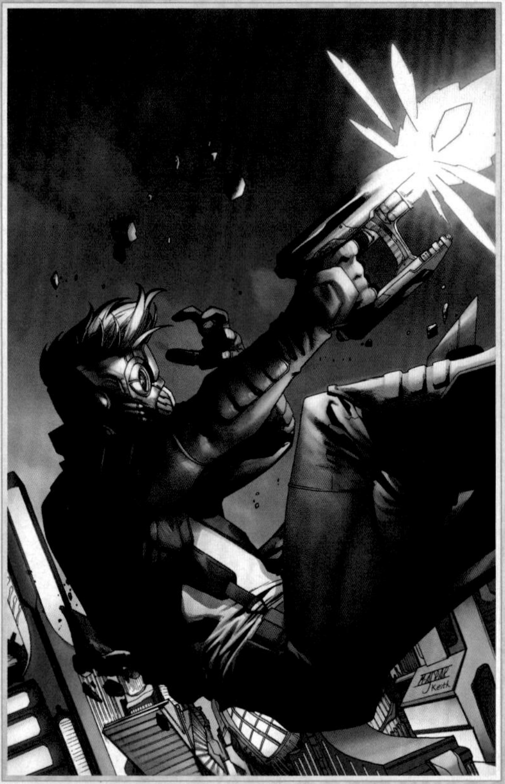

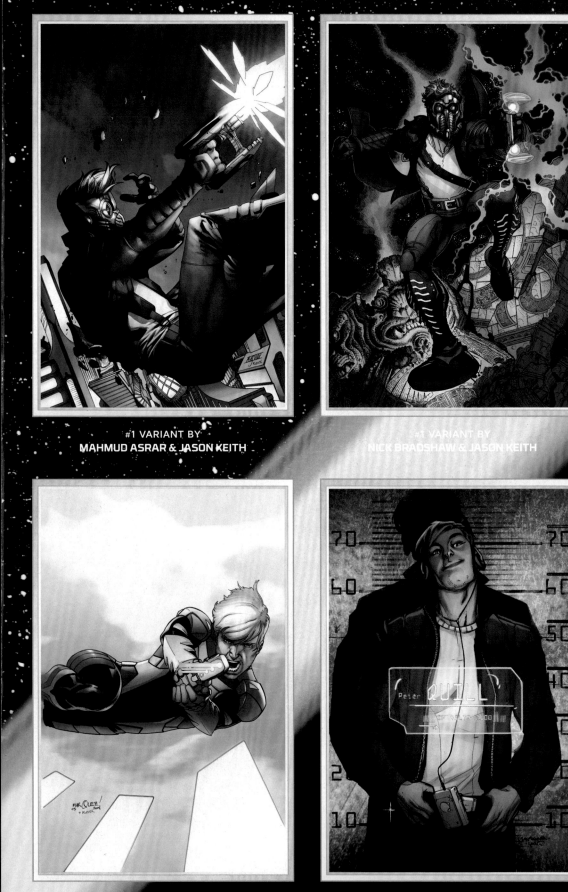

#1 VARIANT BY
MAHMUD ASRAR & JASON KEITH

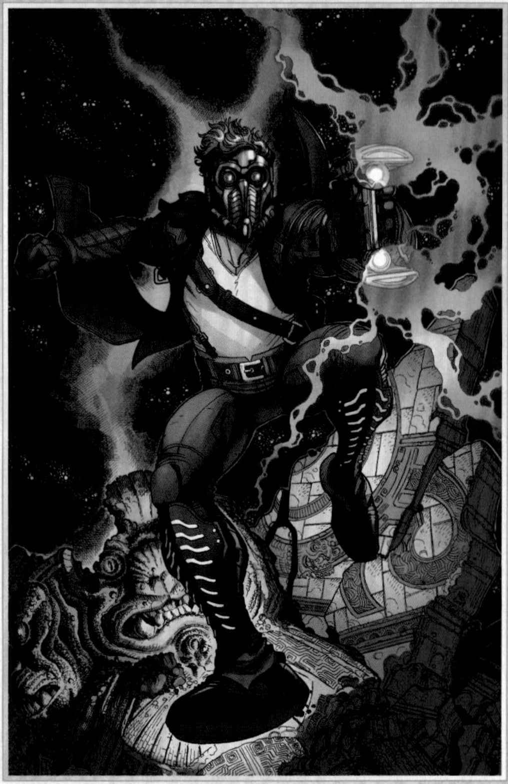

#1 VARIANT BY
NICK BRADSHAW & JASON KEITH

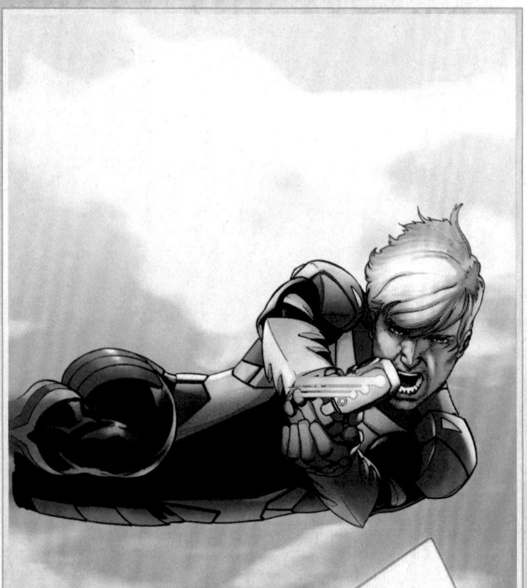

#1 VARIANT BY
DAVID MARQUEZ & JASON KEITH

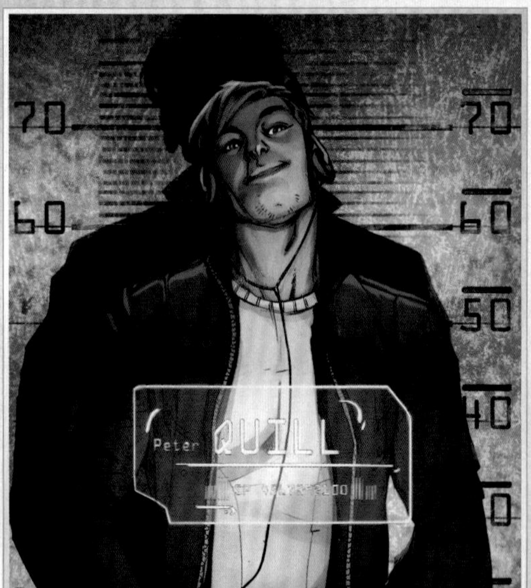
70
60
50
Peter QUILL
10

#1 VARIANT BY
SARA PICHELLI & JASON KEITH

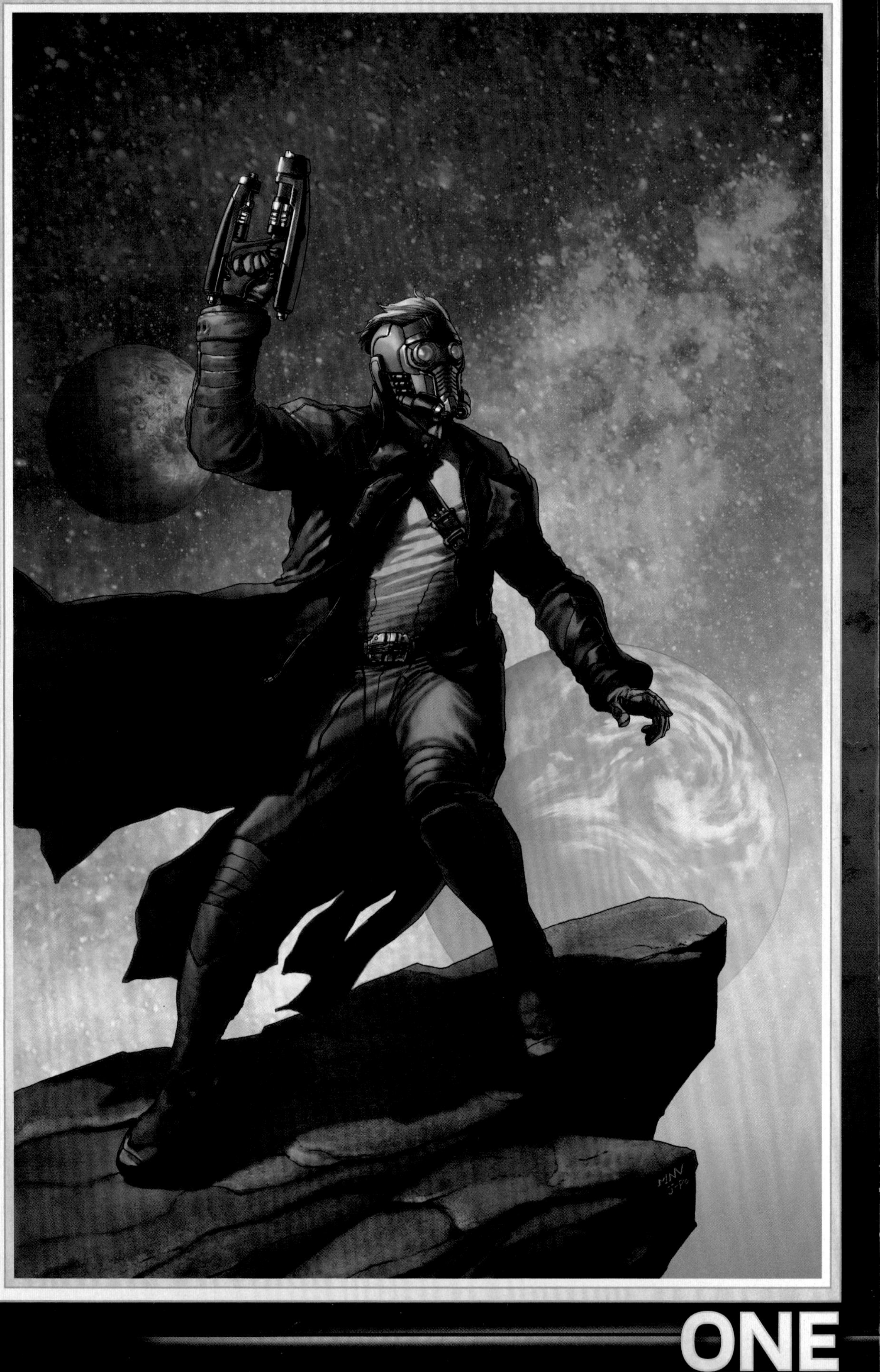

ONE

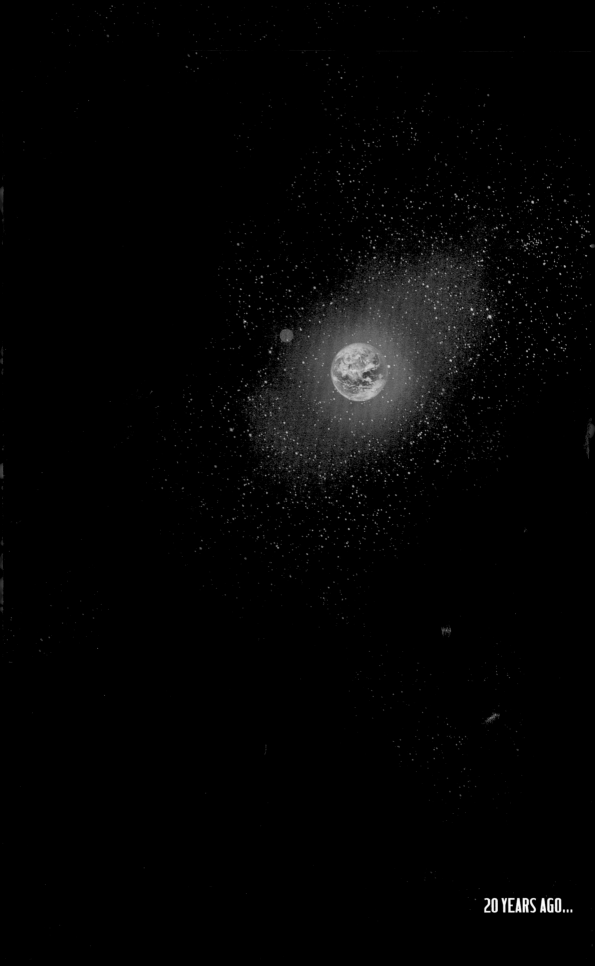

20 YEARS AGO...

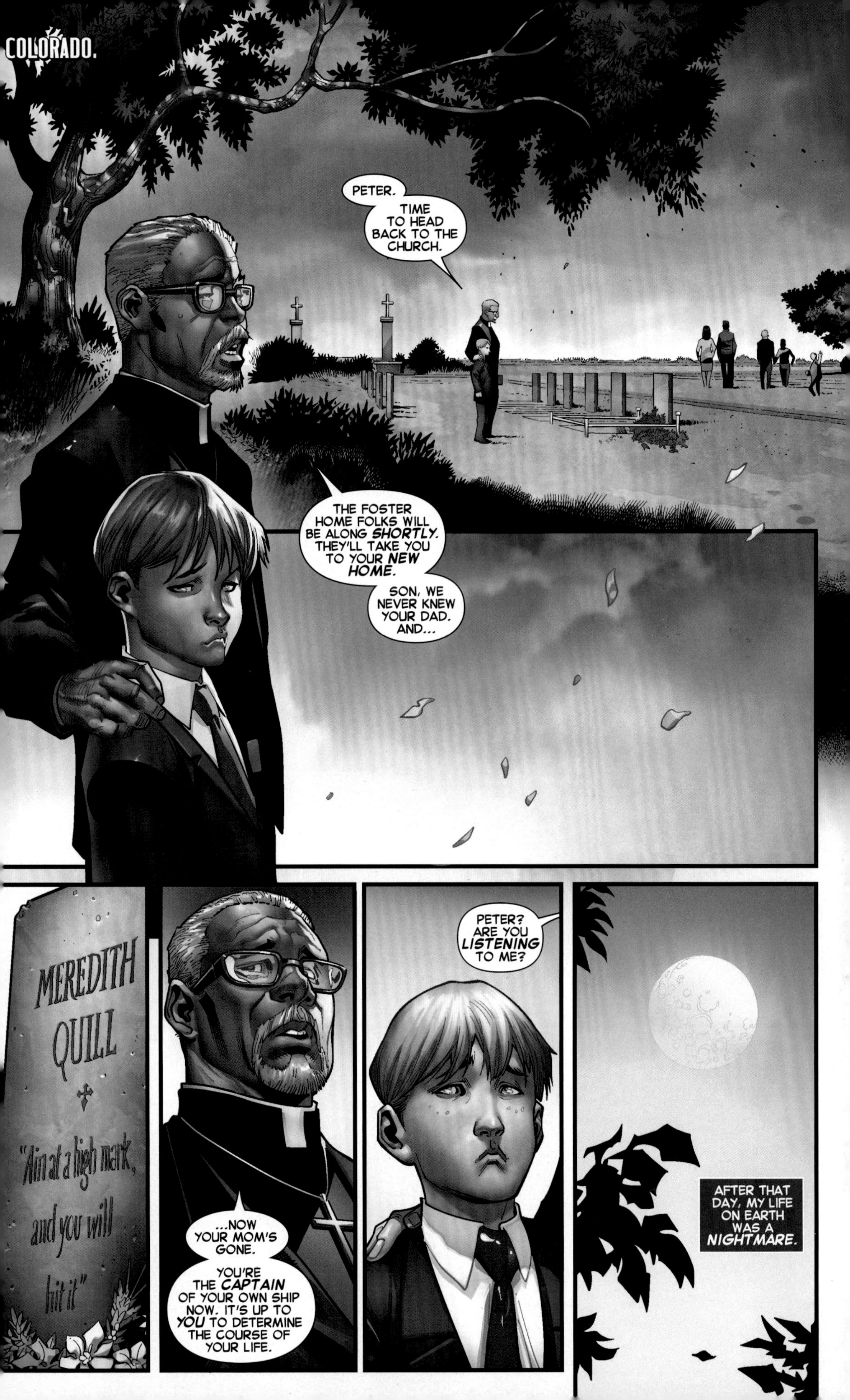
COLORADO.
PETER.
TIME TO HEAD BACK TO THE CHURCH.
THE FOSTER HOME FOLKS WILL BE ALONG SHORTLY. THEY'LL TAKE YOU TO YOUR NEW HOME.
SON, WE NEVER KNEW YOUR DAD. AND...
MEREDITH QUILL
"Aim at a high mark, and you will hit it"
...NOW YOUR MOM'S GONE.
YOU'RE THE CAPTAIN OF YOUR OWN SHIP NOW. IT'S UP TO YOU TO DETERMINE THE COURSE OF YOUR LIFE.
PETER? ARE YOU LISTENING TO ME?
AFTER THAT DAY, MY LIFE ON EARTH WAS A NIGHTMARE.

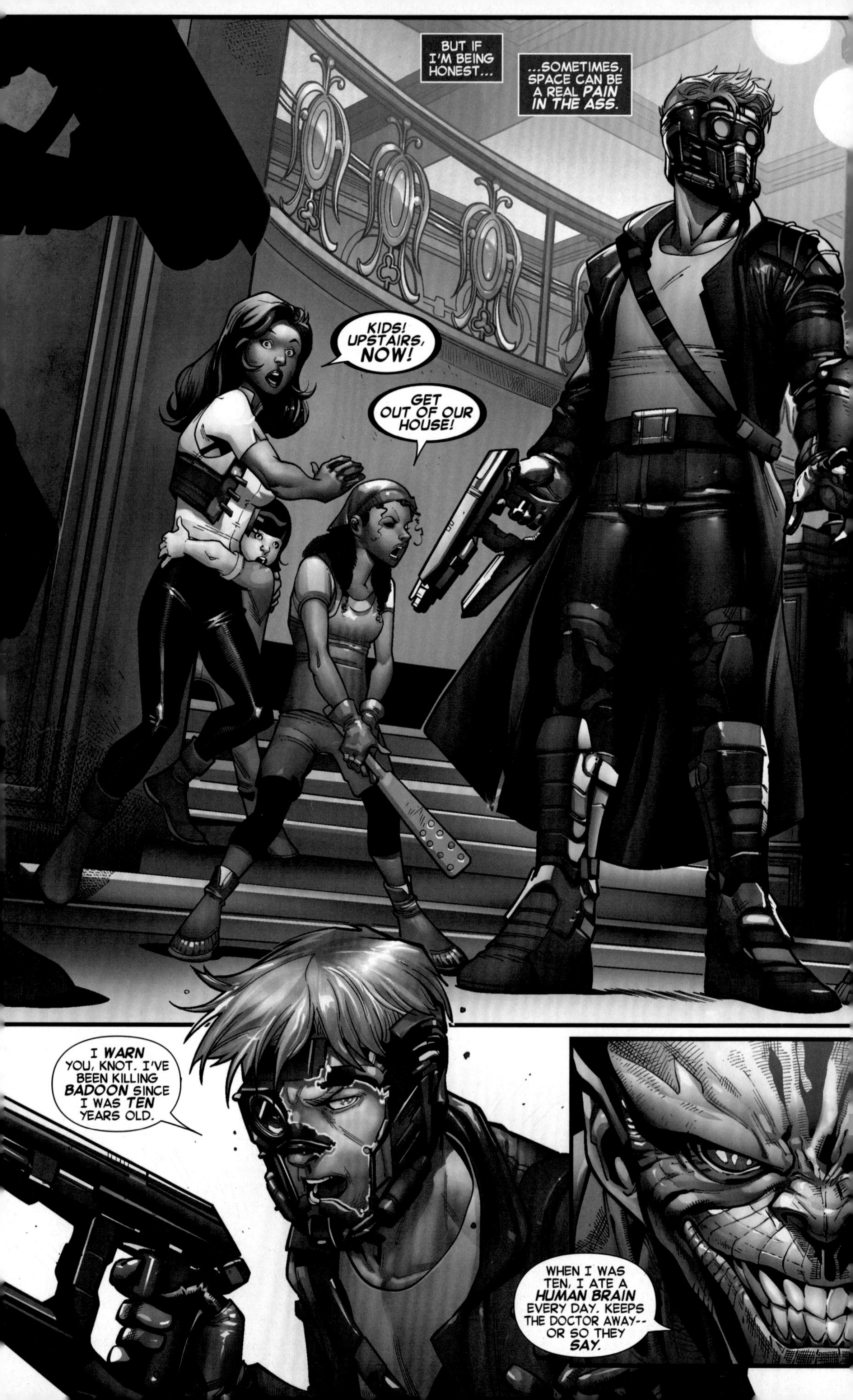
BUT IF I'M BEING HONEST...
...SOMETIMES, SPACE CAN BE A REAL PAIN IN THE ASS.
KIDS! UPSTAIRS, NOW!
GET OUT OF OUR HOUSE!
I WARN YOU, KNOT. I'VE BEEN KILLING BADOON SINCE I WAS TEN YEARS OLD.
WHEN I WAS TEN, I ATE A HUMAN BRAIN EVERY DAY. KEEPS THE DOCTOR AWAY-- OR SO THEY SAY.

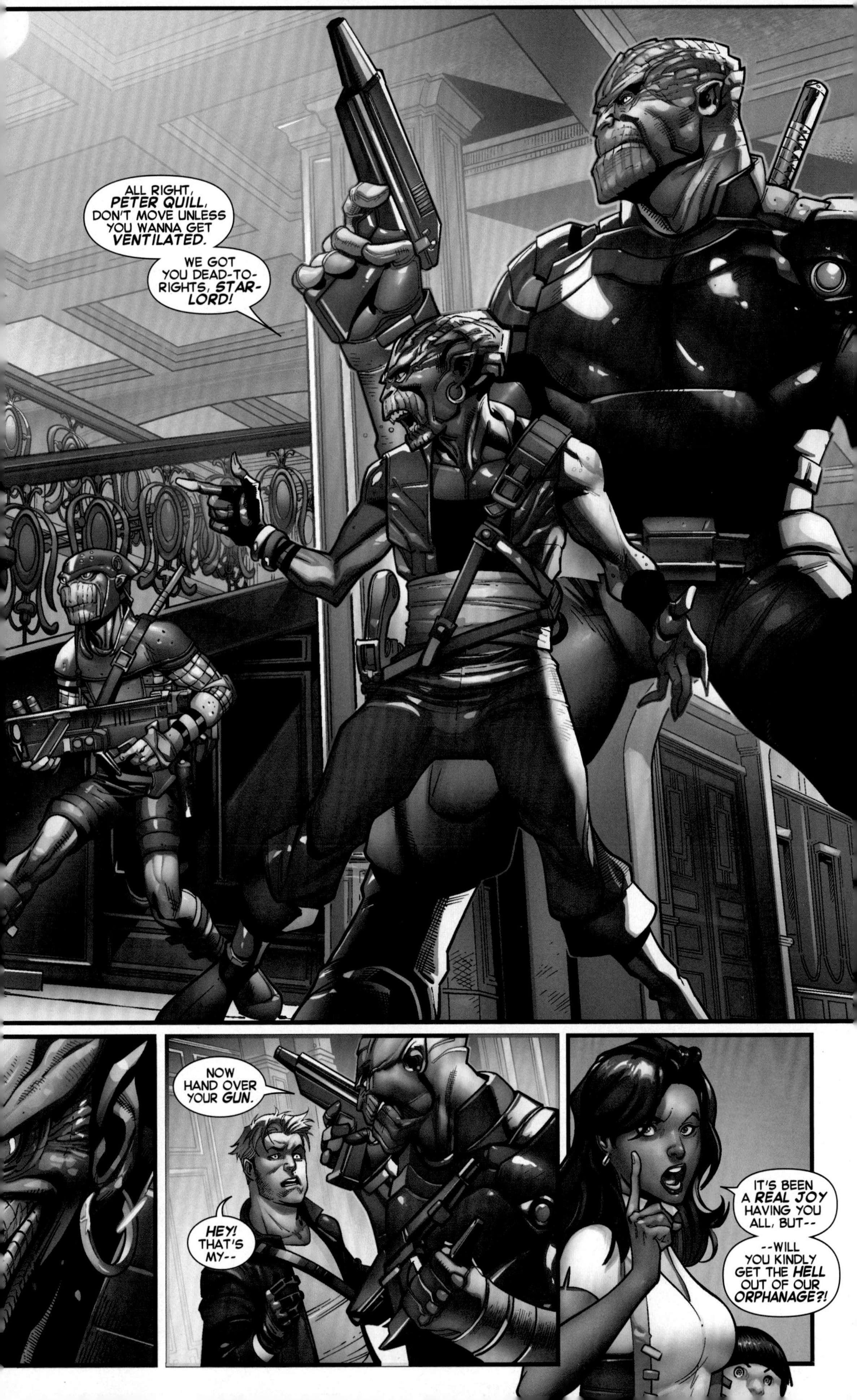
ALL RIGHT, PETER QUILL, DON'T MOVE UNLESS YOU WANNA GET VENTILATED.
WE GOT YOU DEAD-TO-RIGHTS, STAR-LORD!
NOW HAND OVER YOUR GUN.
HEY! THAT'S MY--
IT'S BEEN A REAL JOY HAVING YOU ALL, BUT--
--WILL YOU KINDLY GET THE HELL OUT OF OUR ORPHANAGE?!

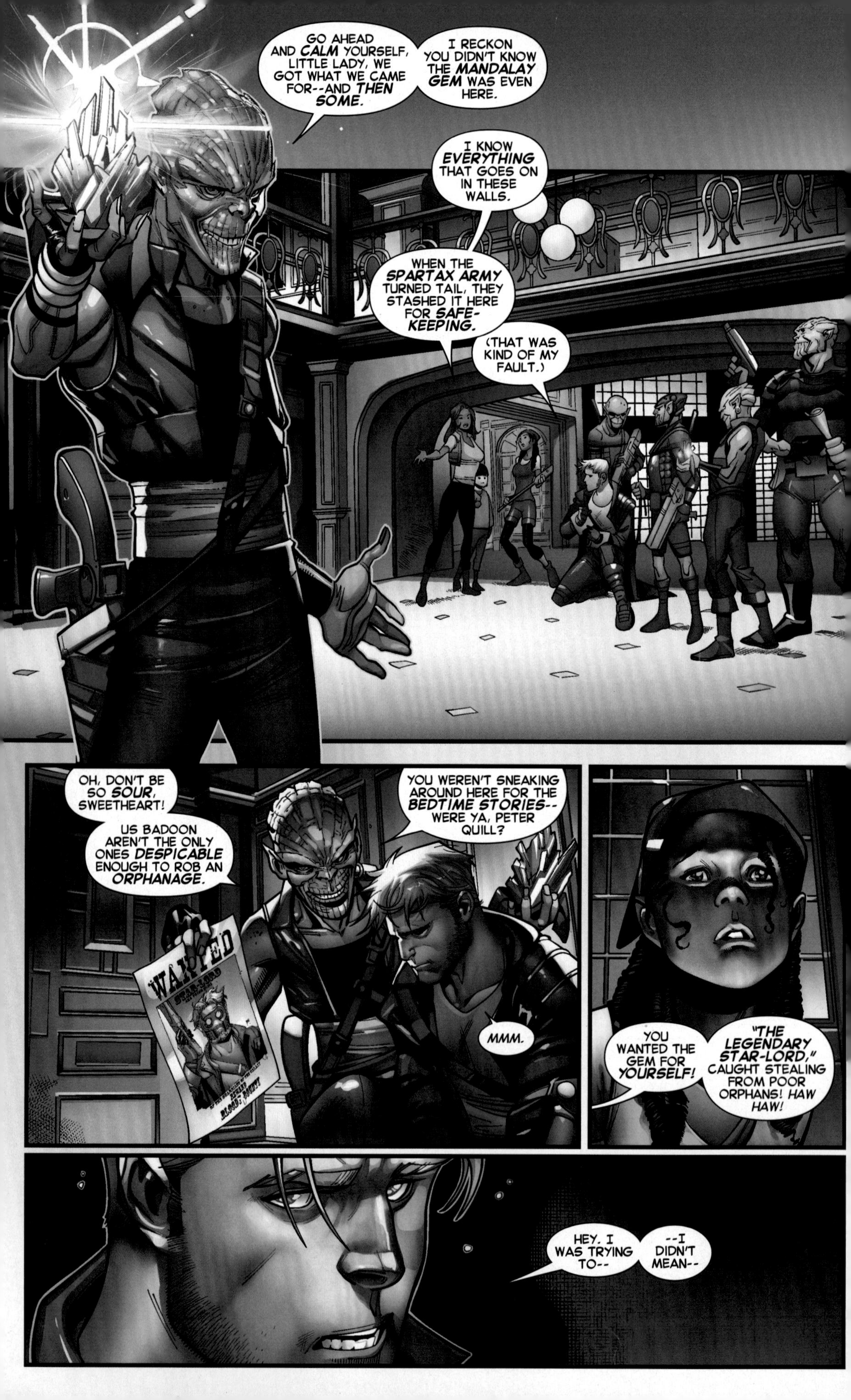
GO AHEAD AND CALM YOURSELF, LITTLE LADY, WE GOT WHAT WE CAME FOR--AND THEN SOME.
I RECKON YOU DIDN'T KNOW THE MANDALAY GEM WAS EVEN HERE.
I KNOW EVERYTHING THAT GOES ON IN THESE WALLS.
WHEN THE SPARTAX ARMY TURNED TAIL, THEY STASHED IT HERE FOR SAFE-KEEPING.
(THAT WAS KIND OF MY FAULT.)
OH, DON'T BE SO SOUR, SWEETHEART!
US BADOON AREN'T THE ONLY ONES DESPICABLE ENOUGH TO ROB AN ORPHANAGE.
YOU WEREN'T SNEAKING AROUND HERE FOR THE BEDTIME STORIES--WERE YA, PETER QUILL?
WANTED
STAR-LORD
MMM.
YOU WANTED THE GEM FOR YOURSELF!
"THE LEGENDARY STAR-LORD," CAUGHT STEALING FROM POOR ORPHANS! HAW HAW!
HEY. I WAS TRYING TO--
--I DIDN'T MEAN--

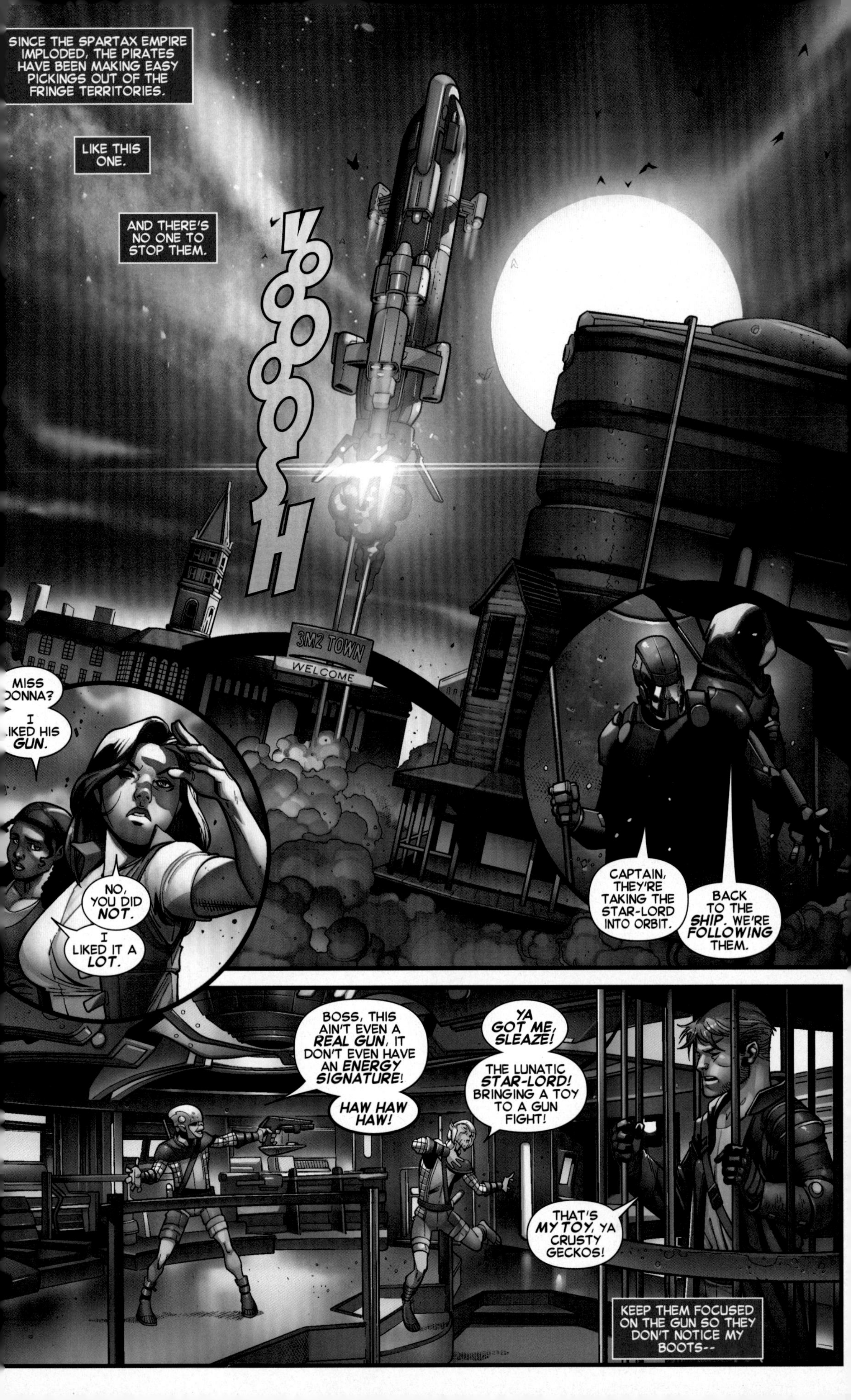
SINCE THE SPARTAX EMPIRE IMPLODED, THE PIRATES HAVE BEEN MAKING EASY PICKINGS OUT OF THE FRINGE TERRITORIES.
LIKE THIS ONE.
AND THERE'S NO ONE TO STOP THEM.
VOOOOOSH
3M2 TOWN
WELCOME
CAPTAIN, THEY'RE TAKING THE STAR-LORD INTO ORBIT.
BACK TO THE SHIP. WE'RE FOLLOWING THEM.
NO, YOU DID NOT.
I LIKED IT A LOT.
BOSS, THIS AIN'T EVEN A REAL GUN, IT DON'T EVEN HAVE AN ENERGY SIGNATURE!
HAW HAW HAW!
YA GOT ME, SLEAZE!
THE LUNATIC STAR-LORD! BRINGING A TOY TO A GUN FIGHT!
THAT'S MY TOY, YA CRUSTY GECKOS!
KEEP THEM FOCUSED ON THE GUN SO THEY DON'T NOTICE MY BOOTS--

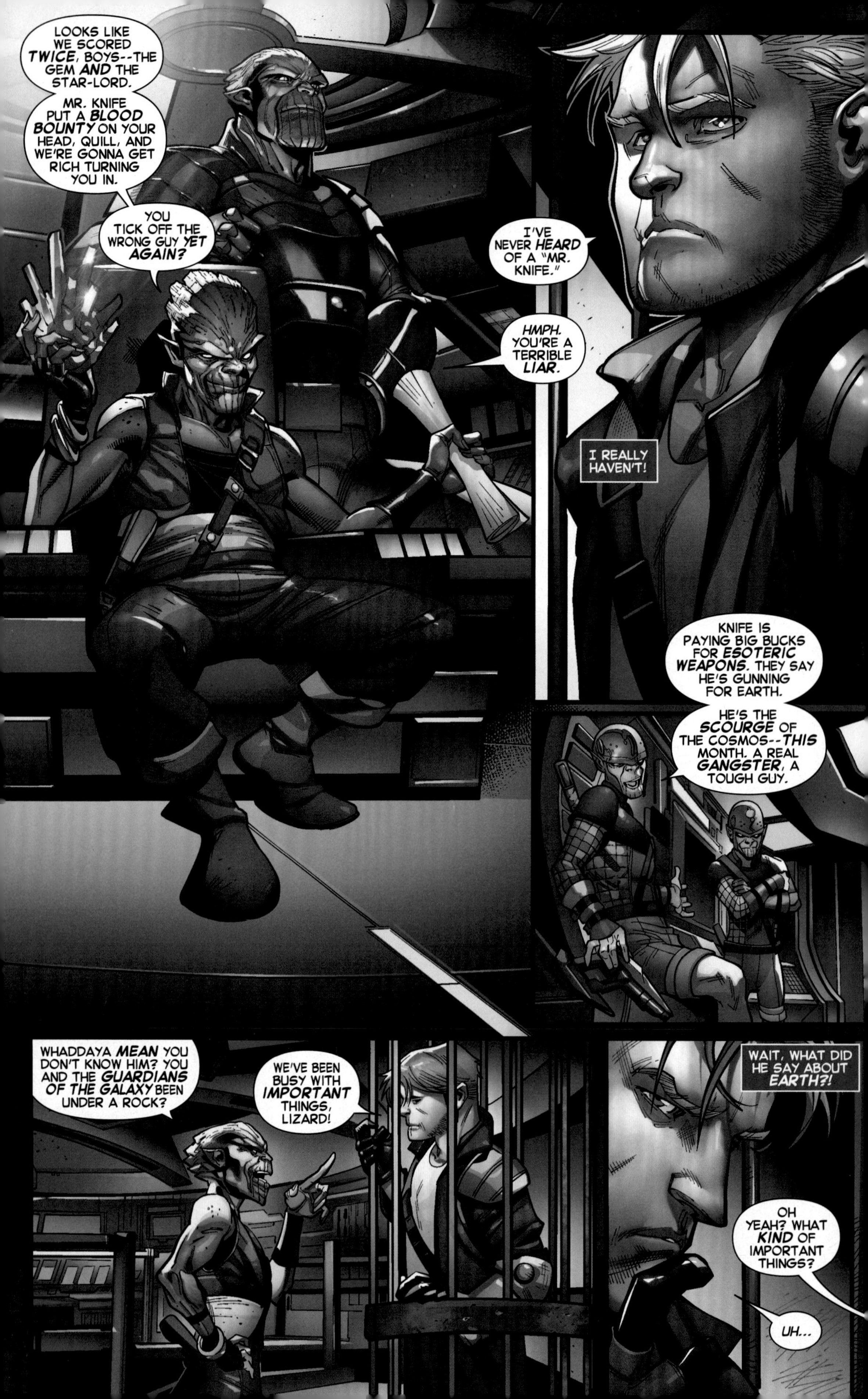
LOOKS LIKE WE SCORED *TWICE*, BOYS--THE GEM *AND* THE STAR-LORD.
MR. KNIFE PUT A *BLOOD BOUNTY* ON YOUR HEAD, QUILL, AND WE'RE GONNA GET RICH TURNING YOU IN.
YOU TICK OFF THE WRONG GUY *YET AGAIN?*
I'VE NEVER *HEARD* OF A "MR. KNIFE."
HMPH. YOU'RE A TERRIBLE *LIAR.*
I REALLY HAVEN'T!
KNIFE IS PAYING BIG BUCKS FOR *ESOTERIC WEAPONS.* THEY SAY HE'S GUNNING FOR EARTH.
HE'S THE *SCOURGE* OF THE COSMOS--*THIS* MONTH. A REAL *GANGSTER*, A TOUGH GUY.
WHADDAYA *MEAN* YOU DON'T KNOW HIM? YOU AND THE *GUARDIANS OF THE GALAXY* BEEN UNDER A ROCK?
WE'VE BEEN BUSY WITH *IMPORTANT* THINGS, LIZARD!
WAIT, WHAT DID HE SAY ABOUT *EARTH?!*
OH YEAH? WHAT *KIND* OF IMPORTANT THINGS?
UH...

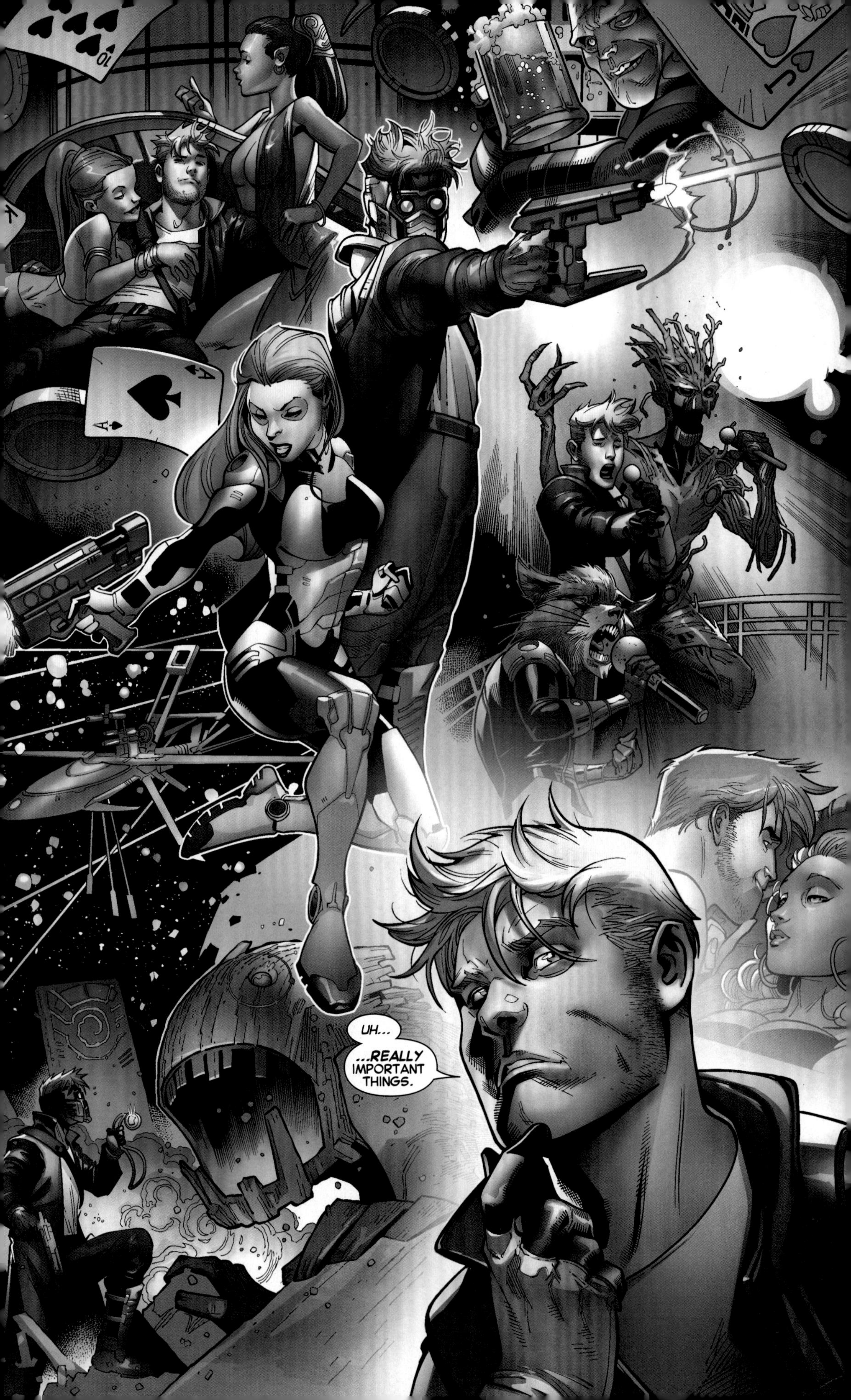
UH...
...REALLY IMPORTANT THINGS.

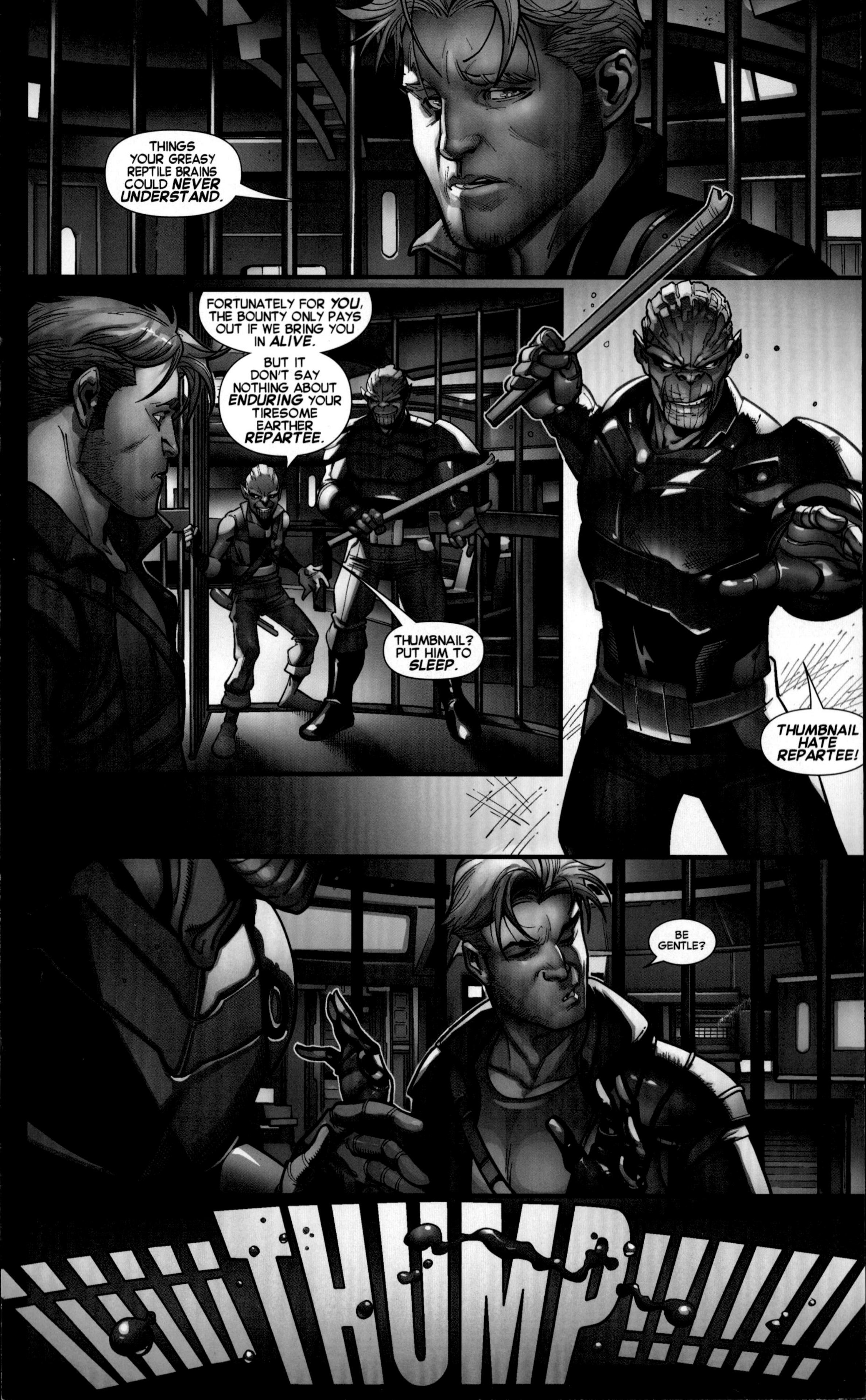
THINGS YOUR GREASY REPTILE BRAINS COULD NEVER UNDERSTAND.
FORTUNATELY FOR YOU, THE BOUNTY ONLY PAYS OUT IF WE BRING YOU IN ALIVE.
BUT IT DON'T SAY NOTHING ABOUT ENDURING YOUR TIRESOME EARTHER REPARTEE.
THUMBNAIL? PUT HIM TO SLEEP.
THUMBNAIL HATE REPARTEE!
BE GENTLE?
THUMP!!!!!!

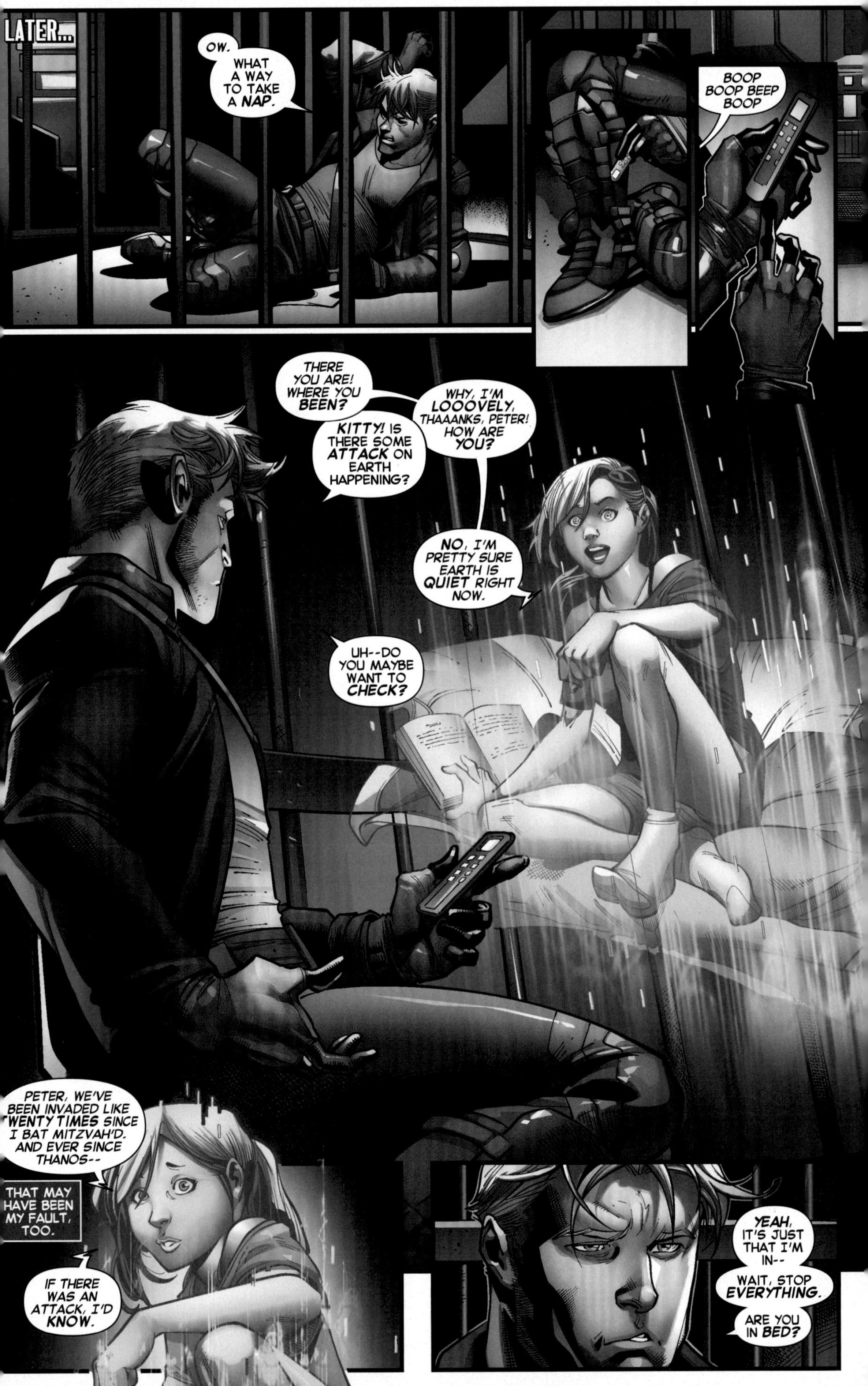
LATER...
OW. WHAT A WAY TO TAKE A NAP.
BOOP BOOP BEEP BOOP
THERE YOU ARE! WHERE YOU BEEN?
WHY, I'M LOOOVELY, THAAANKS, PETER! HOW ARE YOU?
KITTY! IS THERE SOME ATTACK ON EARTH HAPPENING?
NO, I'M PRETTY SURE EARTH IS QUIET RIGHT NOW.
UH--DO YOU MAYBE WANT TO CHECK?
PETER, WE'VE BEEN INVADED LIKE TWENTY TIMES SINCE I BAT MITZVAH'D. AND EVER SINCE THANOS--
THAT MAY HAVE BEEN MY FAULT, TOO.
IF THERE WAS AN ATTACK, I'D KNOW.
YEAH, IT'S JUST THAT I'M IN--
WAIT, STOP EVERYTHING.
ARE YOU IN BED?

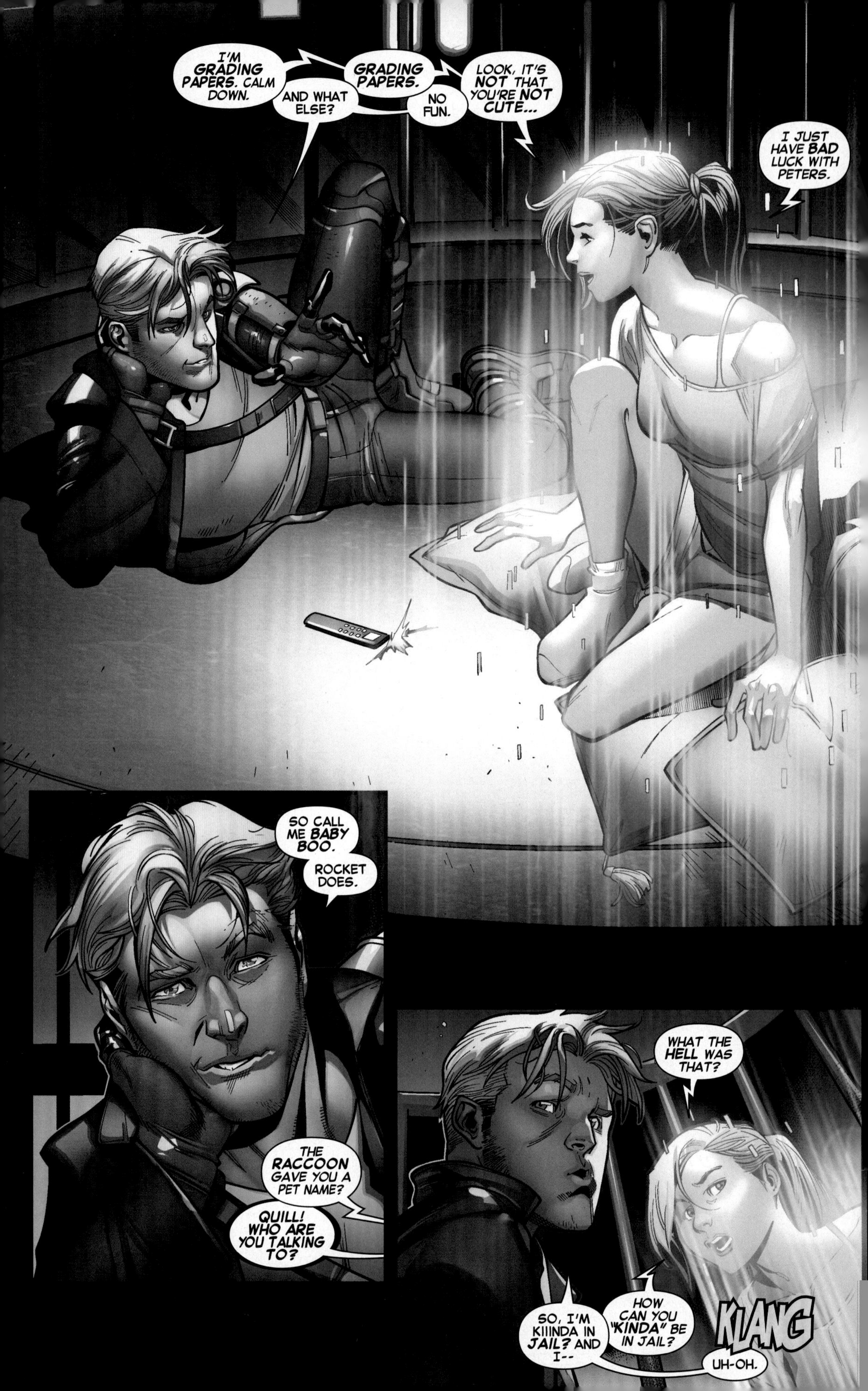
I'M GRADING PAPERS. CALM DOWN.
AND WHAT ELSE?
GRADING PAPERS.
NO FUN.
LOOK, IT'S NOT THAT YOU'RE NOT CUTE...
I JUST HAVE BAD LUCK WITH PETERS.
SO CALL ME BABY BOO.
ROCKET DOES.
THE RACCOON GAVE YOU A PET NAME?
QUILL! WHO ARE YOU TALKING TO?
WHAT THE HELL WAS THAT?
SO, I'M KIIINDA IN JAIL? AND I--
HOW CAN YOU "KINDA" BE IN JAIL?
KLANG
UH-OH.

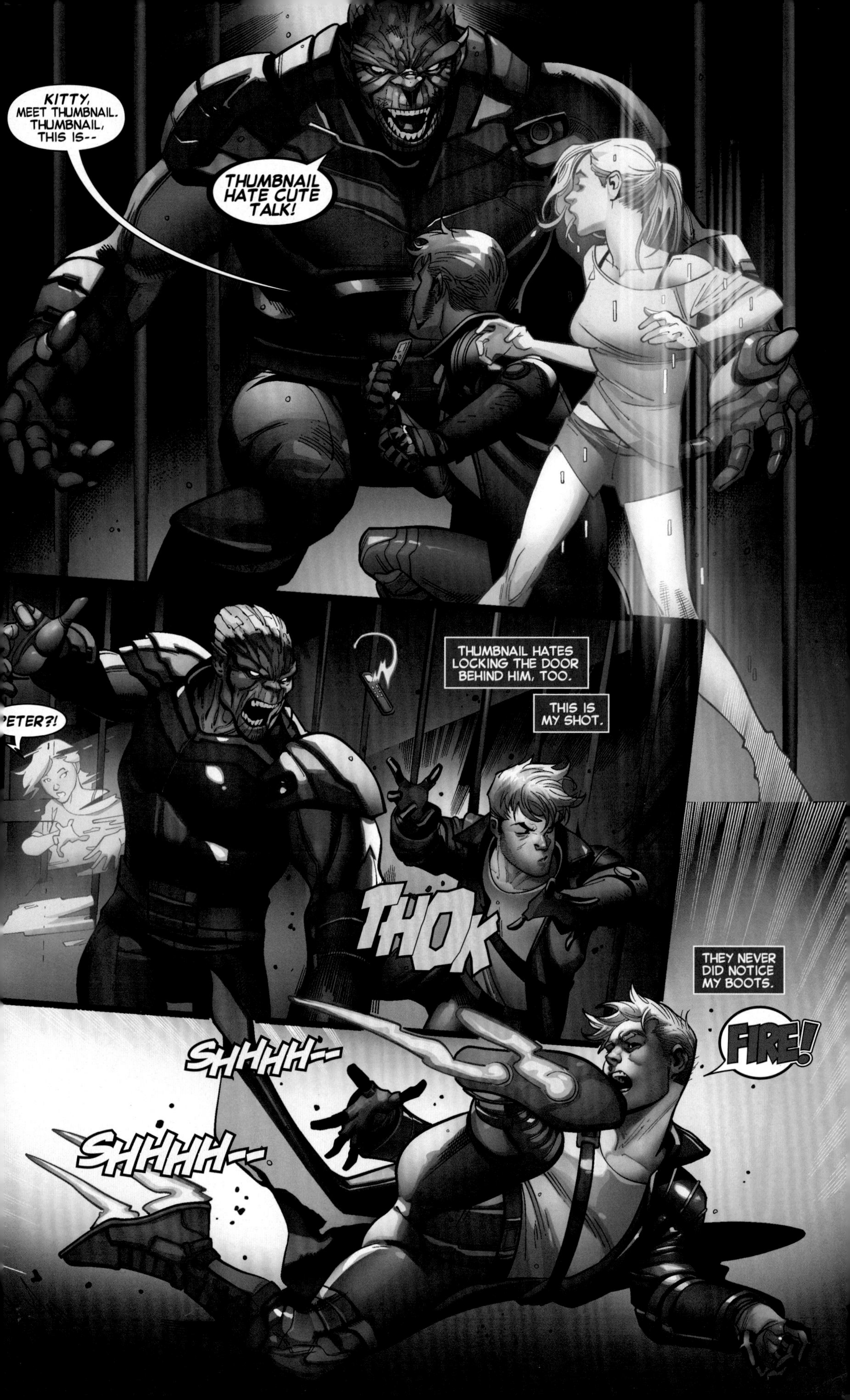
KITTY, MEET THUMBNAIL. THUMBNAIL, THIS IS--
THUMBNAIL HATE CUTE TALK!
THUMBNAIL HATES LOCKING THE DOOR BEHIND HIM, TOO.
THIS IS MY SHOT.
PETER?!
THOK
THEY NEVER DID NOTICE MY BOOTS.
FIRE!
SHHHH--
SHHHH--

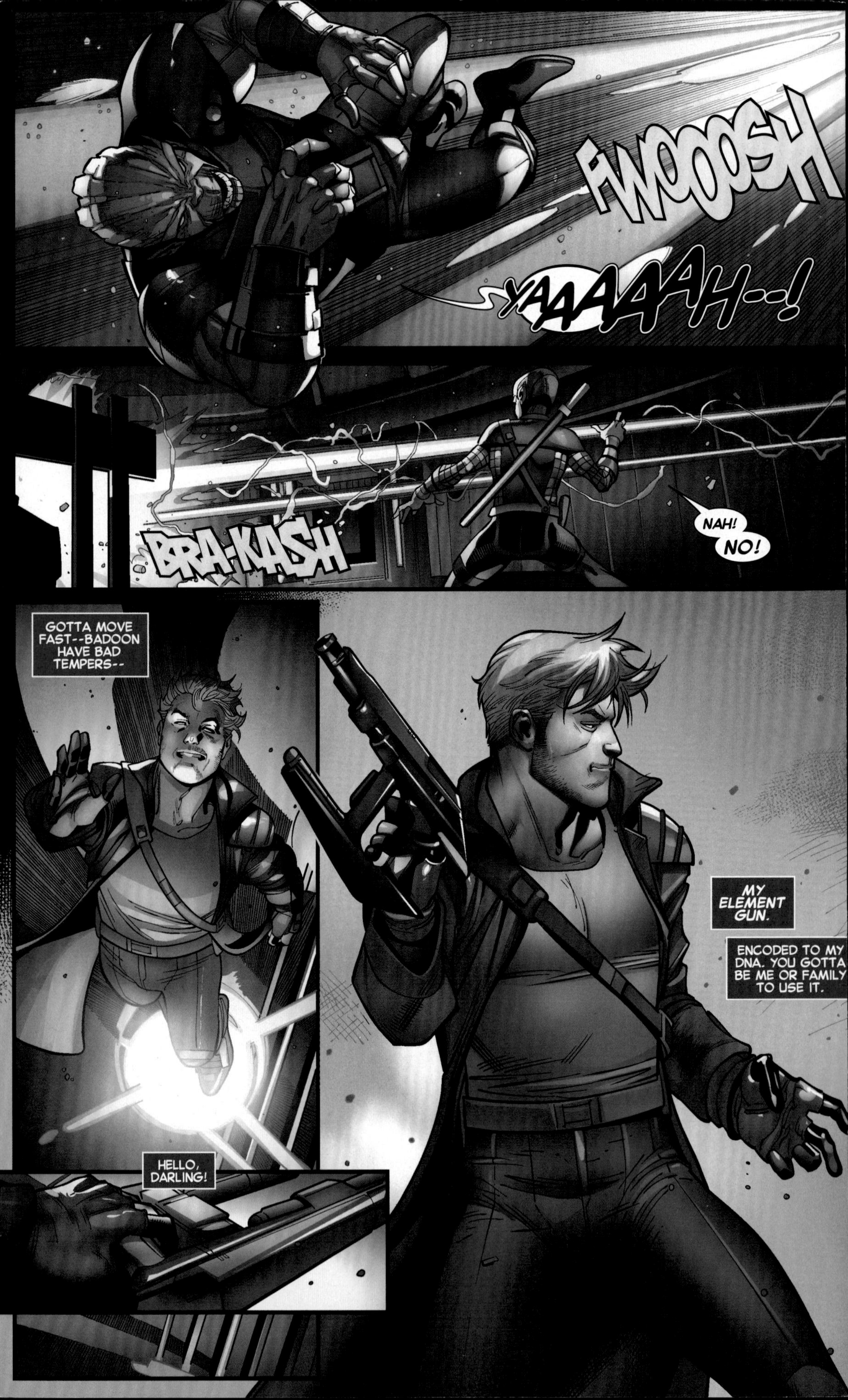
FWOOOSH
YAAAAAH--!
BRA-KASH
NAH! NO!
GOTTA MOVE FAST--BADOON HAVE BAD TEMPERS--
HELLO, DARLING!
MY ELEMENT GUN.
ENCODED TO MY DNA. YOU GOTTA BE ME OR FAMILY TO USE IT.

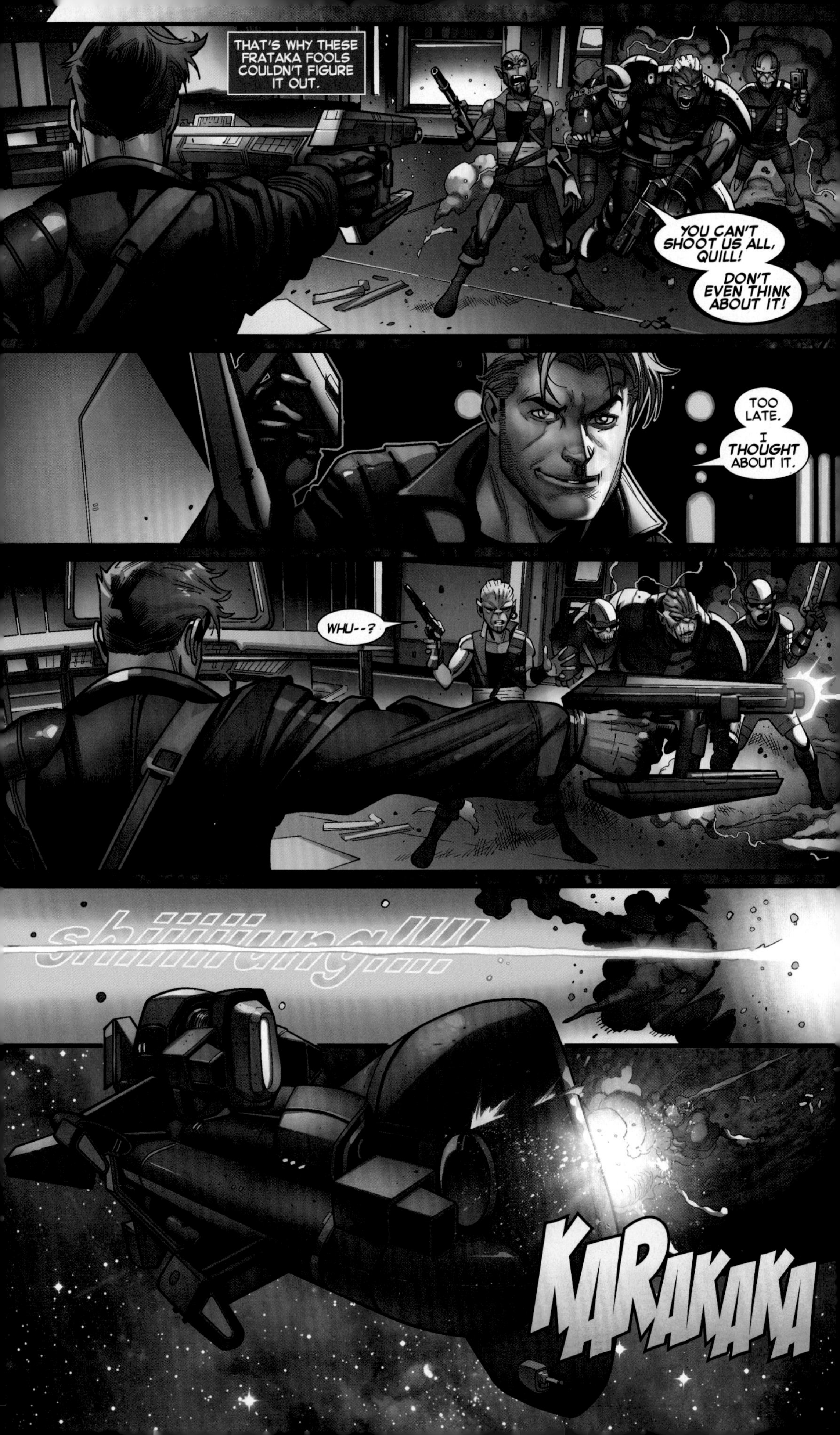
THAT'S WHY THESE FRATAKA FOOLS COULDN'T FIGURE IT OUT.
YOU CAN'T SHOOT US ALL, QUILL!
DON'T EVEN THINK ABOUT IT!
TOO LATE.
I THOUGHT ABOUT IT.
WHU--?
shiiiiing!!!!
KARAKAKA

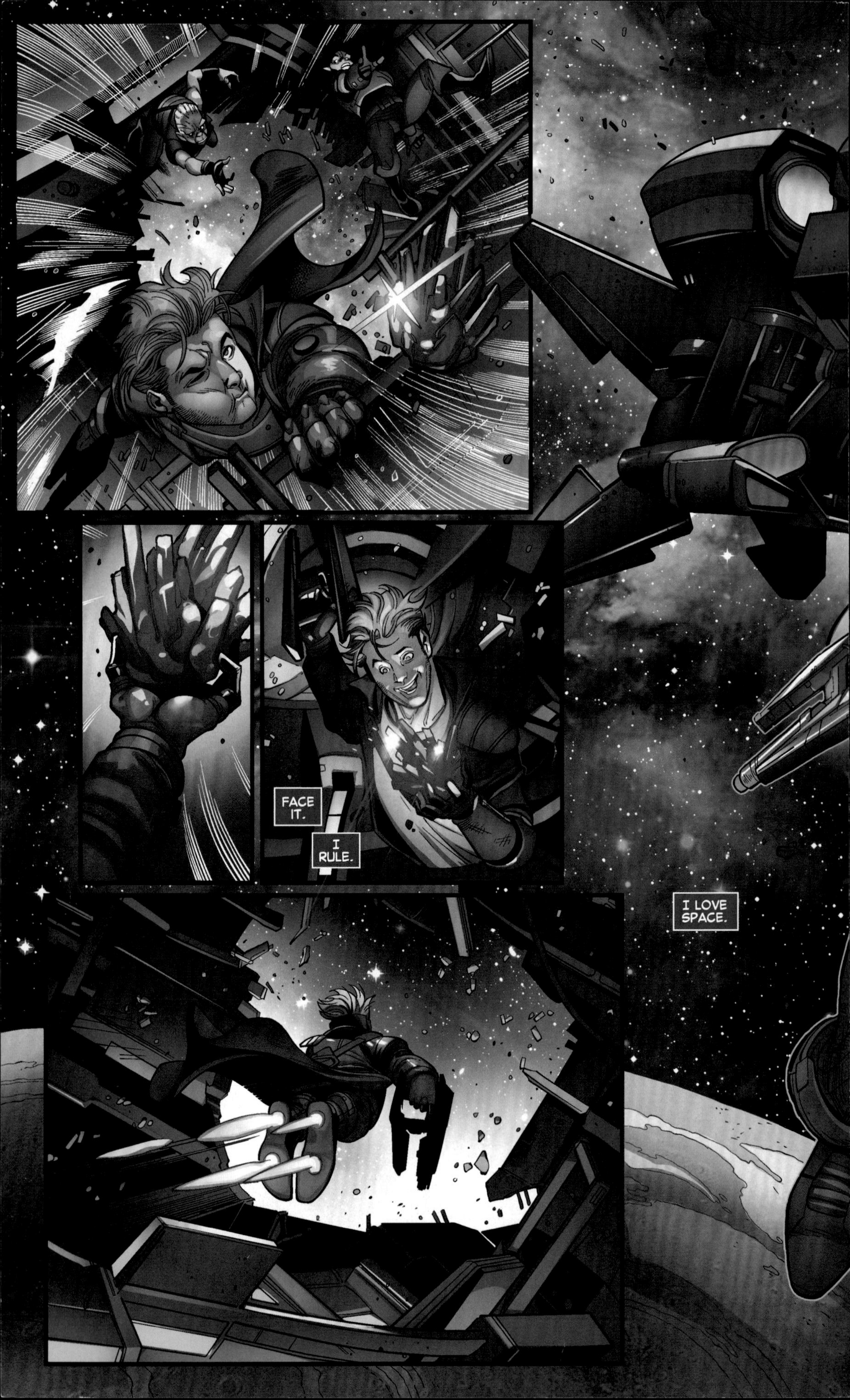
FACE IT.
I RULE.
I LOVE SPACE.

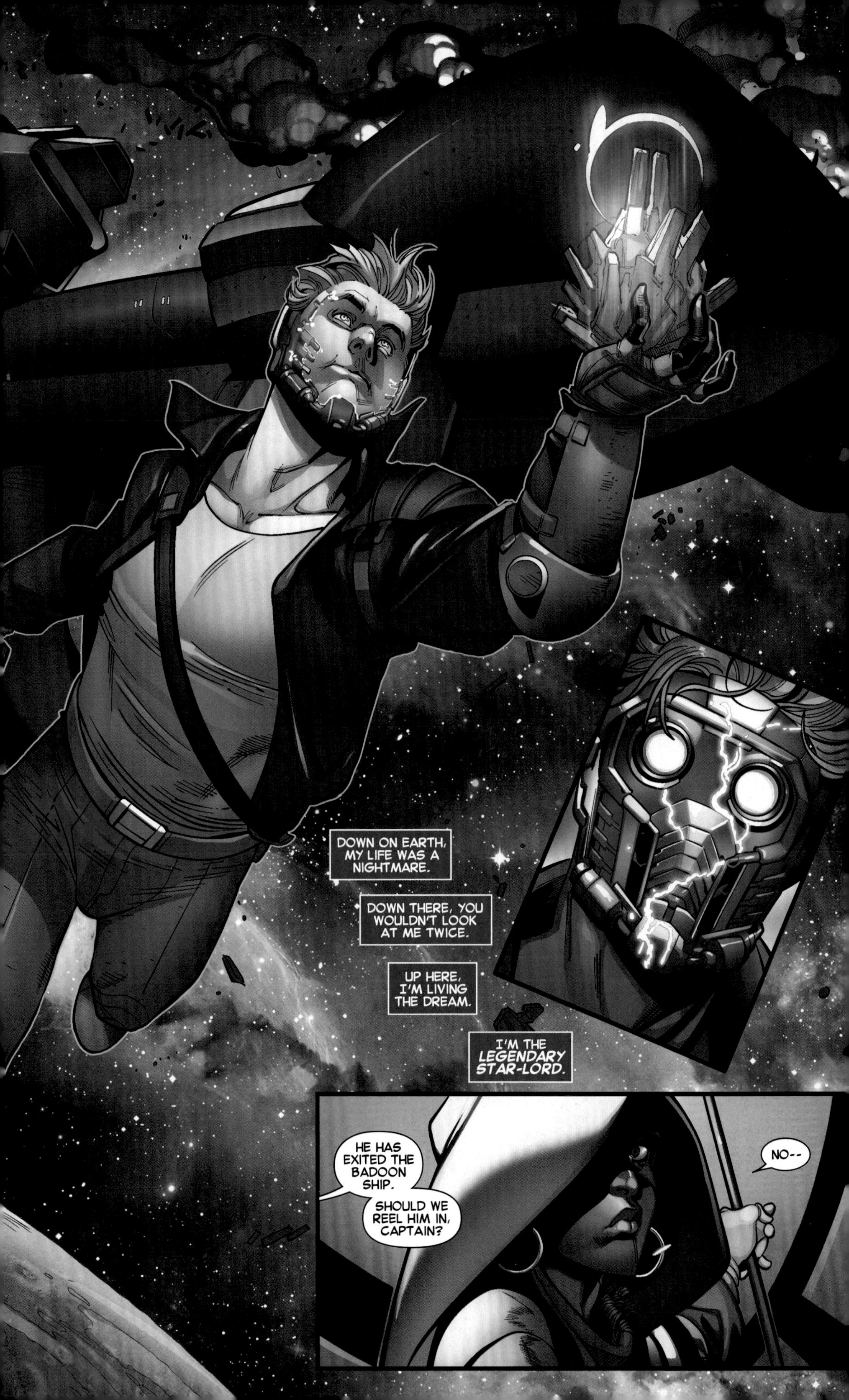
DOWN ON EARTH, MY LIFE WAS A NIGHTMARE.
DOWN THERE, YOU WOULDN'T LOOK AT ME TWICE.
UP HERE, I'M LIVING THE DREAM.
I'M THE *LEGENDARY STAR-LORD.*
HE HAS EXITED THE BADOON SHIP.
SHOULD WE REEL HIM IN, CAPTAIN?
NO--

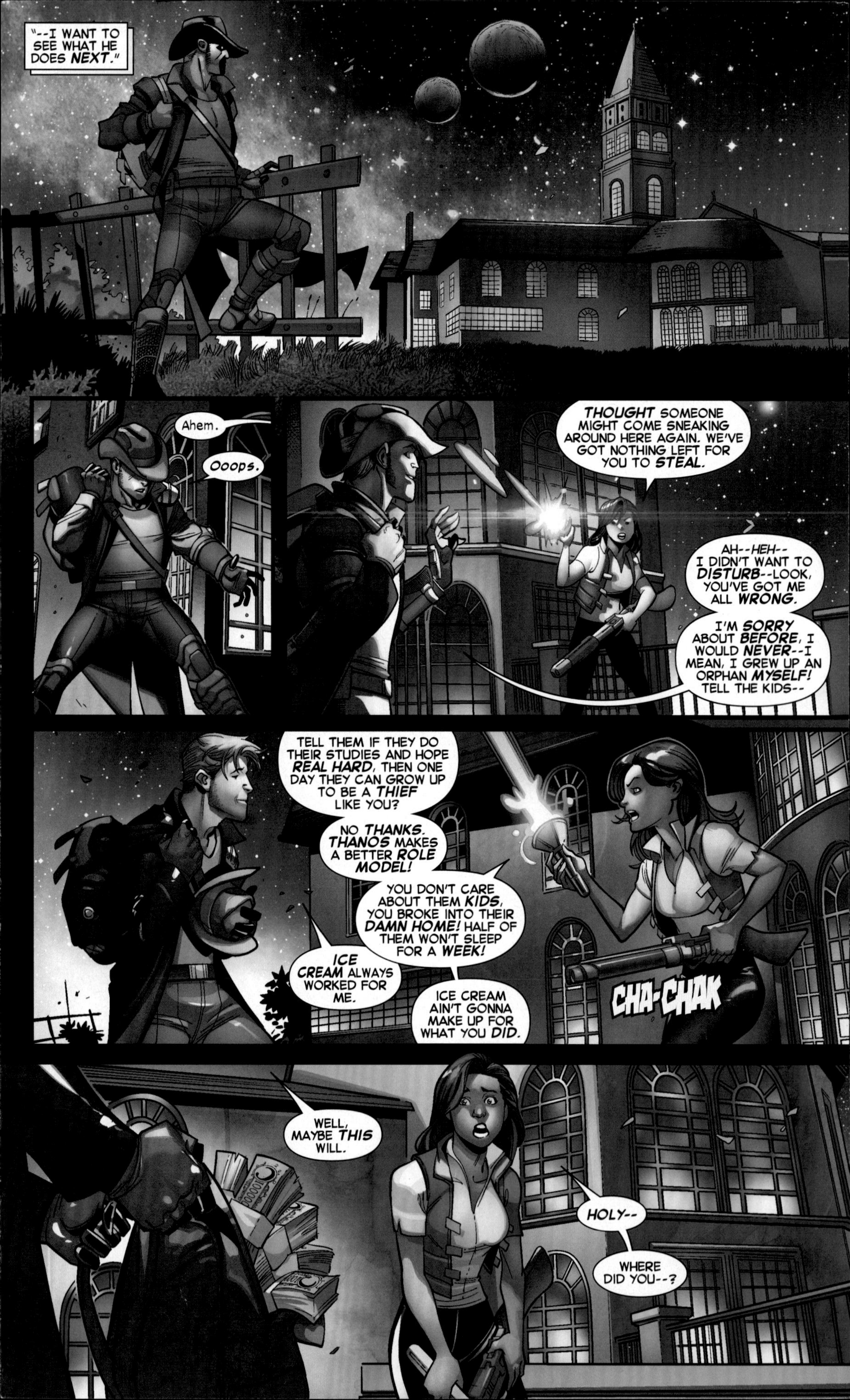
"--I WANT TO SEE WHAT HE DOES NEXT."
Ahem.
Ooops.
THOUGHT SOMEONE MIGHT COME SNEAKING AROUND HERE AGAIN. WE'VE GOT NOTHING LEFT FOR YOU TO STEAL.
AH--HEH-- I DIDN'T WANT TO DISTURB--LOOK, YOU'VE GOT ME ALL WRONG.
I'M SORRY ABOUT BEFORE, I WOULD NEVER--I MEAN, I GREW UP AN ORPHAN MYSELF! TELL THE KIDS--
TELL THEM IF THEY DO THEIR STUDIES AND HOPE REAL HARD, THEN ONE DAY THEY CAN GROW UP TO BE A THIEF LIKE YOU?
NO THANKS. THANOS MAKES A BETTER ROLE MODEL!
YOU DON'T CARE ABOUT THEM KIDS, YOU BROKE INTO THEIR DAMN HOME! HALF OF THEM WON'T SLEEP FOR A WEEK!
ICE CREAM ALWAYS WORKED FOR ME.
ICE CREAM AIN'T GONNA MAKE UP FOR WHAT YOU DID.
CHA-CHAK
WELL, MAYBE THIS WILL.
HOLY--
WHERE DID YOU--?

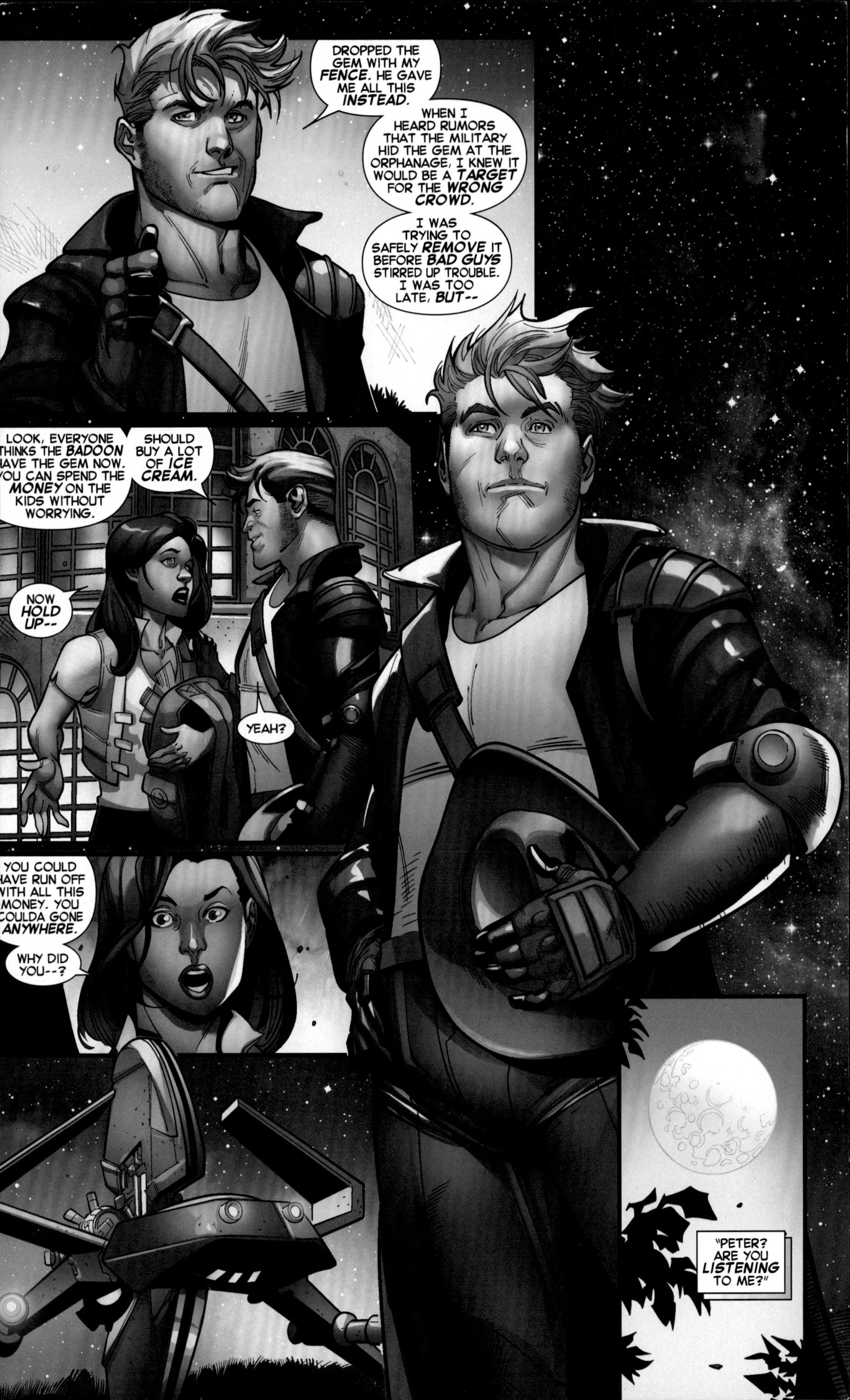
DROPPED THE GEM WITH MY FENCE. HE GAVE ME ALL THIS INSTEAD.
WHEN I HEARD RUMORS THAT THE MILITARY HID THE GEM AT THE ORPHANAGE, I KNEW IT WOULD BE A TARGET FOR THE WRONG CROWD.
I WAS TRYING TO SAFELY REMOVE IT BEFORE BAD GUYS STIRRED UP TROUBLE. I WAS TOO LATE, BUT--
LOOK, EVERYONE THINKS THE BADOON HAVE THE GEM NOW. YOU CAN SPEND THE MONEY ON THE KIDS WITHOUT WORRYING.
SHOULD BUY A LOT OF ICE CREAM.
NOW HOLD UP--
YEAH?
YOU COULD HAVE RUN OFF WITH ALL THIS MONEY. YOU COULDA GONE ANYWHERE.
WHY DID YOU--?
"PETER? ARE YOU LISTENING TO ME?"

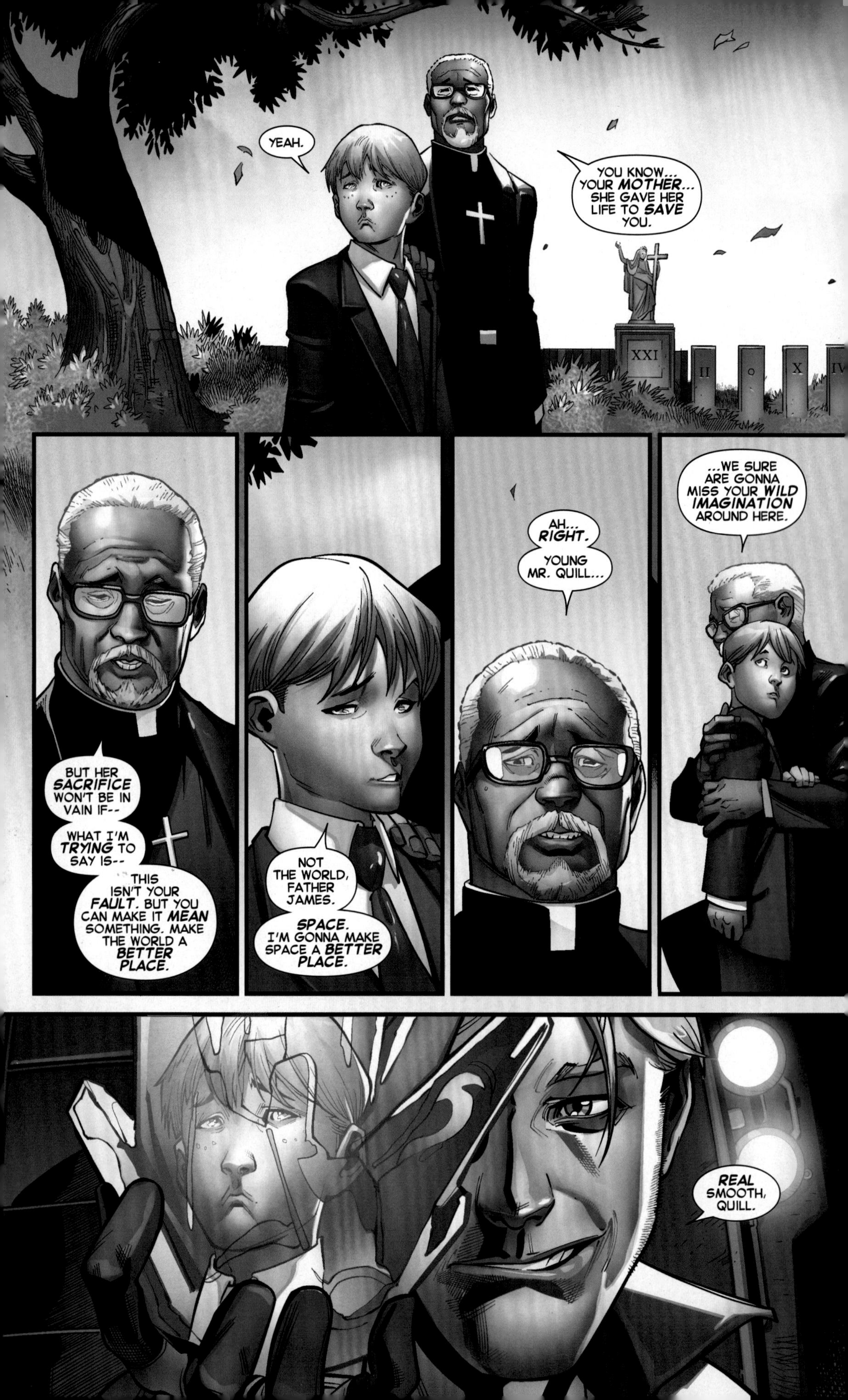
YEAH.
YOU KNOW... YOUR MOTHER... SHE GAVE HER LIFE TO SAVE YOU.
XXI
II
X
IV
BUT HER SACRIFICE WON'T BE IN VAIN IF--
WHAT I'M TRYING TO SAY IS--
THIS ISN'T YOUR FAULT. BUT YOU CAN MAKE IT MEAN SOMETHING. MAKE THE WORLD A BETTER PLACE.
NOT THE WORLD, FATHER JAMES.
SPACE. I'M GONNA MAKE SPACE A BETTER PLACE.
AH... RIGHT.
YOUNG MR. QUILL...
...WE SURE ARE GONNA MISS YOUR WILD IMAGINATION AROUND HERE.
REAL SMOOTH, QUILL.

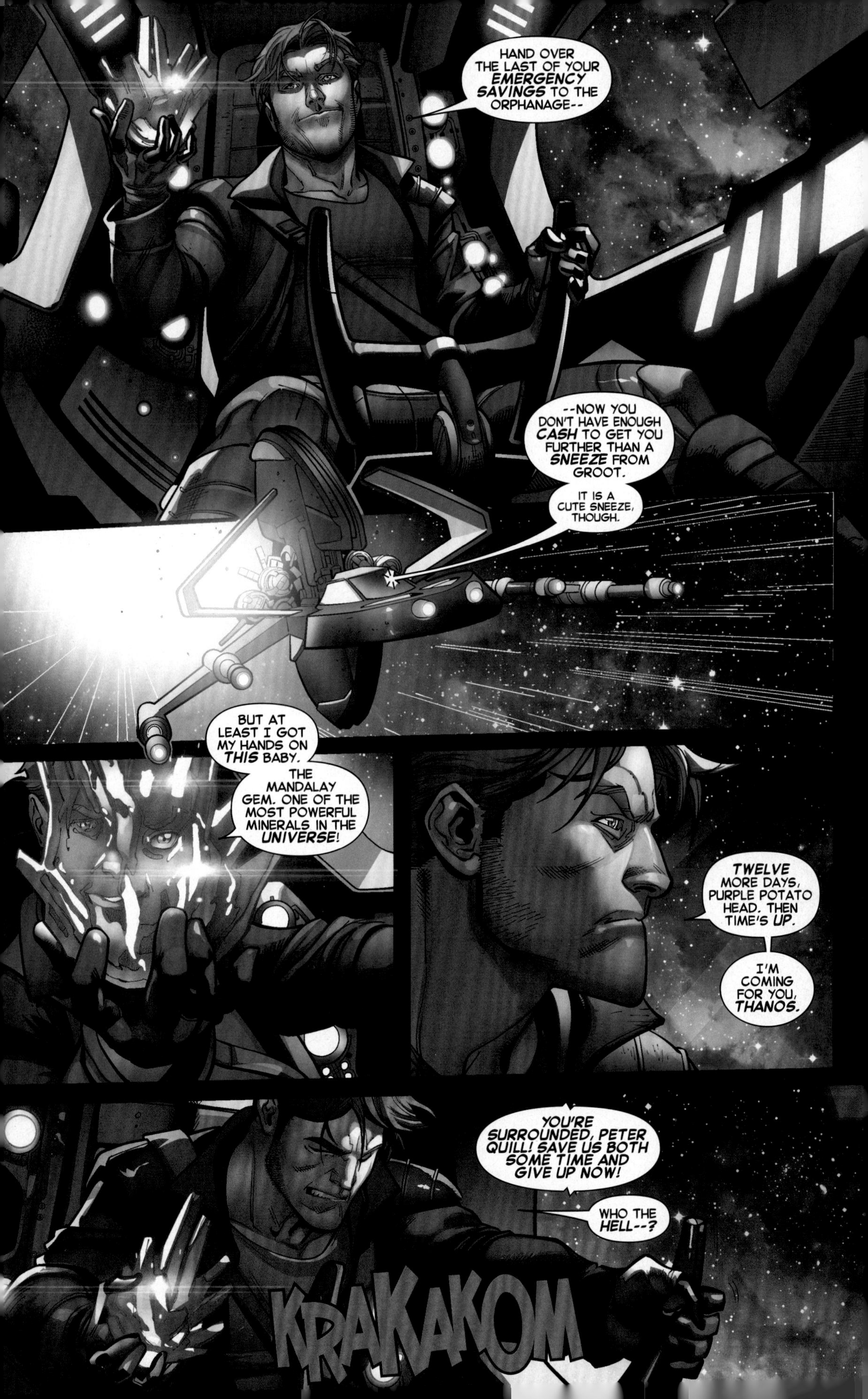
HAND OVER THE LAST OF YOUR EMERGENCY SAVINGS TO THE ORPHANAGE--
--NOW YOU DON'T HAVE ENOUGH CASH TO GET YOU FURTHER THAN A SNEEZE FROM GROOT.
IT IS A CUTE SNEEZE, THOUGH.
BUT AT LEAST I GOT MY HANDS ON THIS BABY.
THE MANDALAY GEM. ONE OF THE MOST POWERFUL MINERALS IN THE UNIVERSE!
TWELVE MORE DAYS, PURPLE POTATO HEAD. THEN TIME'S UP.
I'M COMING FOR YOU, THANOS.
YOU'RE SURROUNDED, PETER QUILL! SAVE US BOTH SOME TIME AND GIVE UP NOW!
WHO THE HELL--?
KRAKAKOM

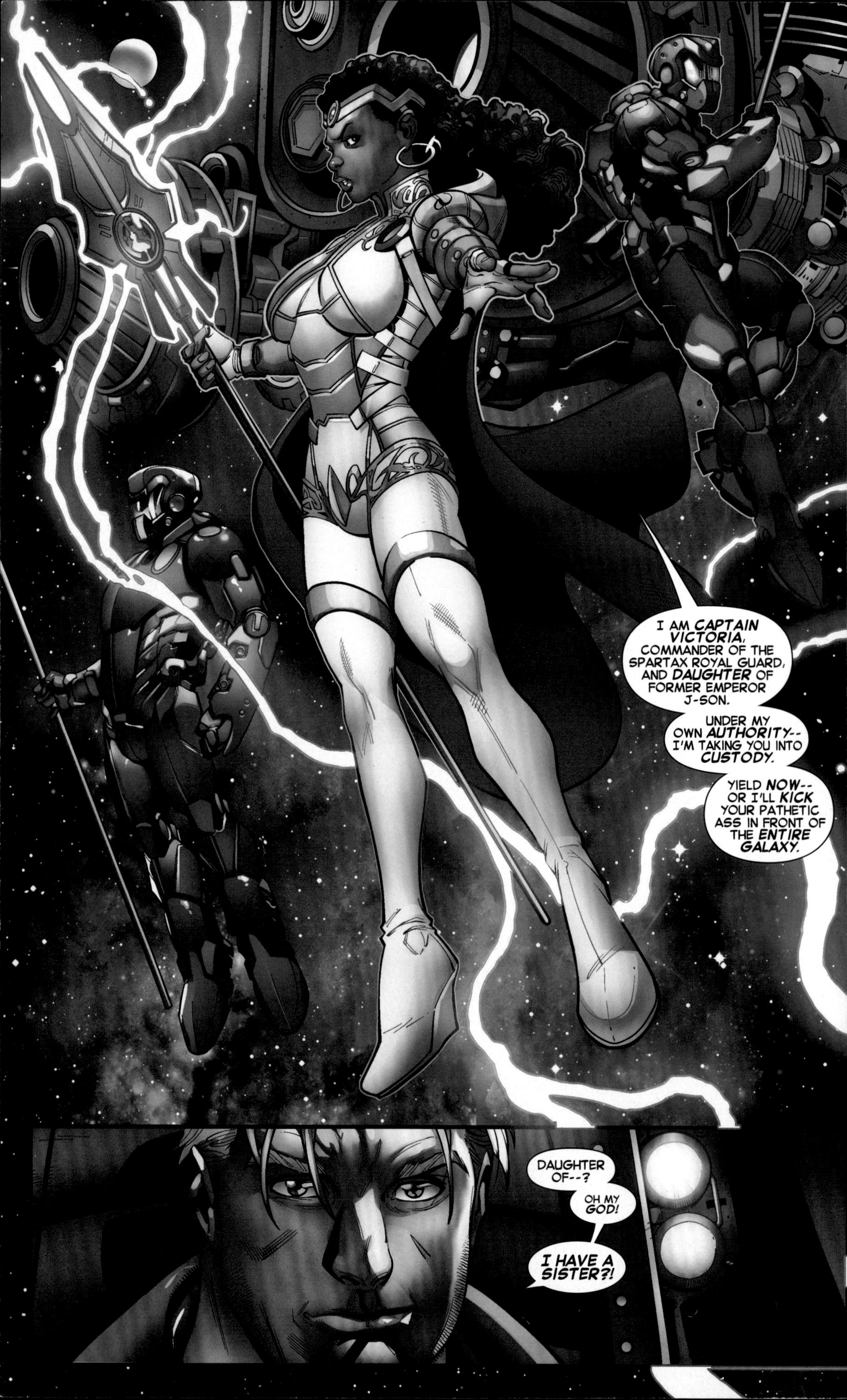
I AM CAPTAIN VICTORIA, COMMANDER OF THE SPARTAX ROYAL GUARD, AND DAUGHTER OF FORMER EMPEROR J-SON.
UNDER MY OWN AUTHORITY-- I'M TAKING YOU INTO CUSTODY.
YIELD NOW-- OR I'LL KICK YOUR PATHETIC ASS IN FRONT OF THE ENTIRE GALAXY.
DAUGHTER OF--?
OH MY GOD!
I HAVE A SISTER?!

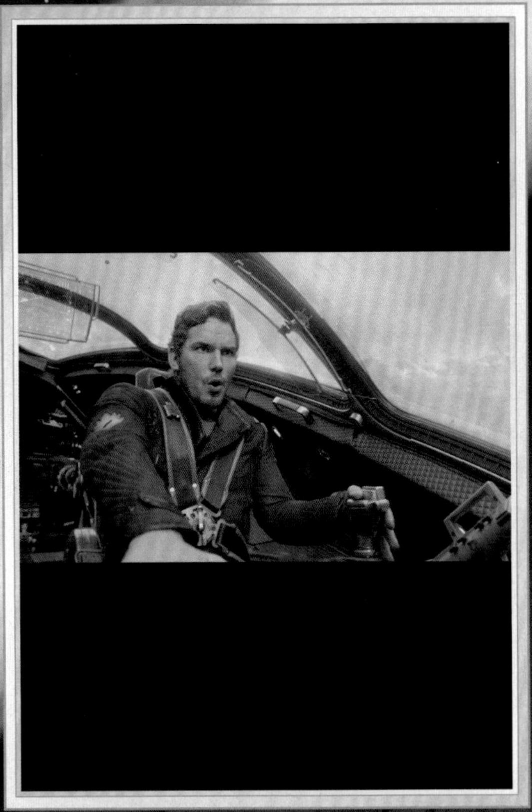

#1 MOVIE VARIANT

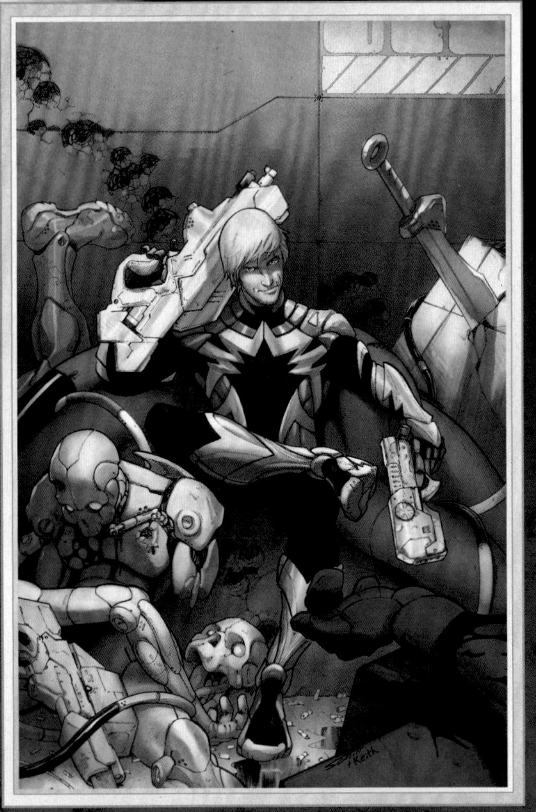

#1 VARIANT BY
VALERIO SCHITI & JASON KEITH

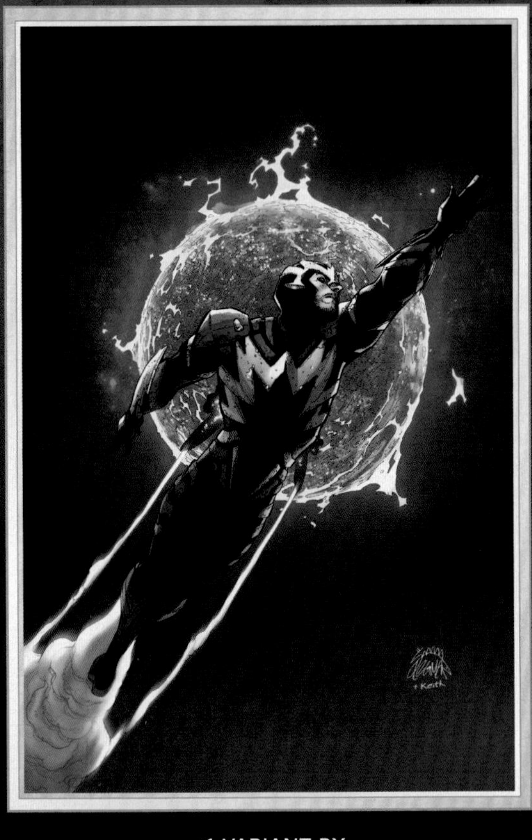

#1 VARIANT BY
RYAN STEGMAN & JASON KEITH

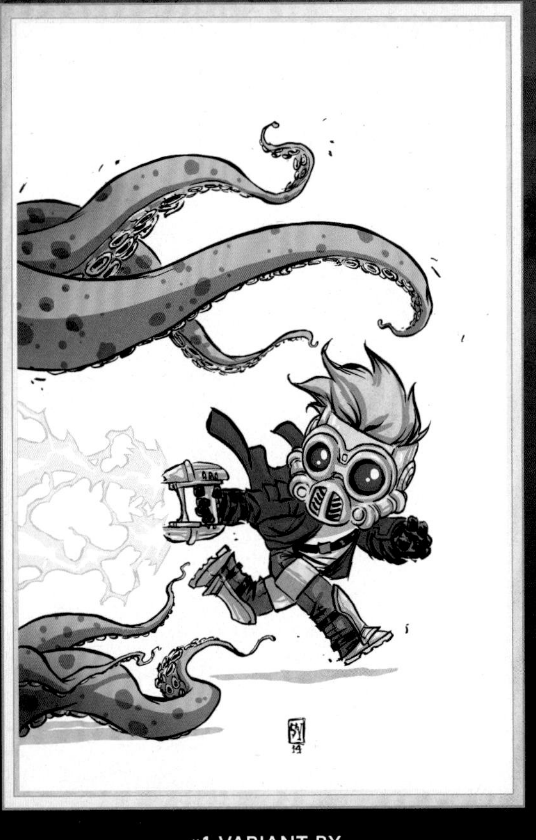

#1 VARIANT BY
SKOTTIE YOUNG

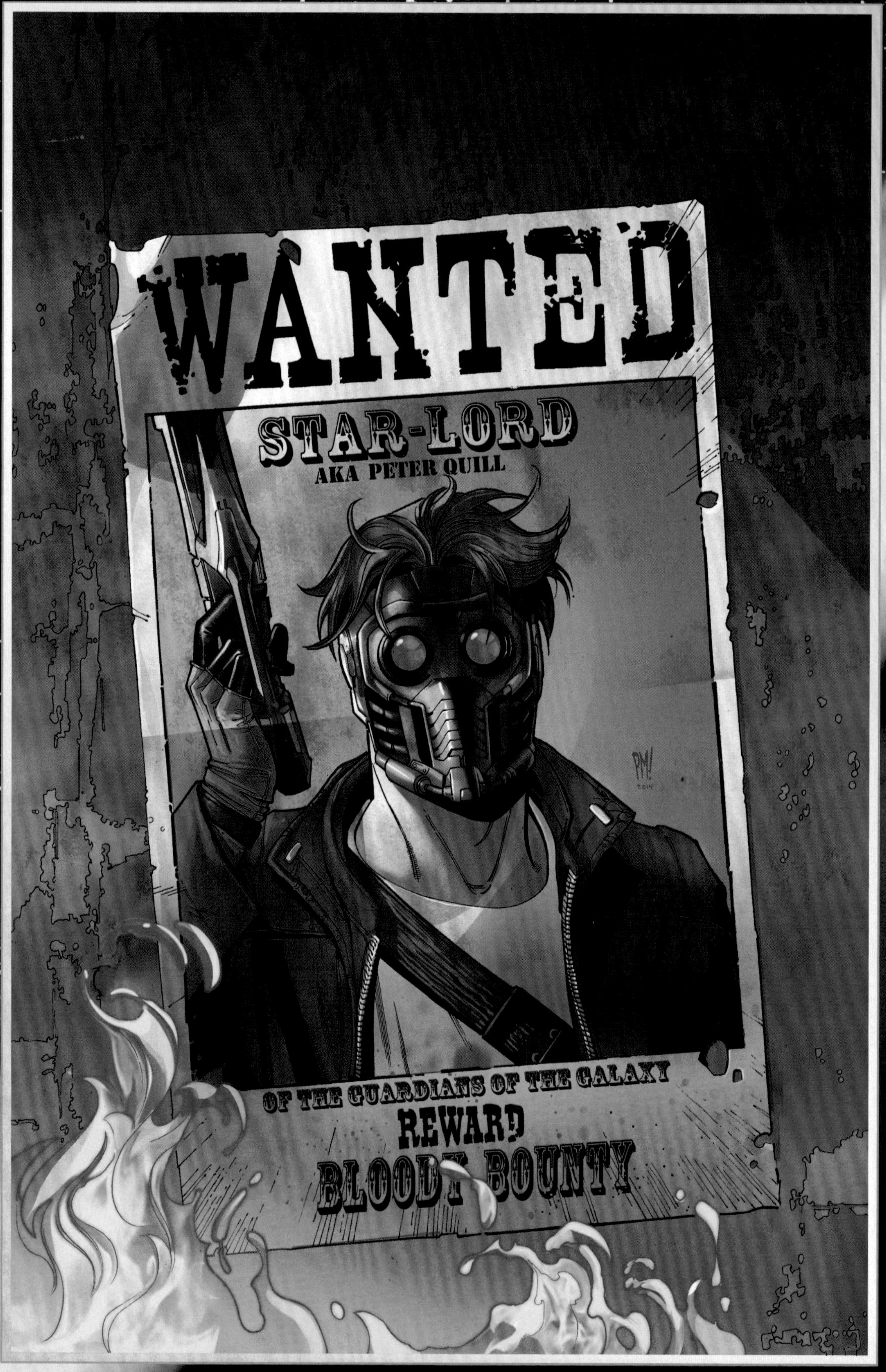
WANTED
STAR-LORD
AKA PETER QUILL
OF THE GUARDIANS OF THE GALAXY
REWARD
BLOODY BOUNTY

TWO

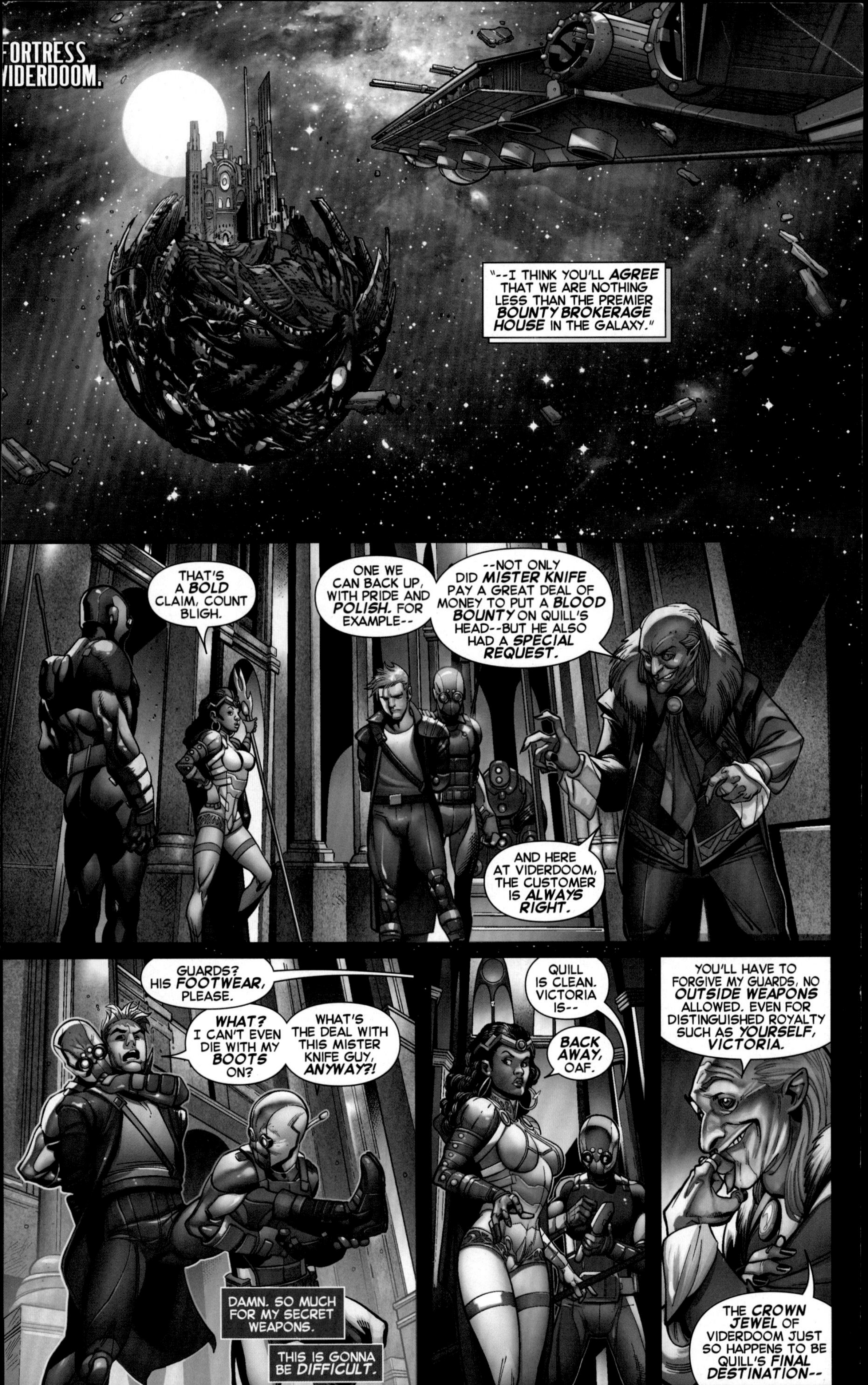
FORTRESS VIDERDOOM.
"--I THINK YOU'LL AGREE THAT WE ARE NOTHING LESS THAN THE PREMIER BOUNTY BROKERAGE HOUSE IN THE GALAXY."
THAT'S A BOLD CLAIM, COUNT BLIGH.
ONE WE CAN BACK UP, WITH PRIDE AND POLISH. FOR EXAMPLE--
--NOT ONLY DID MISTER KNIFE PAY A GREAT DEAL OF MONEY TO PUT A BLOOD BOUNTY ON QUILL'S HEAD--BUT HE ALSO HAD A SPECIAL REQUEST.
AND HERE AT VIDERDOOM, THE CUSTOMER IS ALWAYS RIGHT.
GUARDS? HIS FOOTWEAR, PLEASE.
WHAT? I CAN'T EVEN DIE WITH MY BOOTS ON?
WHAT'S THE DEAL WITH THIS MISTER KNIFE GUY, ANYWAY?!
DAMN. SO MUCH FOR MY SECRET WEAPONS.
THIS IS GONNA BE DIFFICULT.
QUILL IS CLEAN. VICTORIA IS--
BACK AWAY, OAF.
YOU'LL HAVE TO FORGIVE MY GUARDS, NO OUTSIDE WEAPONS ALLOWED. EVEN FOR DISTINGUISHED ROYALTY SUCH AS YOURSELF, VICTORIA.
THE CROWN JEWEL OF VIDERDOOM JUST SO HAPPENS TO BE QUILL'S FINAL DESTINATION--

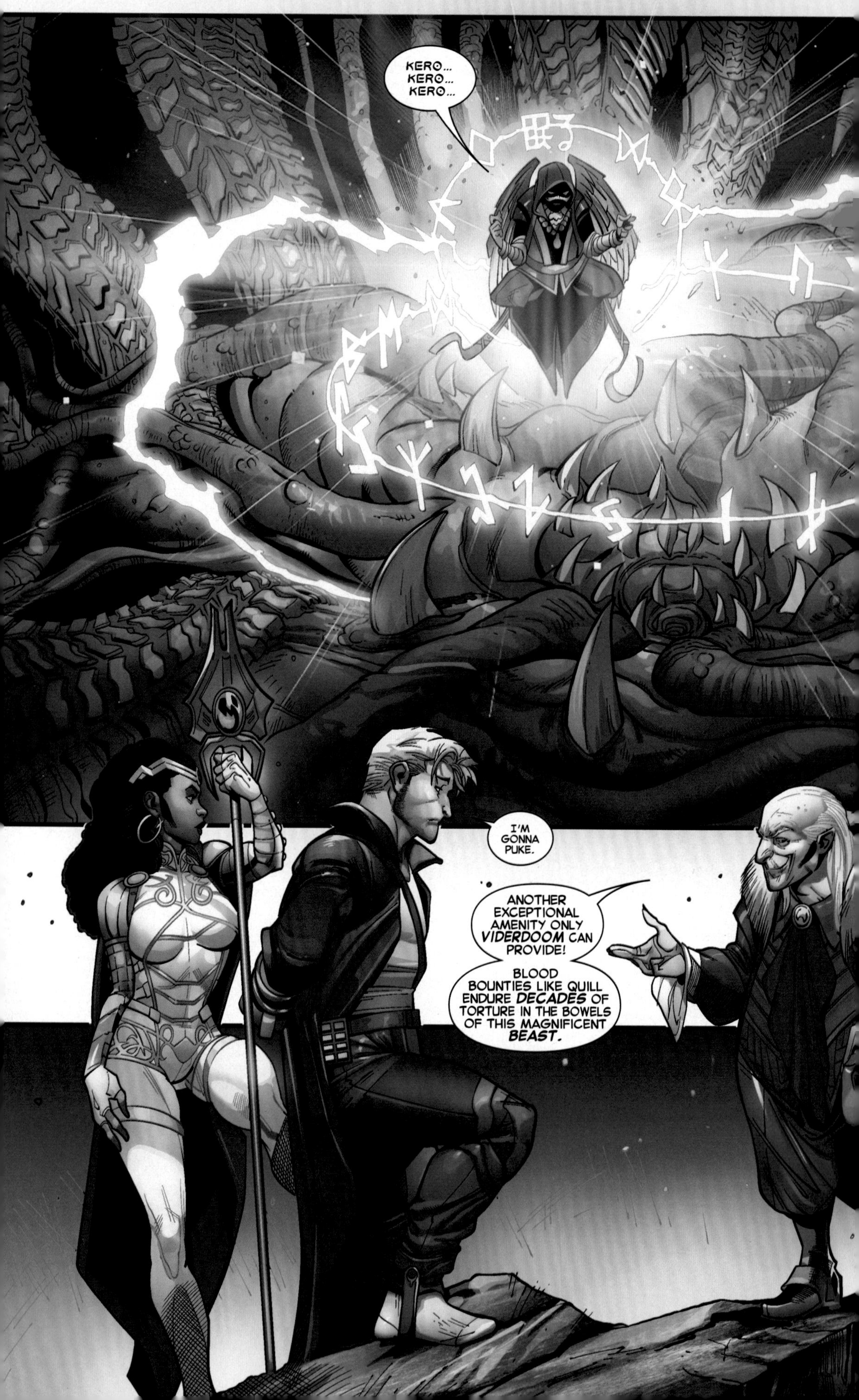
KERO... KERO... KERO...
I'M GONNA PUKE.
ANOTHER EXCEPTIONAL AMENITY ONLY *VIDERDOOM* CAN PROVIDE!
BLOOD BOUNTIES LIKE QUILL ENDURE *DECADES* OF TORTURE IN THE BOWELS OF THIS MAGNIFICENT *BEAST.*

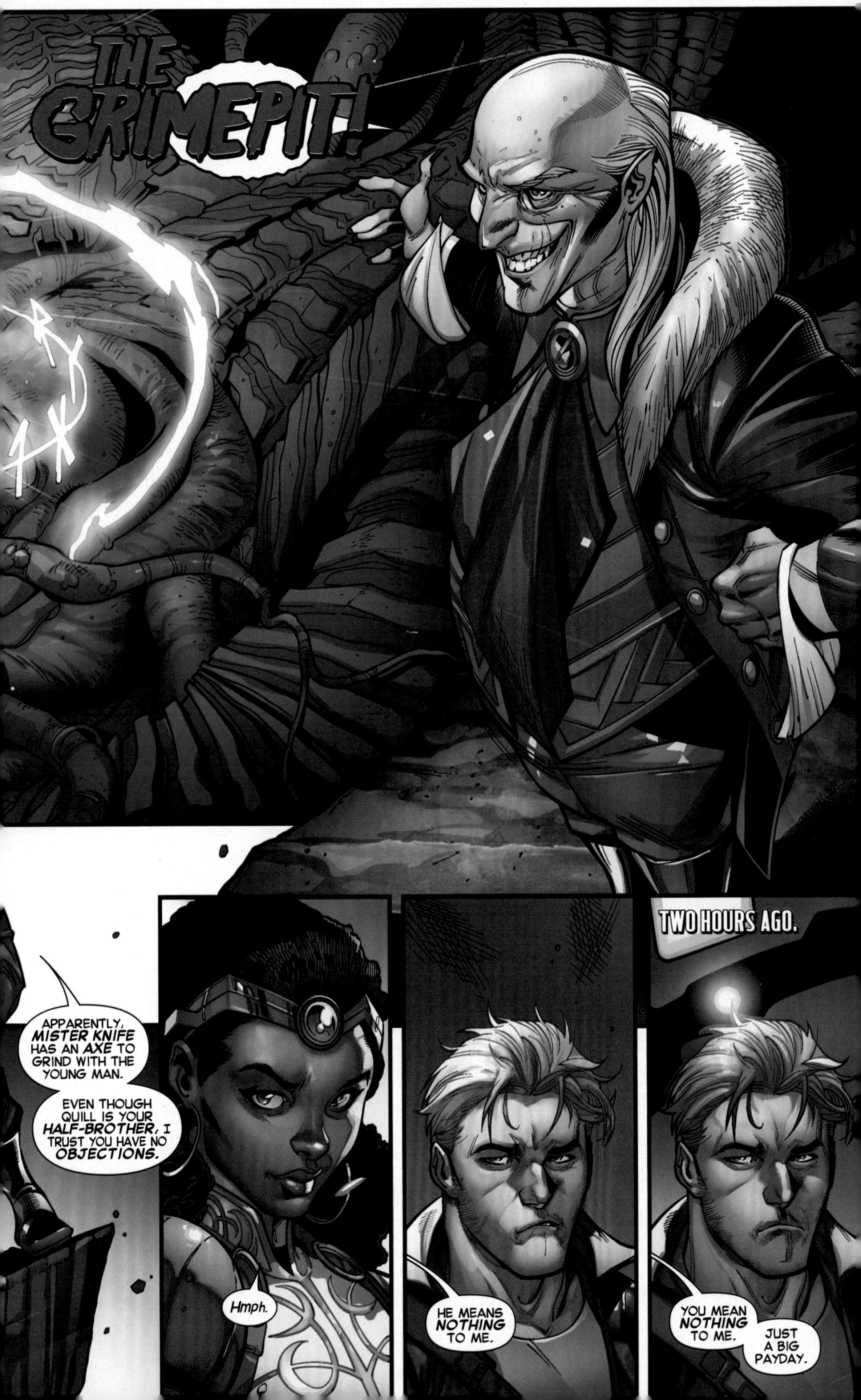
THE GRIMEPIT!
TWO HOURS AGO.
APPARENTLY, MISTER KNIFE HAS AN AXE TO GRIND WITH THE YOUNG MAN.
EVEN THOUGH QUILL IS YOUR HALF-BROTHER, I TRUST YOU HAVE NO OBJECTIONS.
Hmph.
HE MEANS NOTHING TO ME.
YOU MEAN NOTHING TO ME.
JUST A BIG PAYDAY.

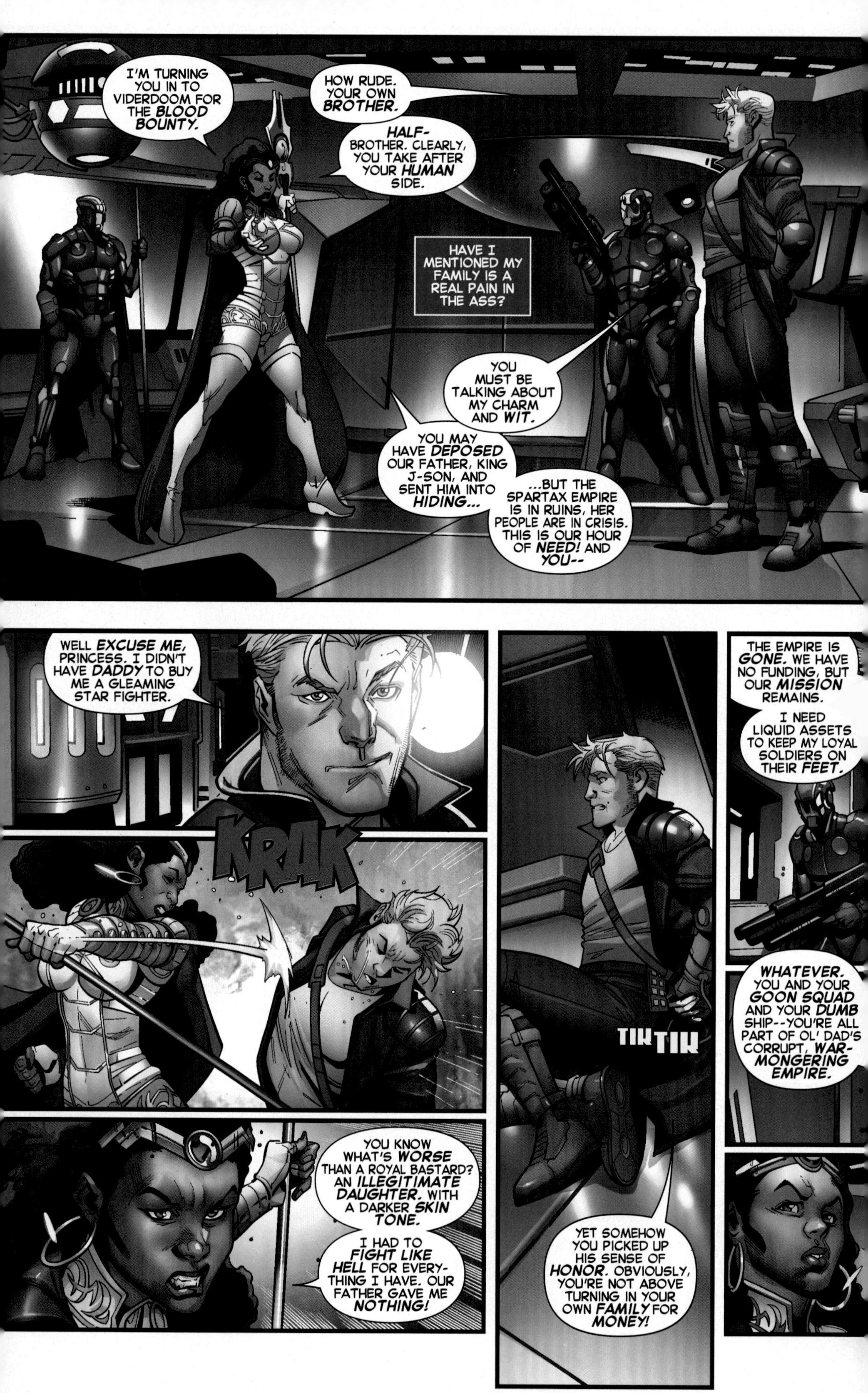
I'M TURNING YOU IN TO VIDERDOOM FOR THE BLOOD BOUNTY.
HOW RUDE. YOUR OWN BROTHER.
HALF-BROTHER. CLEARLY, YOU TAKE AFTER YOUR HUMAN SIDE.
HAVE I MENTIONED MY FAMILY IS A REAL PAIN IN THE ASS?
YOU MUST BE TALKING ABOUT MY CHARM AND WIT.
YOU MAY HAVE DEPOSED OUR FATHER, KING J-SON, AND SENT HIM INTO HIDING...
...BUT THE SPARTAX EMPIRE IS IN RUINS, HER PEOPLE ARE IN CRISIS. THIS IS OUR HOUR OF NEED! AND YOU--
WELL EXCUSE ME, PRINCESS. I DIDN'T HAVE DADDY TO BUY ME A GLEAMING STAR FIGHTER.
KRAK
YOU KNOW WHAT'S WORSE THAN A ROYAL BASTARD? AN ILLEGITIMATE DAUGHTER. WITH A DARKER SKIN TONE.
I HAD TO FIGHT LIKE HELL FOR EVERY-THING I HAVE. OUR FATHER GAVE ME NOTHING!
THE EMPIRE IS GONE. WE HAVE NO FUNDING, BUT OUR MISSION REMAINS.
I NEED LIQUID ASSETS TO KEEP MY LOYAL SOLDIERS ON THEIR FEET.
TIK TIK
WHATEVER. YOU AND YOUR GOON SQUAD AND YOUR DUMB SHIP--YOU'RE ALL PART OF OL' DAD'S CORRUPT, WAR-MONGERING EMPIRE.
YET SOMEHOW YOU PICKED UP HIS SENSE OF HONOR. OBVIOUSLY, YOU'RE NOT ABOVE TURNING IN YOUR OWN FAMILY FOR MONEY!

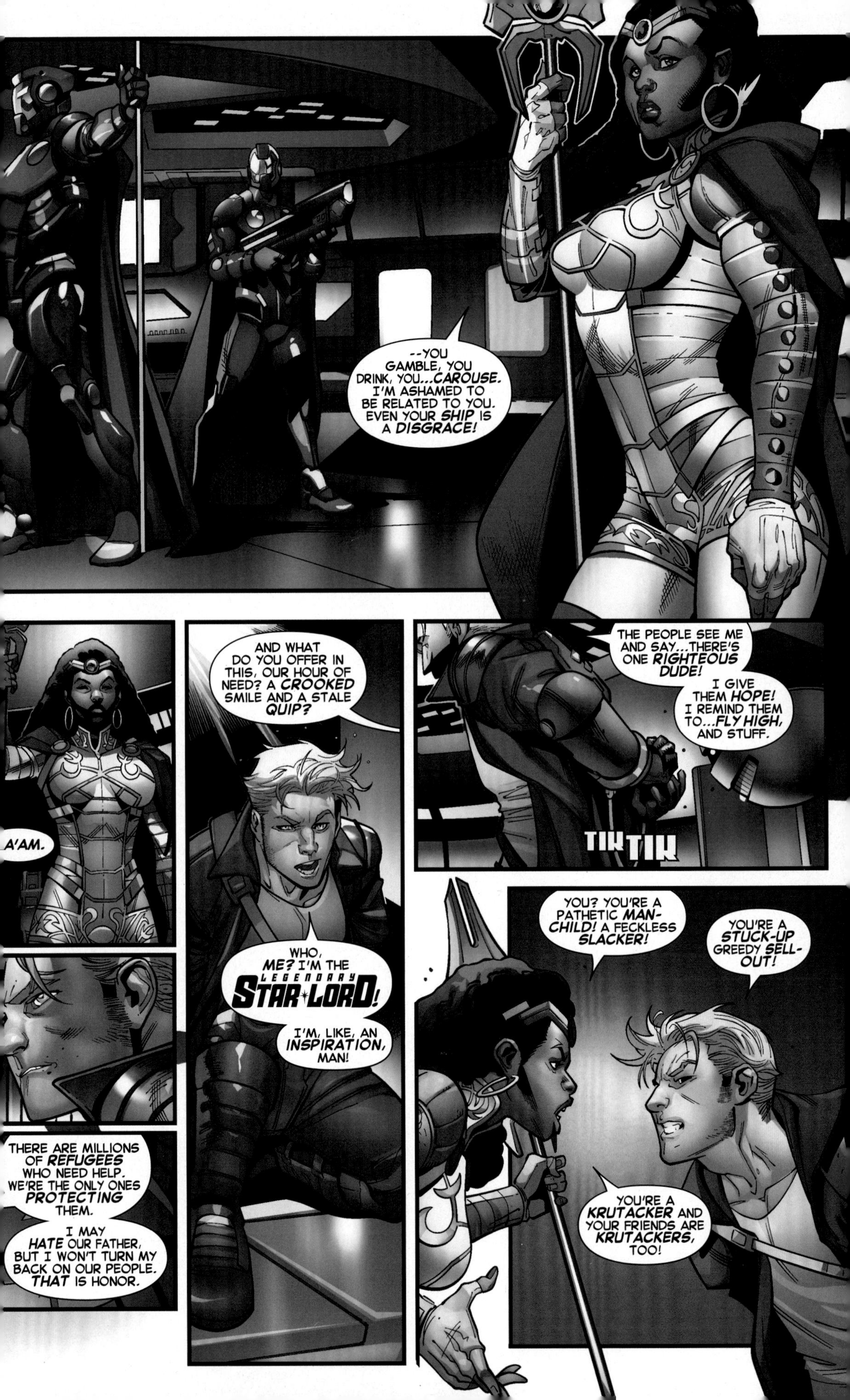
--YOU GAMBLE, YOU DRINK, YOU...CAROUSE. I'M ASHAMED TO BE RELATED TO YOU. EVEN YOUR SHIP IS A DISGRACE!
A'AM.
AND WHAT DO YOU OFFER IN THIS, OUR HOUR OF NEED? A CROOKED SMILE AND A STALE QUIP?
WHO, ME? I'M THE LEGENDARY STAR-LORD!
I'M, LIKE, AN INSPIRATION, MAN!
THE PEOPLE SEE ME AND SAY...THERE'S ONE RIGHTEOUS DUDE!
I GIVE THEM HOPE! I REMIND THEM TO...FLY HIGH, AND STUFF.
TIK TIK
THERE ARE MILLIONS OF REFUGEES WHO NEED HELP. WE'RE THE ONLY ONES PROTECTING THEM.
I MAY HATE OUR FATHER, BUT I WON'T TURN MY BACK ON OUR PEOPLE. THAT IS HONOR.
YOU? YOU'RE A PATHETIC MAN-CHILD! A FECKLESS SLACKER!
YOU'RE A STUCK-UP GREEDY SELL-OUT!
YOU'RE A KRUTACKER AND YOUR FRIENDS ARE KRUTACKERS, TOO!

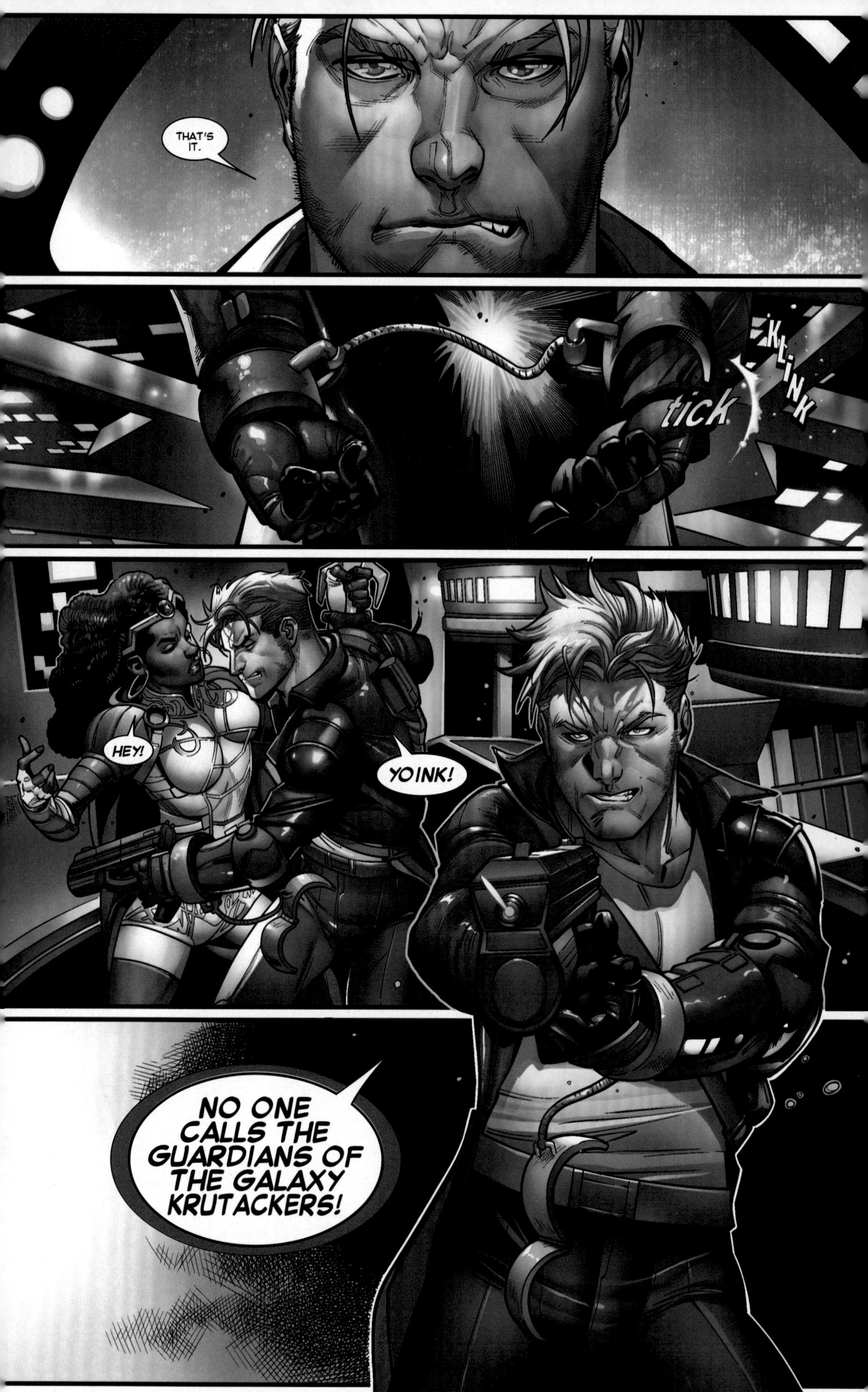
THAT'S IT.
KLINK
tick
HEY!
YOINK!
NO ONE CALLS THE GUARDIANS OF THE GALAXY KRUTACKERS!

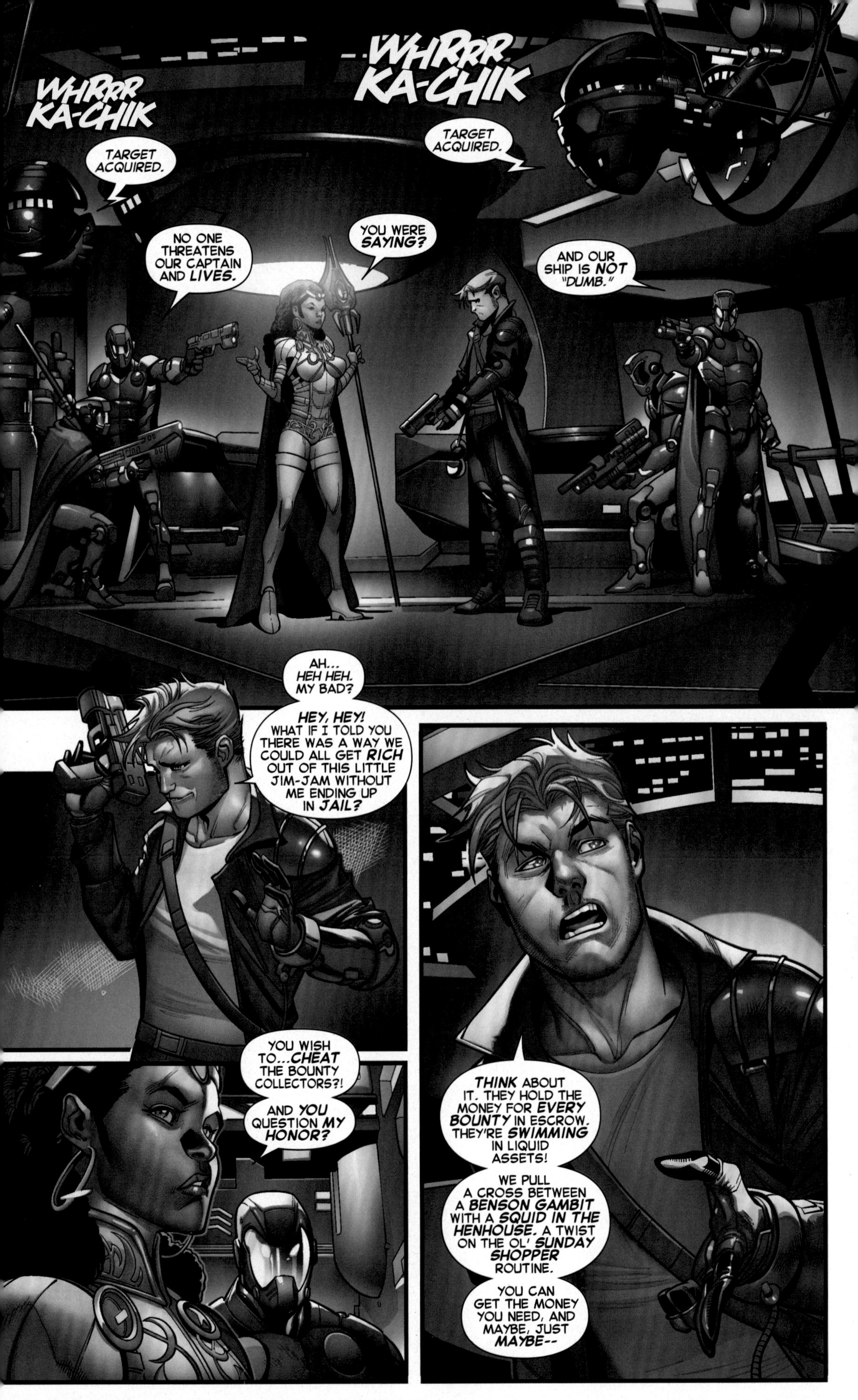
WHRRR KA-CHIK
TARGET ACQUIRED.
WHRRR KA-CHIK
TARGET ACQUIRED.
NO ONE THREATENS OUR CAPTAIN AND LIVES.
YOU WERE SAYING?
AND OUR SHIP IS NOT "DUMB."
AH... HEH HEH. MY BAD?
HEY, HEY! WHAT IF I TOLD YOU THERE WAS A WAY WE COULD ALL GET RICH OUT OF THIS LITTLE JIM-JAM WITHOUT ME ENDING UP IN JAIL?
YOU WISH TO...CHEAT THE BOUNTY COLLECTORS?!
AND YOU QUESTION MY HONOR?
THINK ABOUT IT. THEY HOLD THE MONEY FOR EVERY BOUNTY IN ESCROW. THEY'RE SWIMMING IN LIQUID ASSETS!
WE PULL A CROSS BETWEEN A BENSON GAMBIT WITH A SQUID IN THE HENHOUSE. A TWIST ON THE OL' SUNDAY SHOPPER ROUTINE.
YOU CAN GET THE MONEY YOU NEED, AND MAYBE, JUST MAYBE--

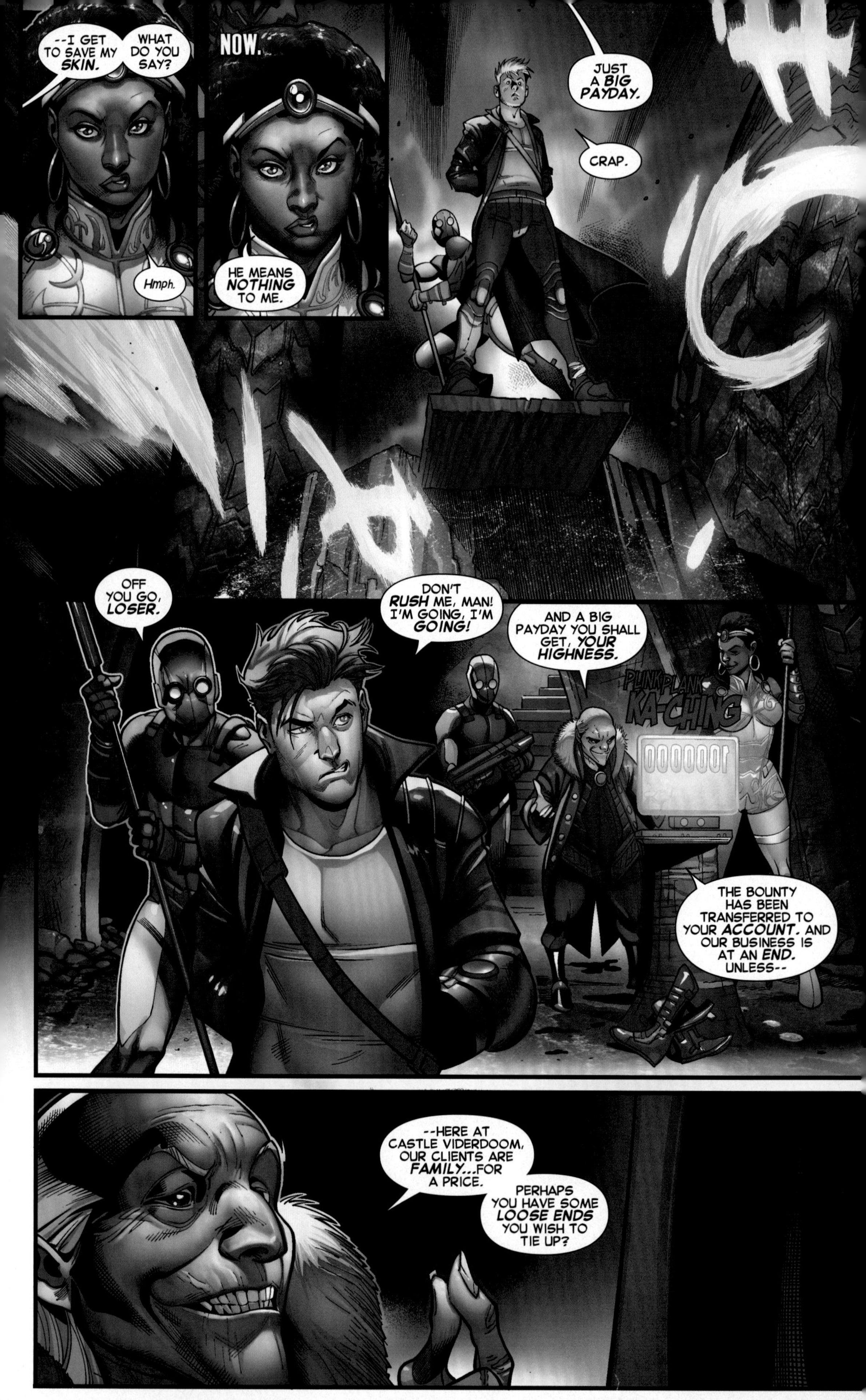
--I GET TO SAVE MY SKIN.
WHAT DO YOU SAY?
Hmph.
NOW.
HE MEANS NOTHING TO ME.
JUST A BIG PAYDAY.
CRAP.
OFF YOU GO, LOSER.
DON'T RUSH ME, MAN! I'M GOING, I'M GOING!
AND A BIG PAYDAY YOU SHALL GET, YOUR HIGHNESS.
PLINK PLANK KA-CHING
THE BOUNTY HAS BEEN TRANSFERRED TO YOUR ACCOUNT. AND OUR BUSINESS IS AT AN END. UNLESS--
--HERE AT CASTLE VIDERDOOM, OUR CLIENTS ARE FAMILY...FOR A PRICE.
PERHAPS YOU HAVE SOME LOOSE ENDS YOU WISH TO TIE UP?

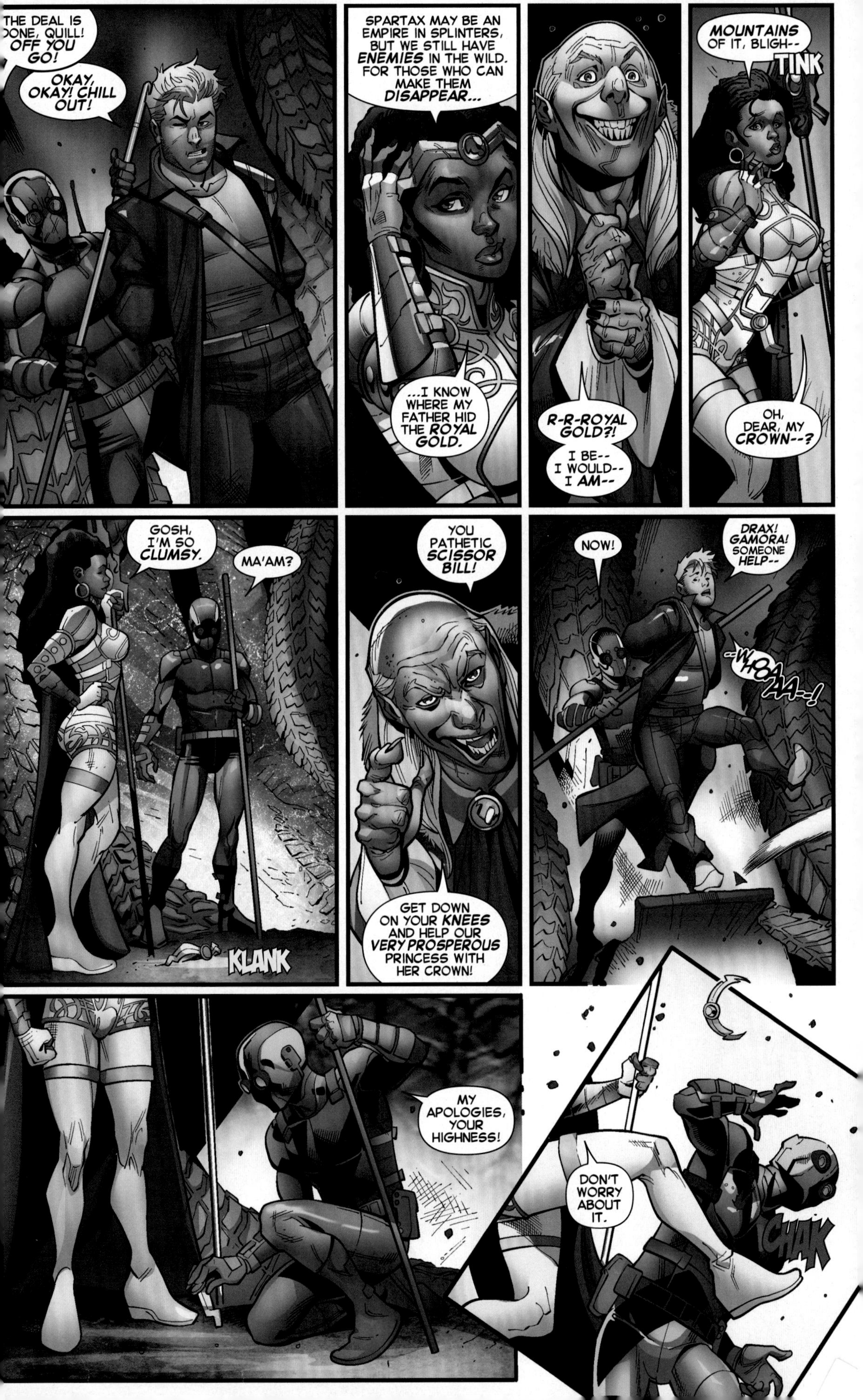
THE DEAL IS DONE, QUILL! OFF YOU GO!
OKAY, OKAY! CHILL OUT!
SPARTAX MAY BE AN EMPIRE IN SPLINTERS, BUT WE STILL HAVE ENEMIES IN THE WILD. FOR THOSE WHO CAN MAKE THEM DISAPPEAR...
...I KNOW WHERE MY FATHER HID THE ROYAL GOLD.
R-R-ROYAL GOLD?!
I BE-- I WOULD-- I AM--
MOUNTAINS OF IT, BLIGH--
TINK
OH, DEAR, MY CROWN--?
GOSH, I'M SO CLUMSY.
MA'AM?
KLANK
YOU PATHETIC SCISSOR BILL!
GET DOWN ON YOUR KNEES AND HELP OUR VERY PROSPEROUS PRINCESS WITH HER CROWN!
NOW!
DRAX! GAMORA! SOMEONE HELP--
--WHOAAAA--!
MY APOLOGIES, YOUR HIGHNESS!
DON'T WORRY ABOUT IT.
CHAK

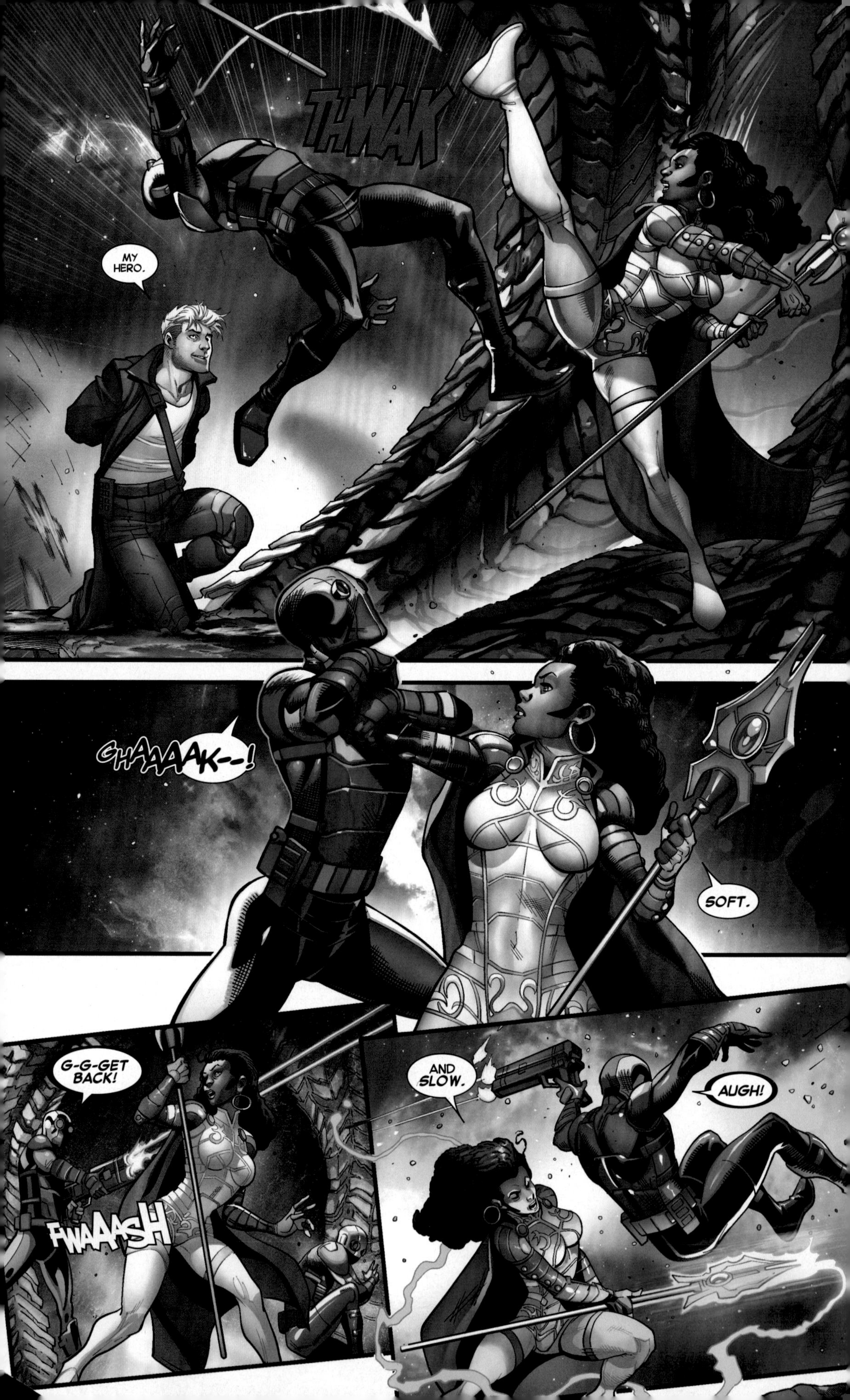
THWAK
MY HERO.
GHAAAAK--!
SOFT.
G-G-GET BACK!
FWAAASH
AND SLOW.
AUGH!

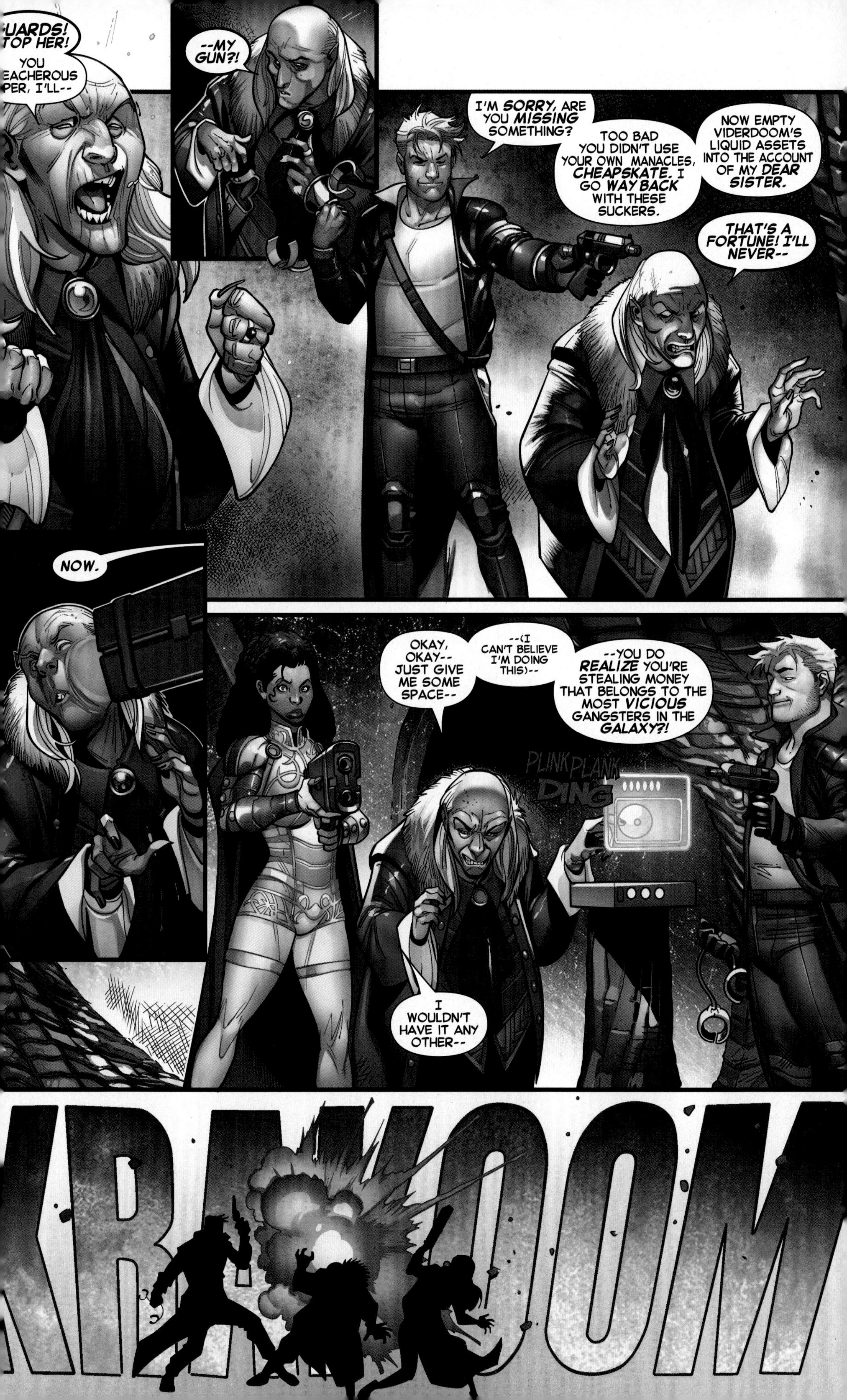
GUARDS! STOP HER! YOU TREACHEROUS ...PER, I'LL--
--MY GUN?!
I'M SORRY, ARE YOU MISSING SOMETHING?
TOO BAD YOU DIDN'T USE YOUR OWN MANACLES, CHEAPSKATE. I GO WAY BACK WITH THESE SUCKERS.
NOW EMPTY VIDERDOOM'S LIQUID ASSETS INTO THE ACCOUNT OF MY DEAR SISTER.
THAT'S A FORTUNE! I'LL NEVER--
NOW.
OKAY, OKAY-- JUST GIVE ME SOME SPACE--
--(I CAN'T BELIEVE I'M DOING THIS)--
--YOU DO REALIZE YOU'RE STEALING MONEY THAT BELONGS TO THE MOST VICIOUS GANGSTERS IN THE GALAXY?!
PLINK PLANK DING
I WOULDN'T HAVE IT ANY OTHER--
KRAKOOM

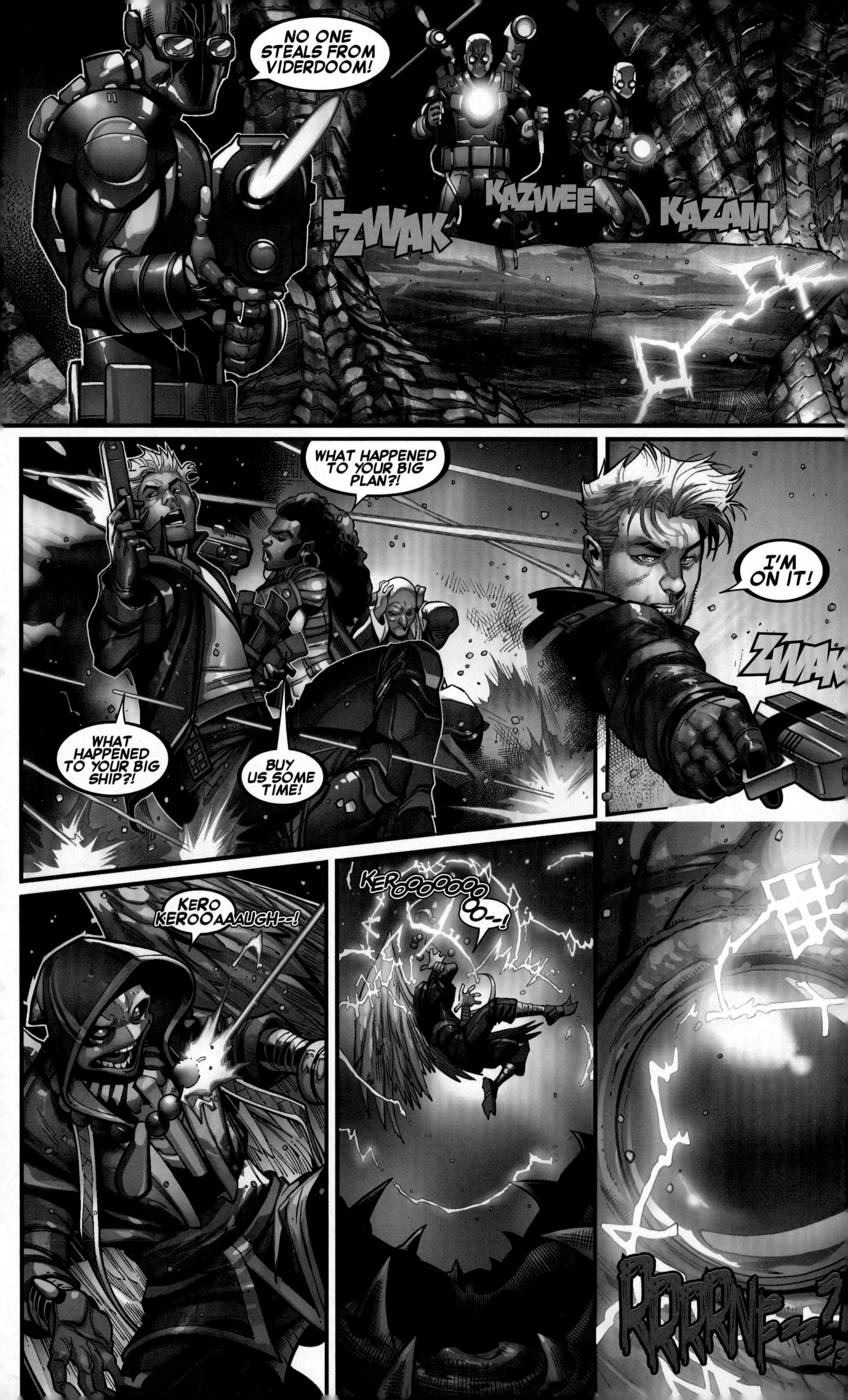
NO ONE STEALS FROM VIDERDOOM!
FZWAK
KAZWEE
KAZAM
WHAT HAPPENED TO YOUR BIG PLAN?!
WHAT HAPPENED TO YOUR BIG SHIP?!
BUY US SOME TIME!
I'M ON IT!
ZWAK
KERO KEROOAAAUGH--!
KEROOOOOOOOOO--!
RRRRN--?

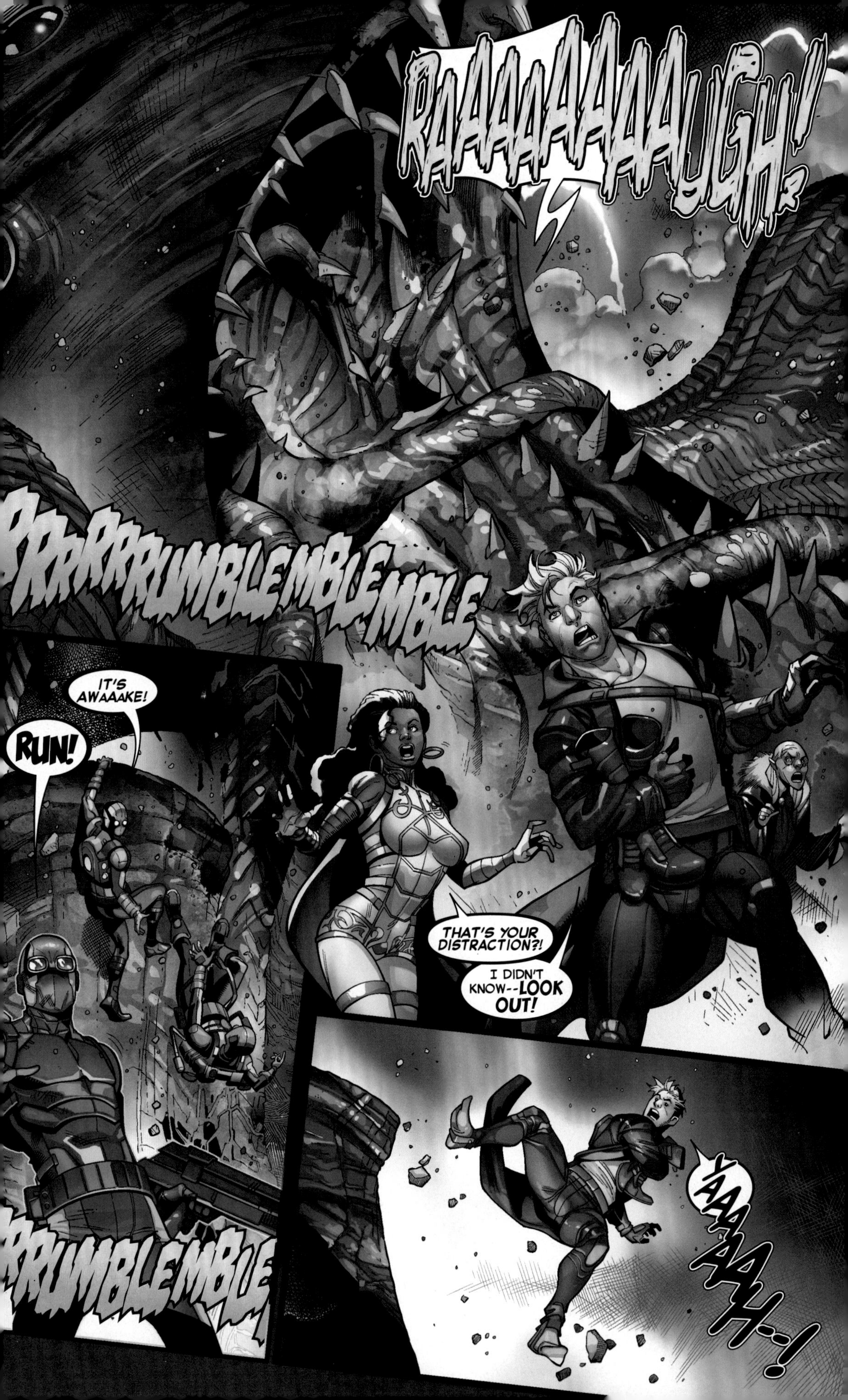
RAAAAAAAAAAUGH!
RRRRRRRUMBLEMBLEMBLE
IT'S AWAAAKE!
RUN!
THAT'S YOUR DISTRACTION?!
I DIDN'T KNOW--LOOK OUT!
RRUMBLEMBLE
YAAAAAH--!

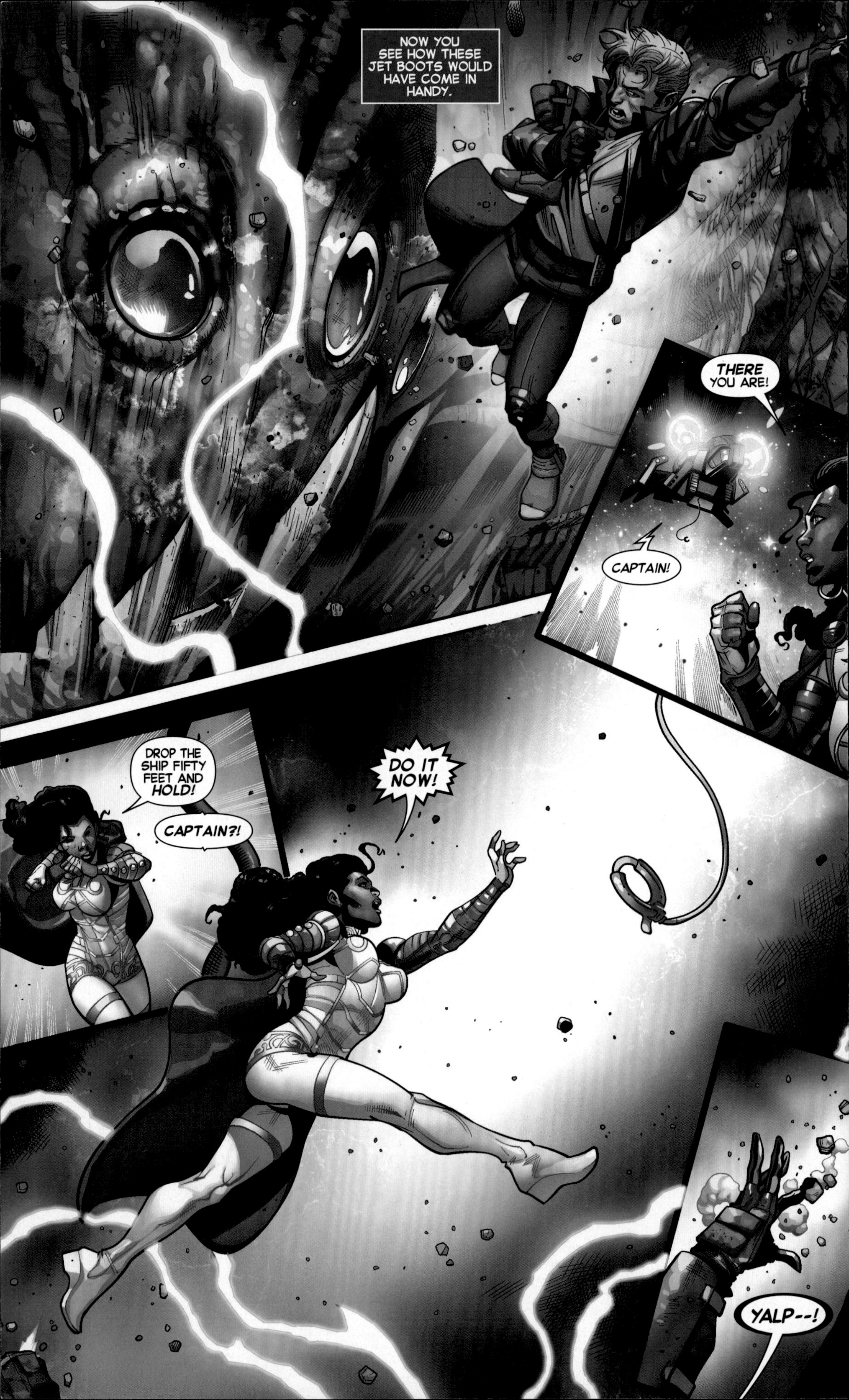
NOW YOU SEE HOW THESE JET BOOTS WOULD HAVE COME IN HANDY.
THERE YOU ARE!
CAPTAIN!
DROP THE SHIP FIFTY FEET AND HOLD!
CAPTAIN?!
DO IT NOW!
YALP--!

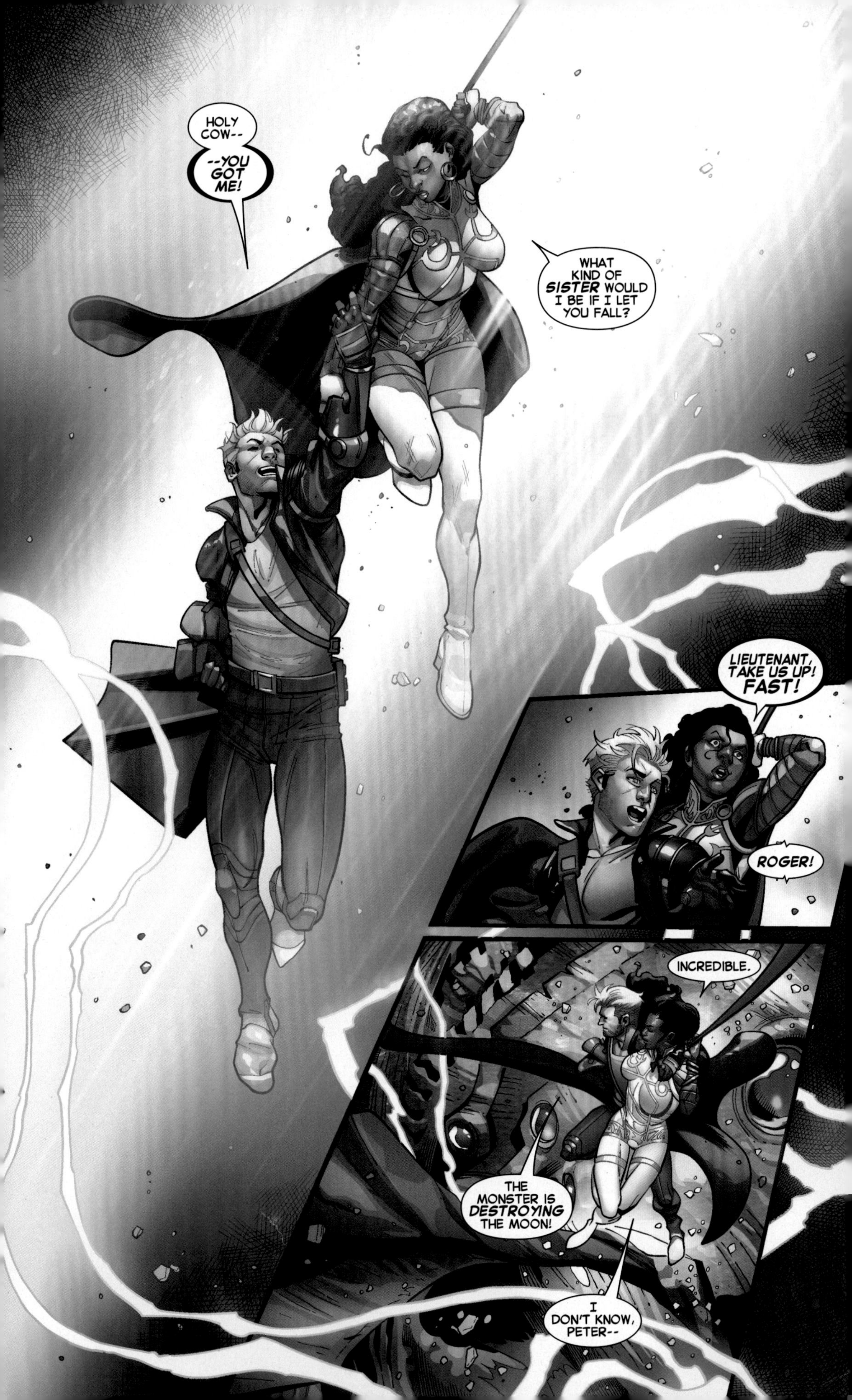
HOLY COW--
--YOU GOT ME!
WHAT KIND OF SISTER WOULD I BE IF I LET YOU FALL?
LIEUTENANT, TAKE US UP! FAST!
ROGER!
INCREDIBLE.
THE MONSTER IS DESTROYING THE MOON!
I DON'T KNOW, PETER--

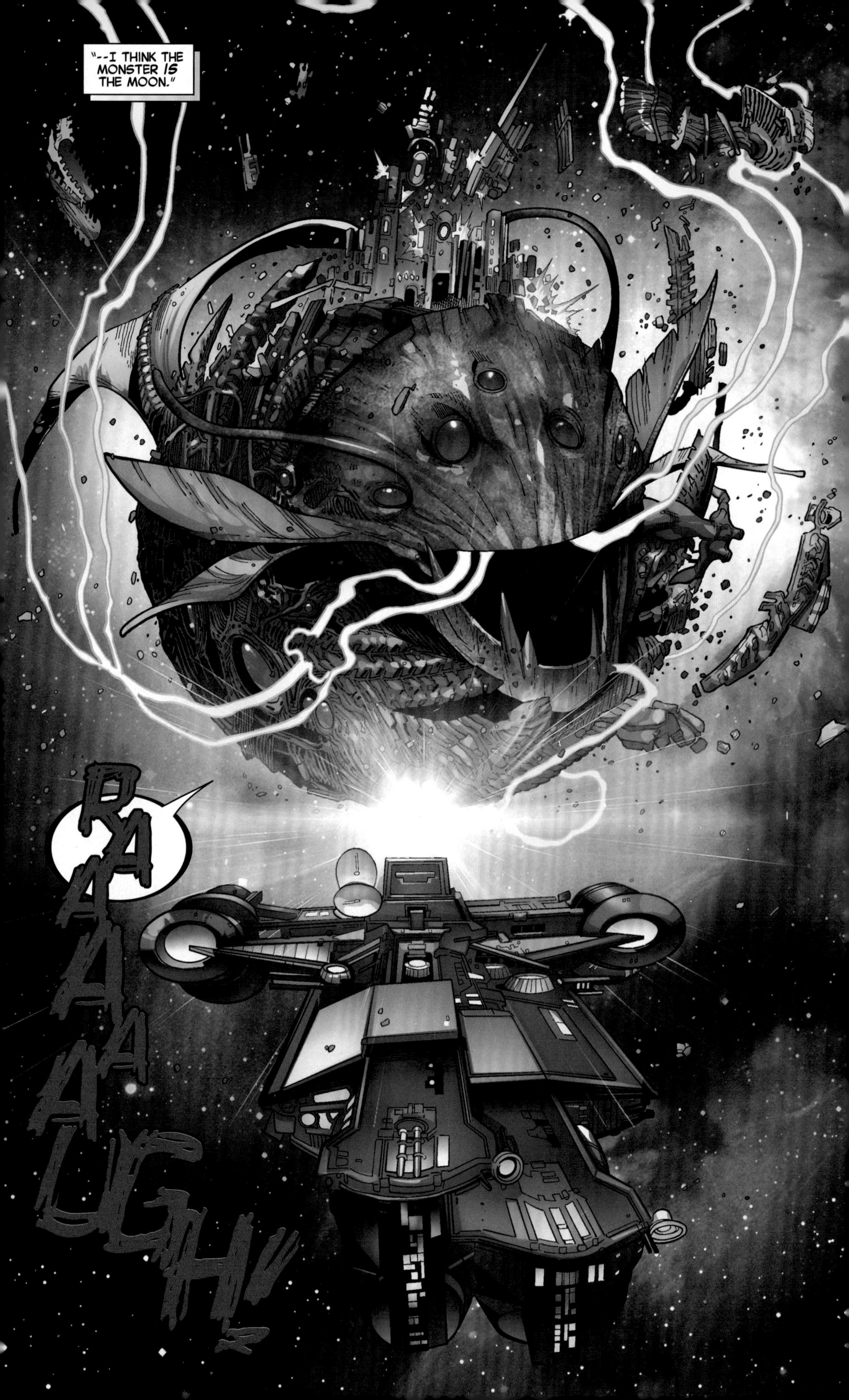
"--I THINK THE MONSTER IS THE MOON."
RAAAAAAAUGH!

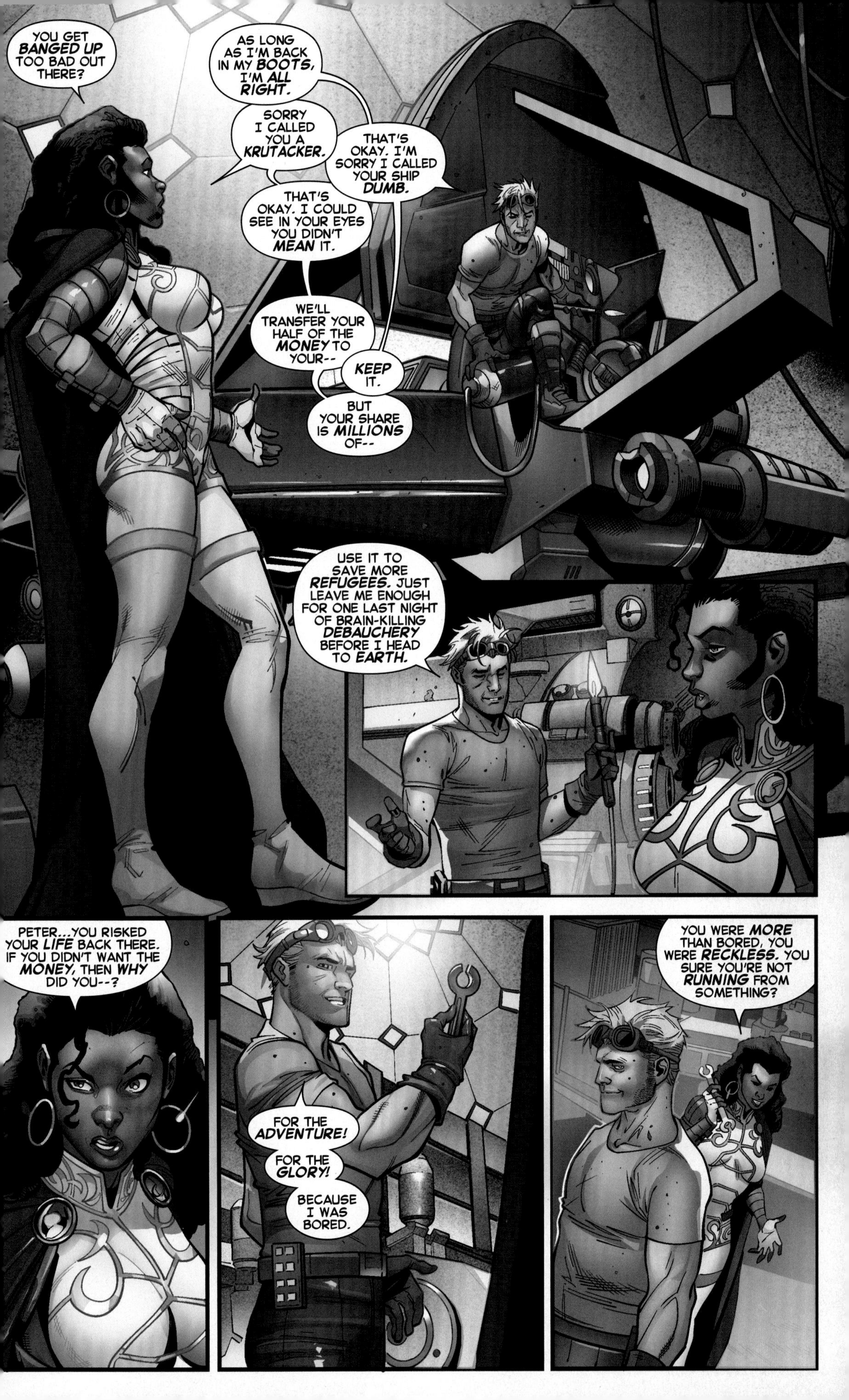
YOU GET BANGED UP TOO BAD OUT THERE?
AS LONG AS I'M BACK IN MY BOOTS, I'M ALL RIGHT.
SORRY I CALLED YOU A KRUTACKER.
THAT'S OKAY. I'M SORRY I CALLED YOUR SHIP DUMB.
THAT'S OKAY. I COULD SEE IN YOUR EYES YOU DIDN'T MEAN IT.
WE'LL TRANSFER YOUR HALF OF THE MONEY TO YOUR--
KEEP IT.
BUT YOUR SHARE IS MILLIONS OF--
USE IT TO SAVE MORE REFUGEES. JUST LEAVE ME ENOUGH FOR ONE LAST NIGHT OF BRAIN-KILLING DEBAUCHERY BEFORE I HEAD TO EARTH.
PETER...YOU RISKED YOUR LIFE BACK THERE. IF YOU DIDN'T WANT THE MONEY, THEN WHY DID YOU--?
FOR THE ADVENTURE!
FOR THE GLORY!
BECAUSE I WAS BORED.
YOU WERE MORE THAN BORED, YOU WERE RECKLESS. YOU SURE YOU'RE NOT RUNNING FROM SOMETHING?

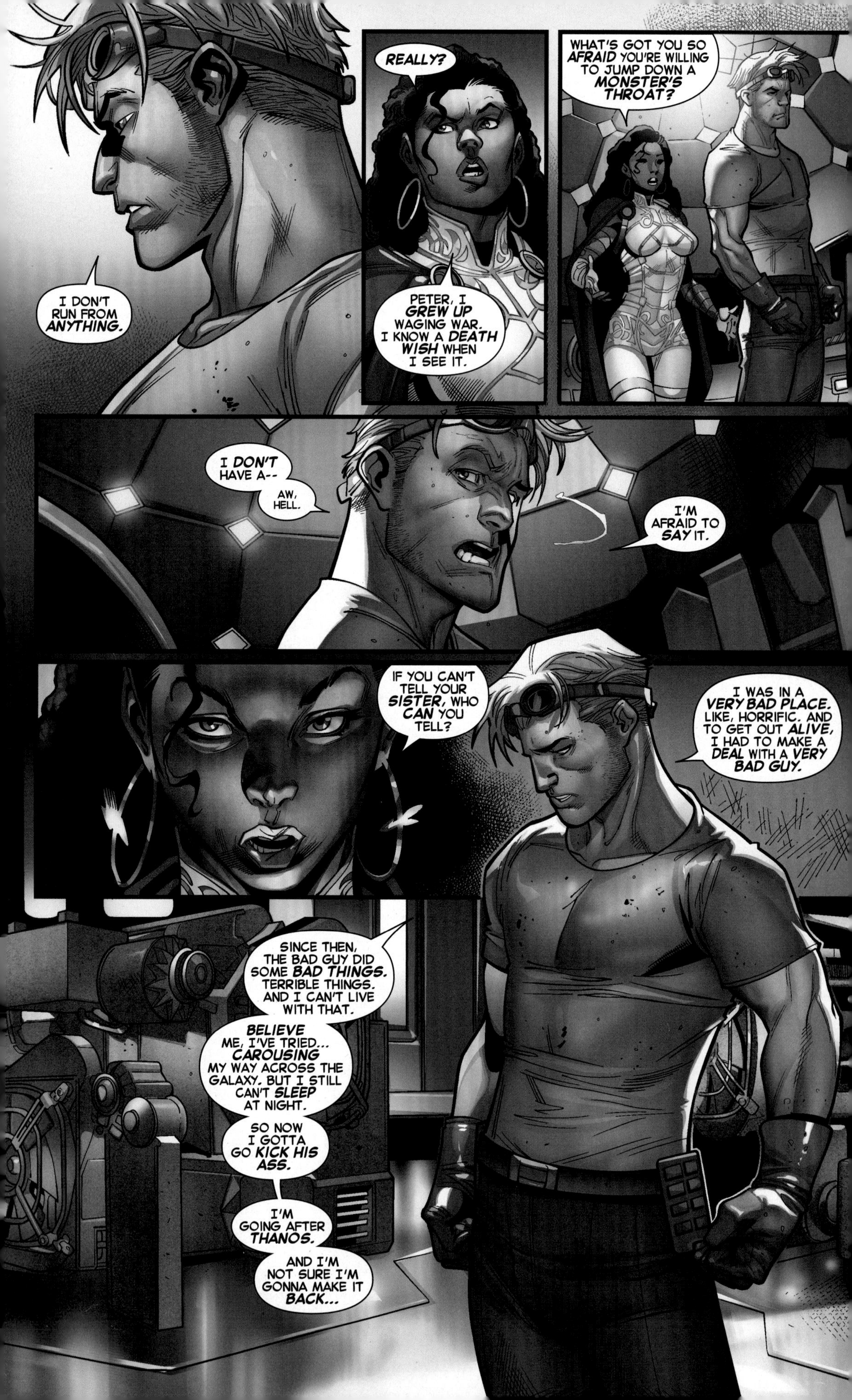
I DON'T RUN FROM ANYTHING.
REALLY?
PETER, I GREW UP WAGING WAR. I KNOW A DEATH WISH WHEN I SEE IT.
WHAT'S GOT YOU SO AFRAID YOU'RE WILLING TO JUMP DOWN A MONSTER'S THROAT?
I DON'T HAVE A--
AW, HELL.
I'M AFRAID TO SAY IT.
IF YOU CAN'T TELL YOUR SISTER, WHO CAN YOU TELL?
I WAS IN A VERY BAD PLACE. LIKE, HORRIFIC. AND TO GET OUT ALIVE, I HAD TO MAKE A DEAL WITH A VERY BAD GUY.
SINCE THEN, THE BAD GUY DID SOME BAD THINGS. TERRIBLE THINGS. AND I CAN'T LIVE WITH THAT.
BELIEVE ME, I'VE TRIED... CAROUSING MY WAY ACROSS THE GALAXY. BUT I STILL CAN'T SLEEP AT NIGHT.
SO NOW I GOTTA GO KICK HIS ASS.
I'M GOING AFTER THANOS.
AND I'M NOT SURE I'M GONNA MAKE IT BACK...

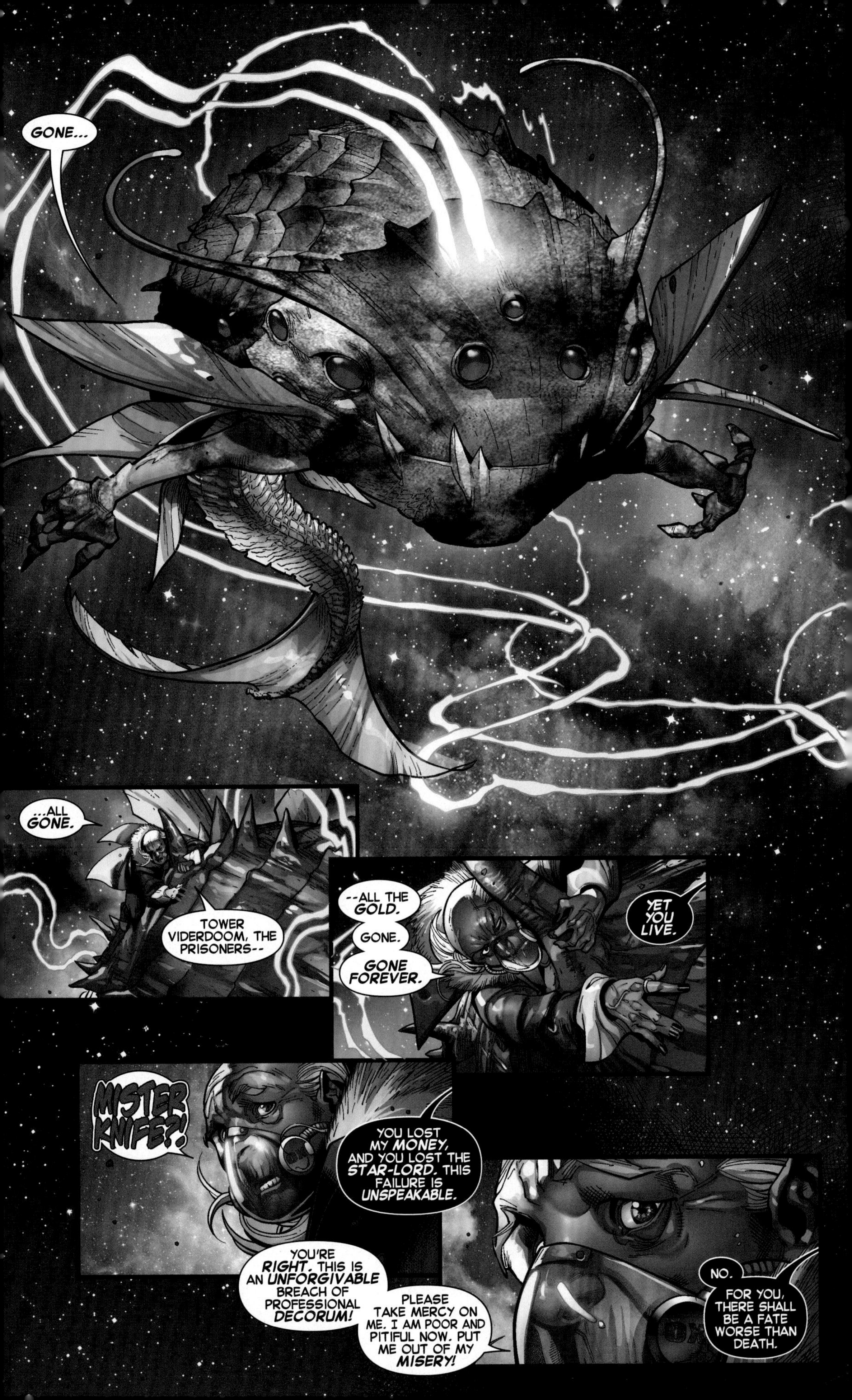
GONE...
...ALL GONE.
TOWER VIDERDOOM, THE PRISONERS--
--ALL THE GOLD.
GONE.
GONE FOREVER.
YET YOU LIVE.
MISTER KNIFE?!
YOU LOST MY MONEY, AND YOU LOST THE STAR-LORD. THIS FAILURE IS UNSPEAKABLE.
YOU'RE RIGHT. THIS IS AN UNFORGIVABLE BREACH OF PROFESSIONAL DECORUM!
PLEASE TAKE MERCY ON ME. I AM POOR AND PITIFUL NOW. PUT ME OUT OF MY MISERY!
NO.
FOR YOU, THERE SHALL BE A FATE WORSE THAN DEATH.

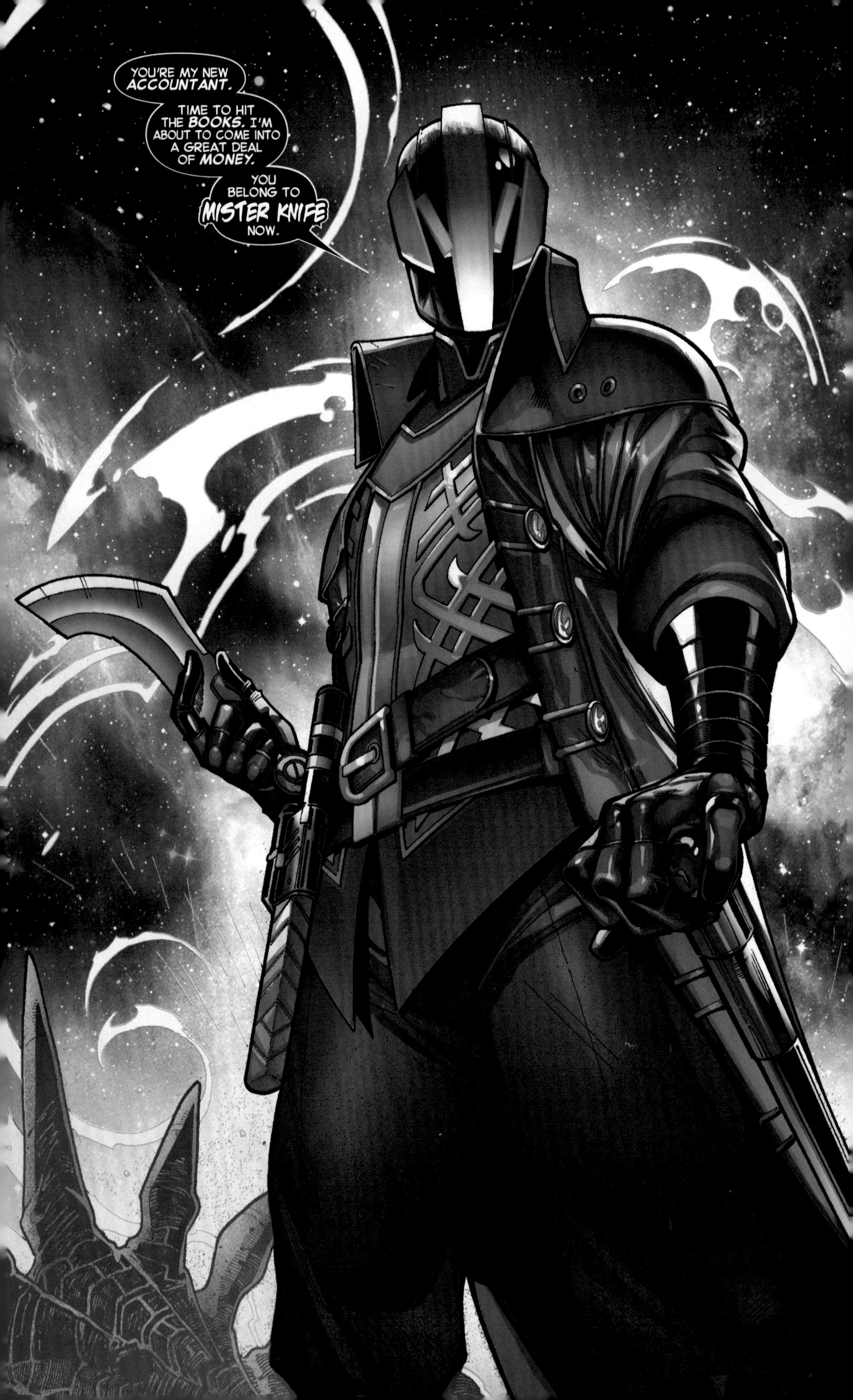
YOU'RE MY NEW ACCOUNTANT.
TIME TO HIT THE BOOKS. I'M ABOUT TO COME INTO A GREAT DEAL OF MONEY.
YOU BELONG TO MISTER KNIFE NOW.

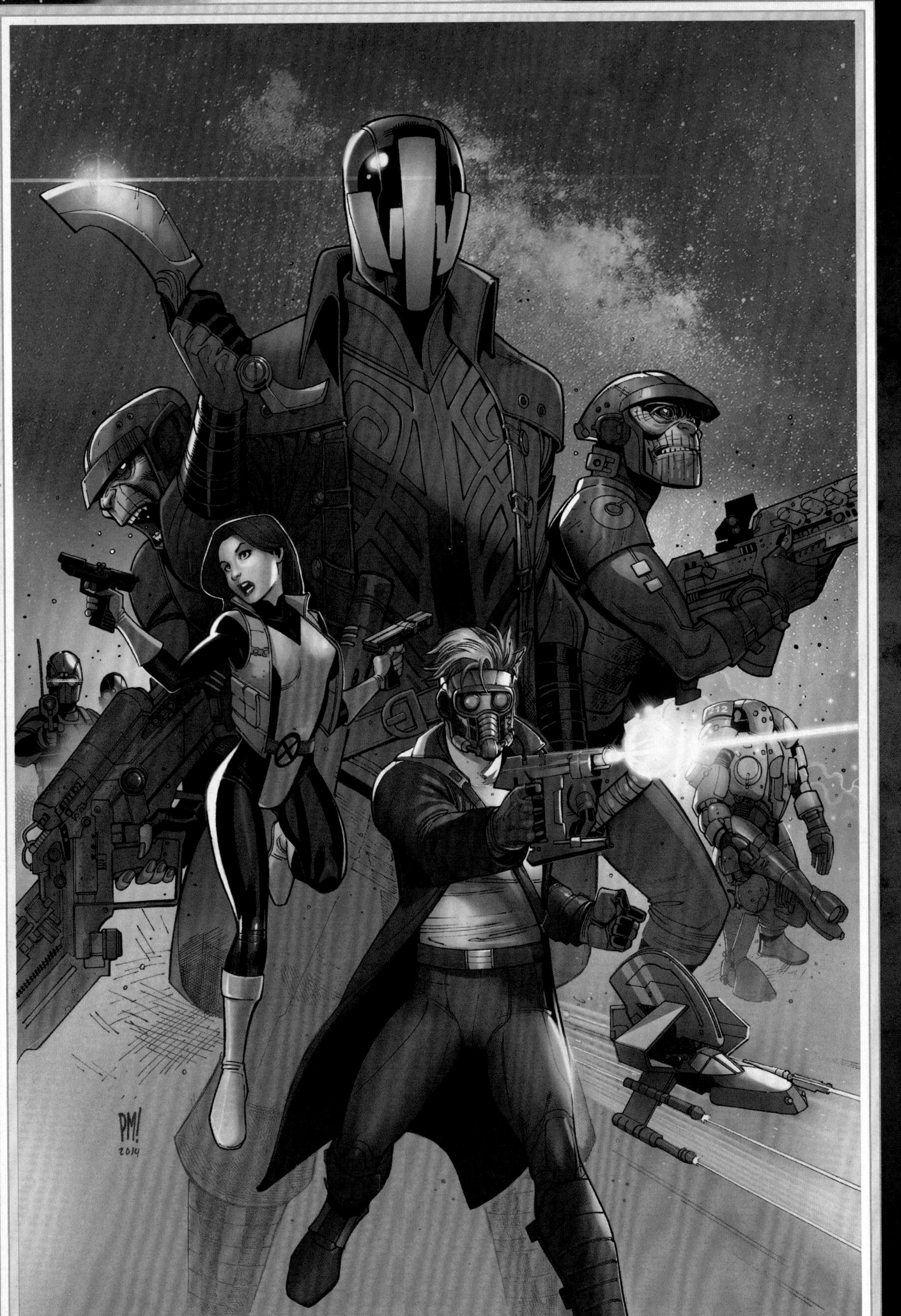

THREE

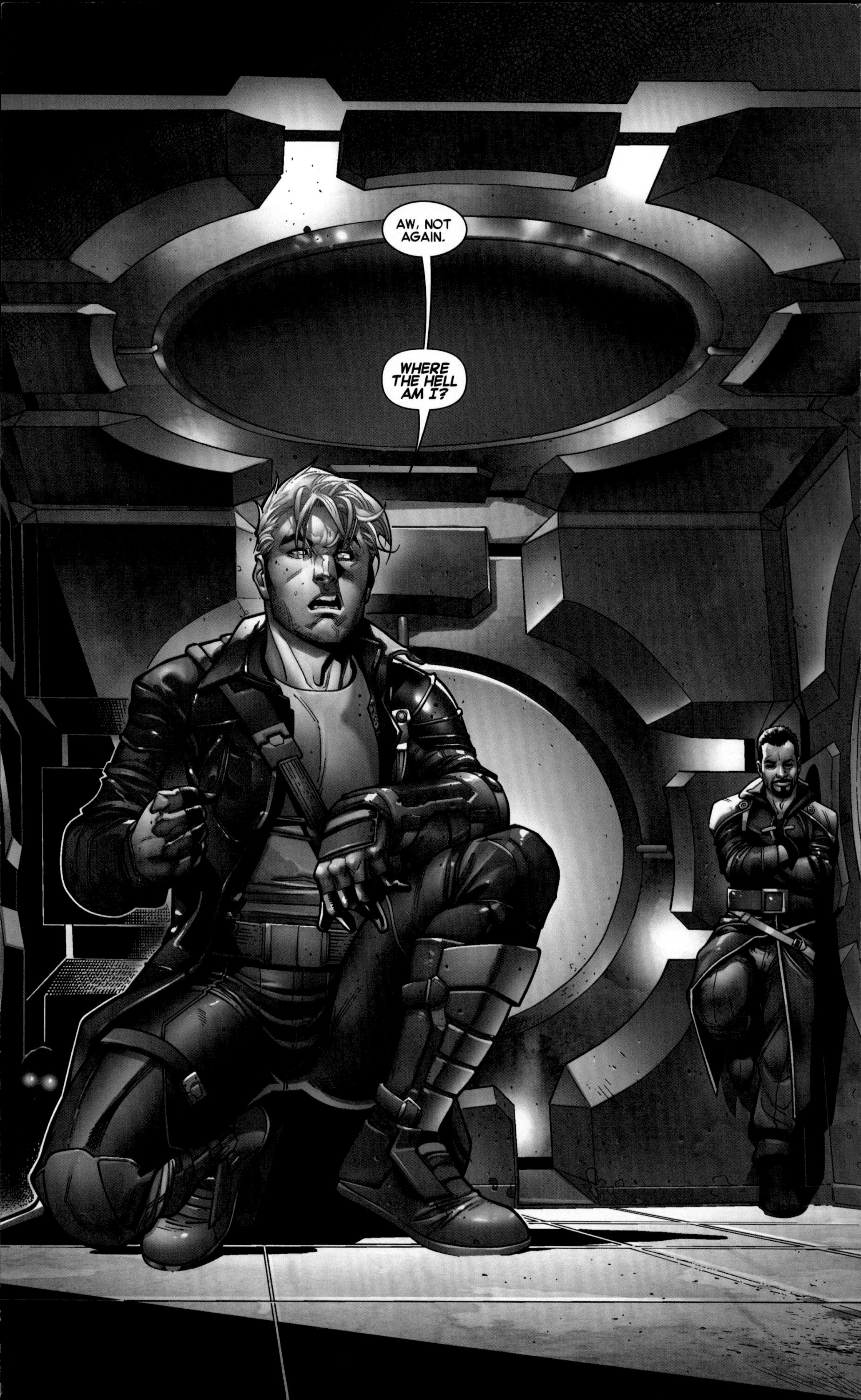
AW, NOT AGAIN.
WHERE THE HELL AM I?

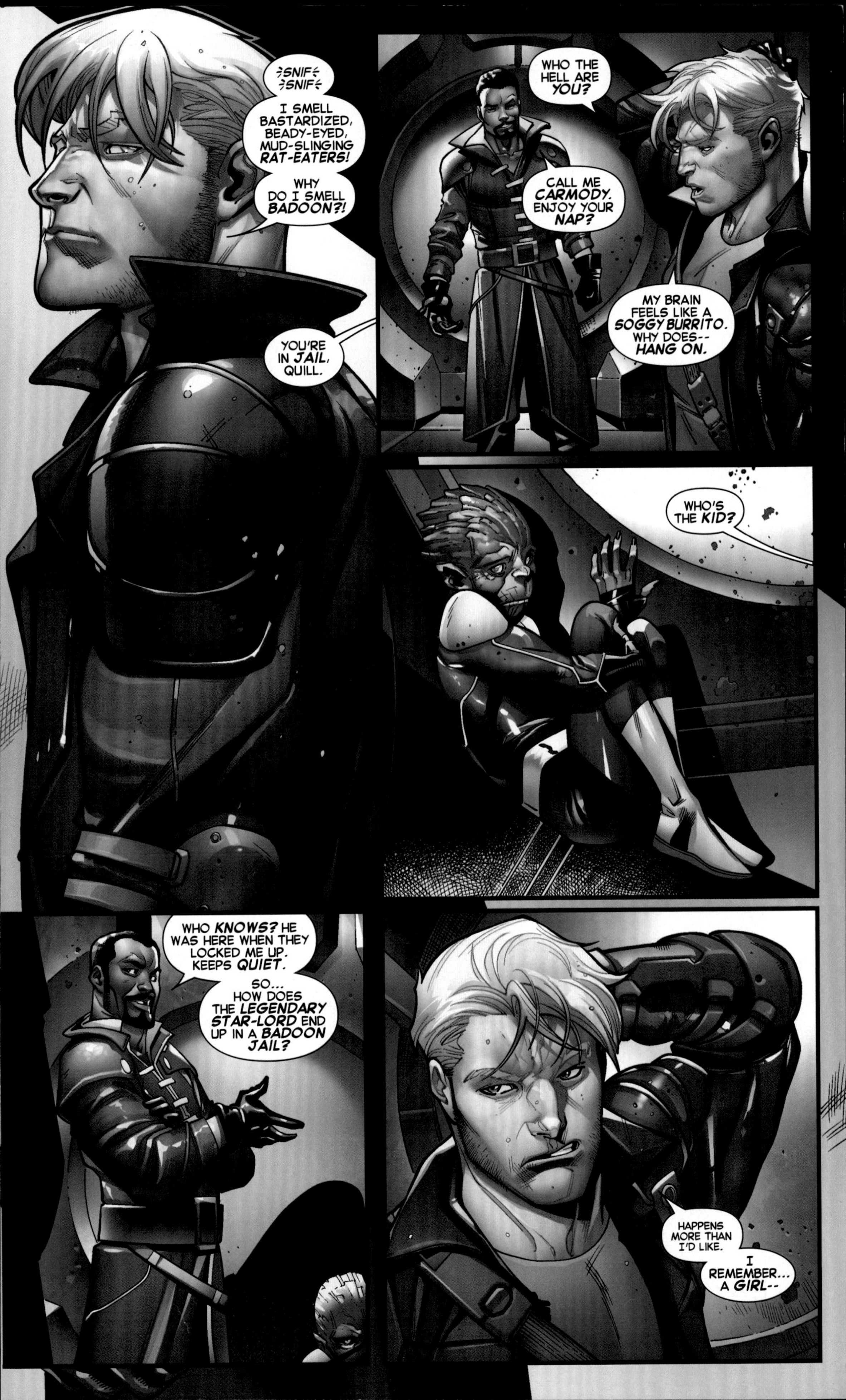

SNIF SNIF
I SMELL BASTARDIZED, BEADY-EYED, MUD-SLINGING RAT-EATERS!
WHY DO I SMELL BADOON?!
YOU'RE IN JAIL, QUILL.
WHO THE HELL ARE YOU?
CALL ME CARMODY. ENJOY YOUR NAP?
MY BRAIN FEELS LIKE A SOGGY BURRITO. WHY DOES-- HANG ON.
WHO'S THE KID?
WHO KNOWS? HE WAS HERE WHEN THEY LOCKED ME UP. KEEPS QUIET.
SO... HOW DOES THE LEGENDARY STAR-LORD END UP IN A BADOON JAIL?
HAPPENS MORE THAN I'D LIKE.
I REMEMBER... A GIRL--

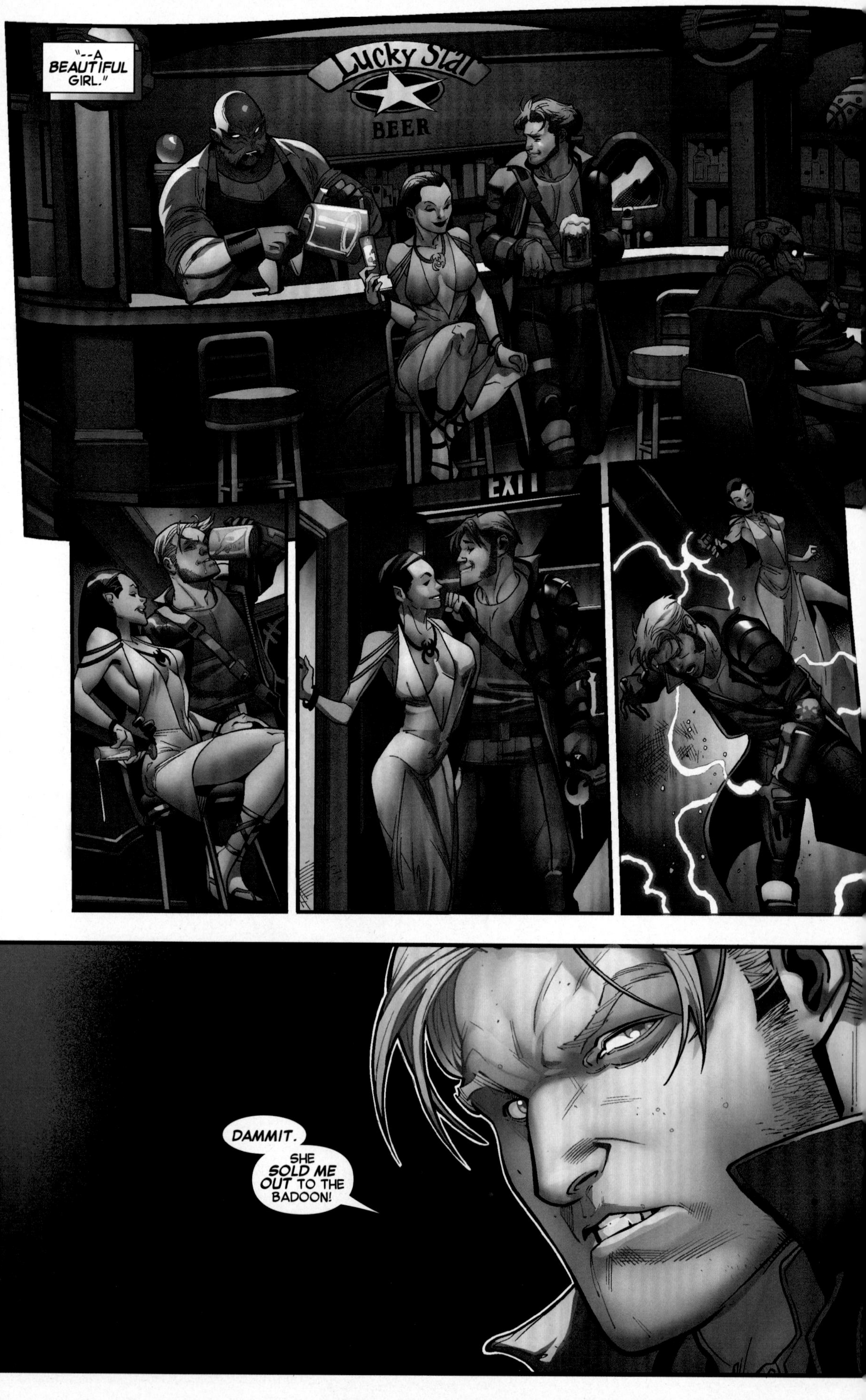
"--A BEAUTIFUL GIRL."
Lucky Star
BEER
EXIT
DAMMIT.
SHE SOLD ME OUT TO THE BADOON!

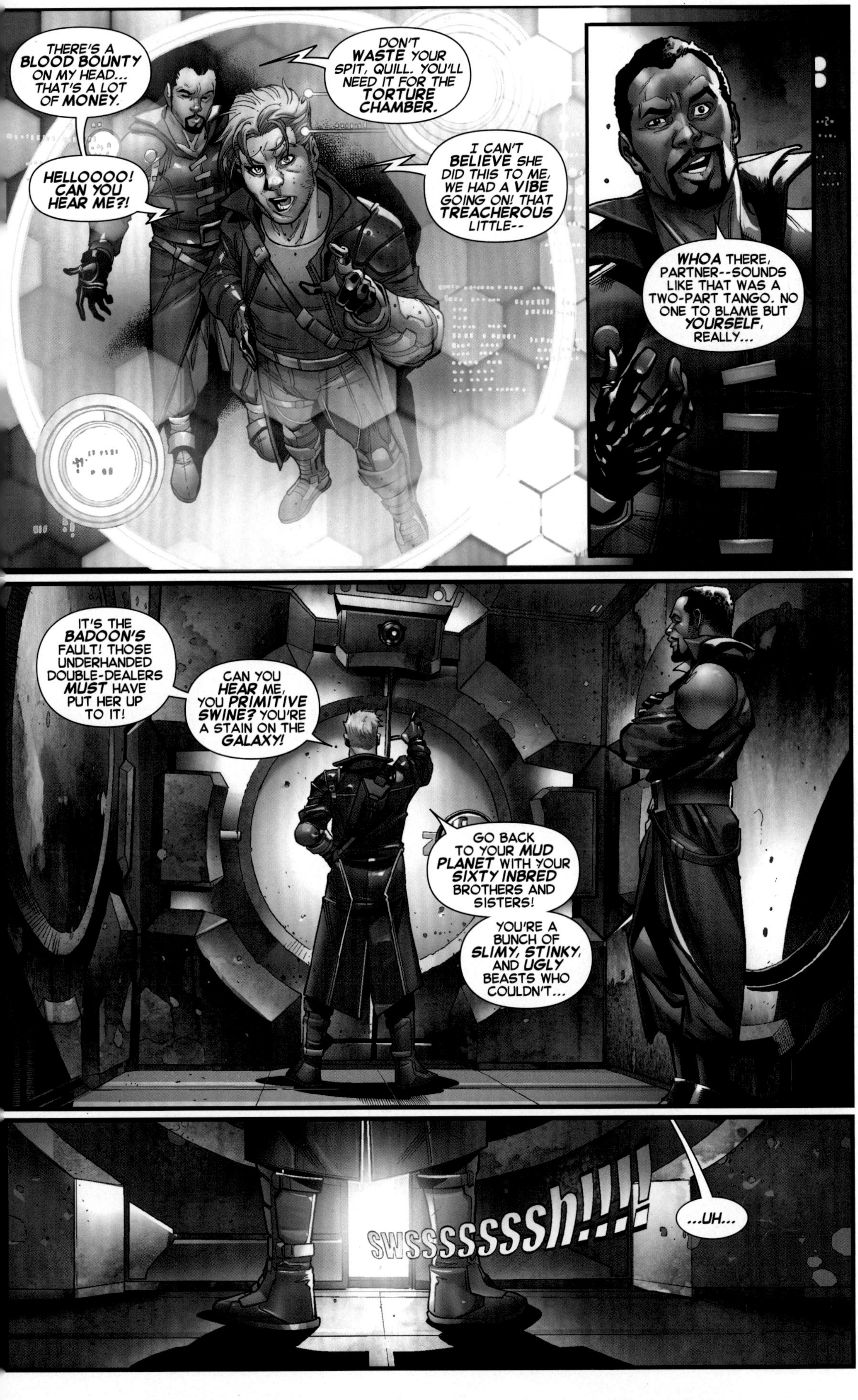
THERE'S A BLOOD BOUNTY ON MY HEAD... THAT'S A LOT OF MONEY.
DON'T WASTE YOUR SPIT, QUILL. YOU'LL NEED IT FOR THE TORTURE CHAMBER.
HELLOOOO! CAN YOU HEAR ME?!
I CAN'T BELIEVE SHE DID THIS TO ME, WE HAD A VIBE GOING ON! THAT TREACHEROUS LITTLE--
WHOA THERE, PARTNER--SOUNDS LIKE THAT WAS A TWO-PART TANGO. NO ONE TO BLAME BUT YOURSELF, REALLY...
IT'S THE BADOON'S FAULT! THOSE UNDERHANDED DOUBLE-DEALERS MUST HAVE PUT HER UP TO IT!
CAN YOU HEAR ME, YOU PRIMITIVE SWINE? YOU'RE A STAIN ON THE GALAXY!
GO BACK TO YOUR MUD PLANET WITH YOUR SIXTY INBRED BROTHERS AND SISTERS!
YOU'RE A BUNCH OF SLIMY, STINKY, AND UGLY BEASTS WHO COULDN'T...
SWSSSSSSSSh!!!!
...UH...

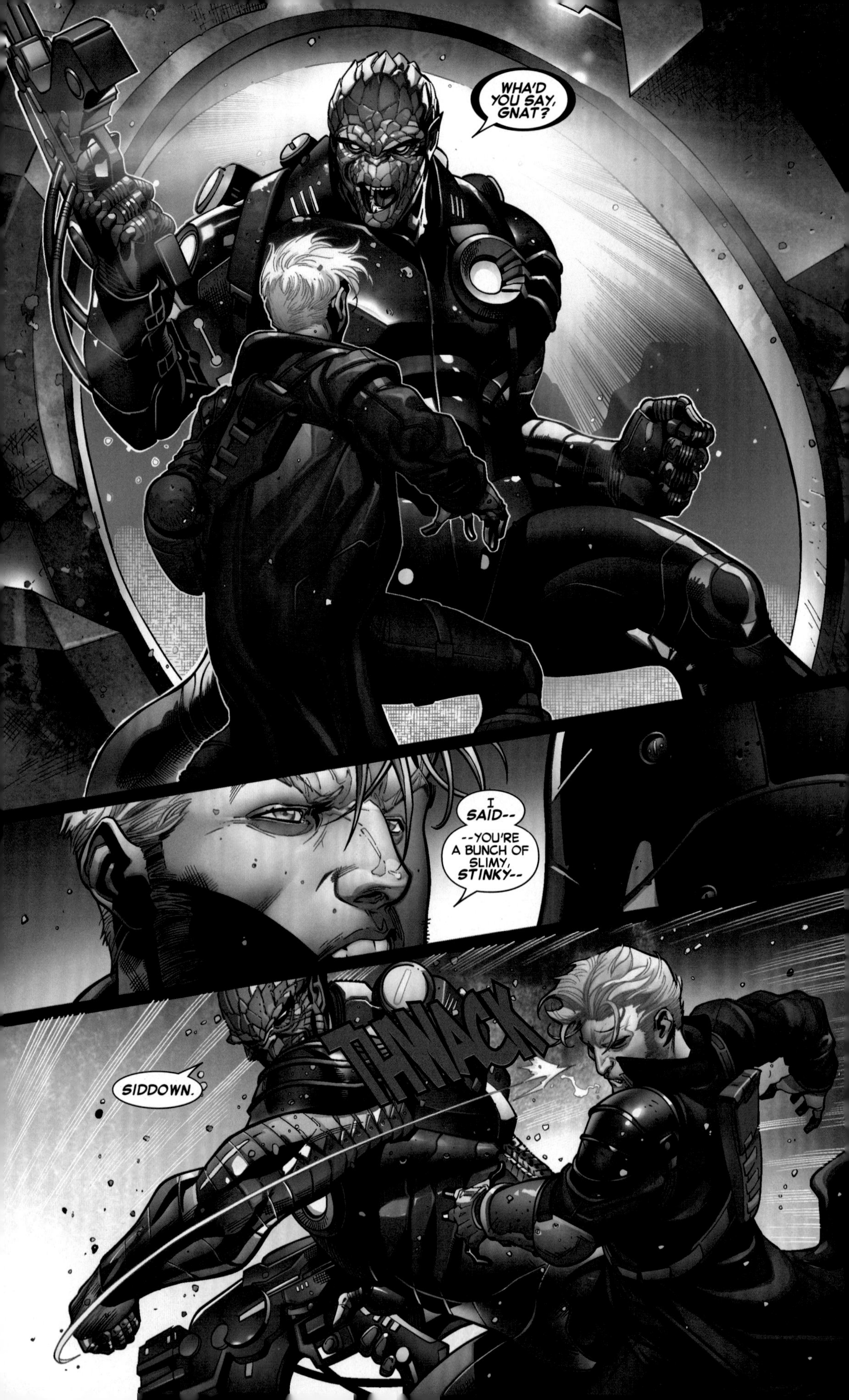
WHA'D YOU SAY, GNAT?
I SAID--
--YOU'RE A BUNCH OF SLIMY, STINKY--
THWACK
SIDDOWN.

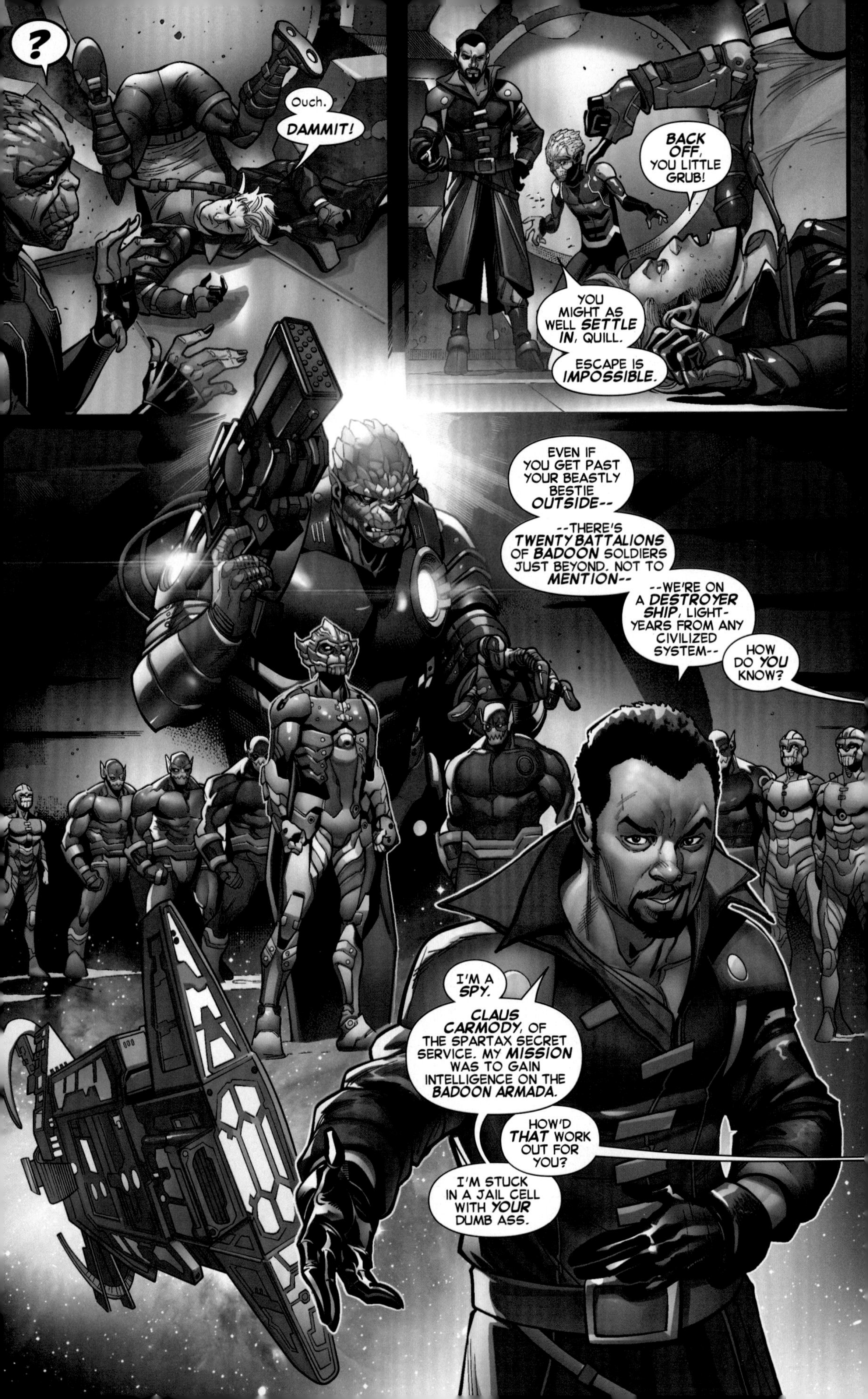
?
Ouch.
DAMMIT!
BACK OFF, YOU LITTLE GRUB!
YOU MIGHT AS WELL SETTLE IN, QUILL.
ESCAPE IS IMPOSSIBLE.
EVEN IF YOU GET PAST YOUR BEASTLY BESTIE OUTSIDE--
--THERE'S TWENTY BATTALIONS OF BADOON SOLDIERS JUST BEYOND. NOT TO MENTION--
--WE'RE ON A DESTROYER SHIP, LIGHT-YEARS FROM ANY CIVILIZED SYSTEM--
HOW DO YOU KNOW?
I'M A SPY.
CLAUS CARMODY, OF THE SPARTAX SECRET SERVICE. MY MISSION WAS TO GAIN INTELLIGENCE ON THE BADOON ARMADA.
HOW'D THAT WORK OUT FOR YOU?
I'M STUCK IN A JAIL CELL WITH YOUR DUMB ASS.

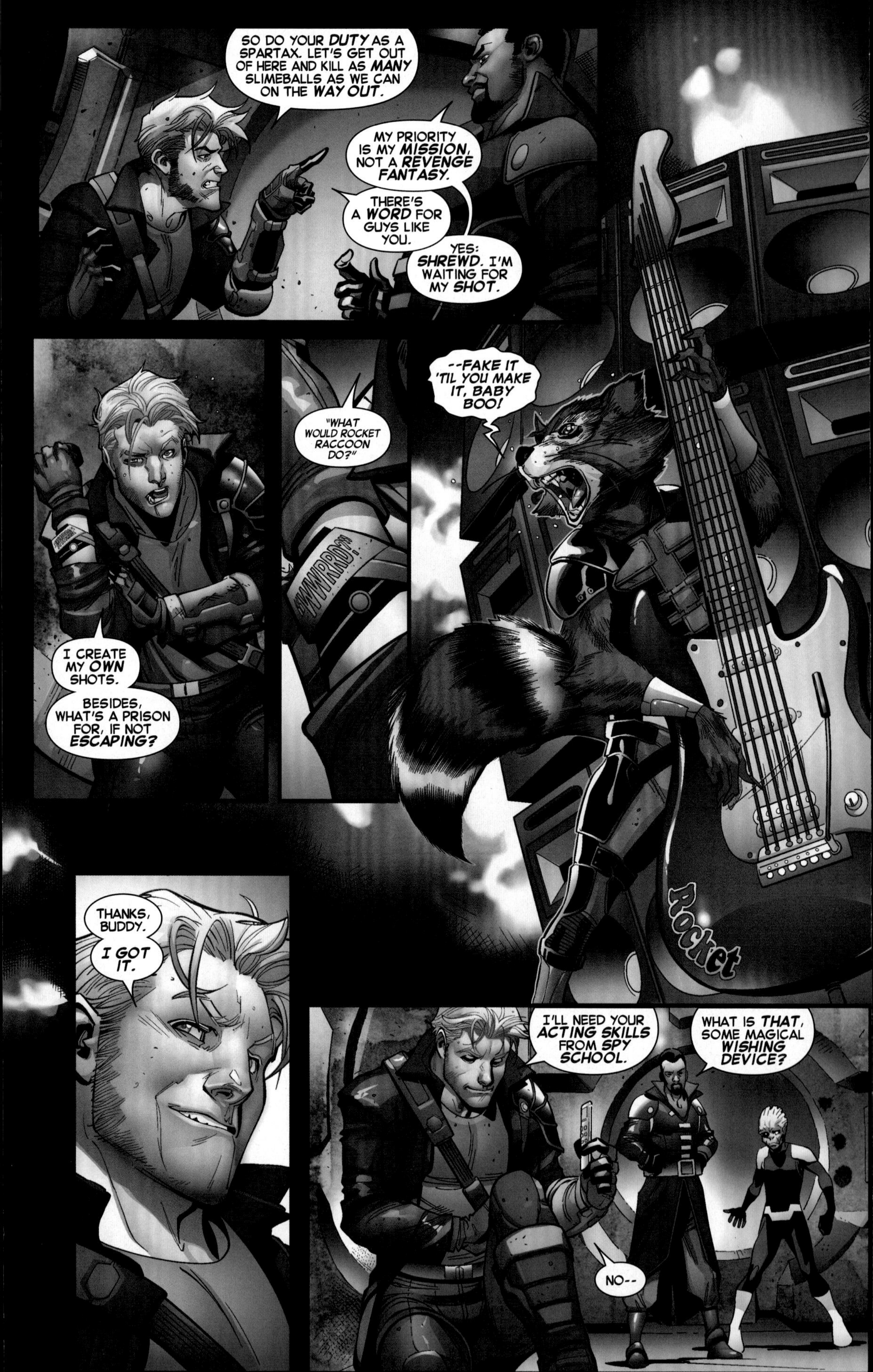

SO DO YOUR DUTY AS A SPARTAX. LET'S GET OUT OF HERE AND KILL AS MANY SLIMEBALLS AS WE CAN ON THE WAY OUT.
MY PRIORITY IS MY MISSION, NOT A REVENGE FANTASY.
THERE'S A WORD FOR GUYS LIKE YOU.
YES: SHREWD. I'M WAITING FOR MY SHOT.
I CREATE MY OWN SHOTS.
BESIDES, WHAT'S A PRISON FOR, IF NOT ESCAPING?
"WHAT WOULD ROCKET RACCOON DO?"
#WWRRD?!
--FAKE IT 'TIL YOU MAKE IT, BABY BOO!
Rocket
THANKS, BUDDY.
I GOT IT.
I'LL NEED YOUR ACTING SKILLS FROM SPY SCHOOL.
WHAT IS THAT, SOME MAGICAL WISHING DEVICE?
NO--

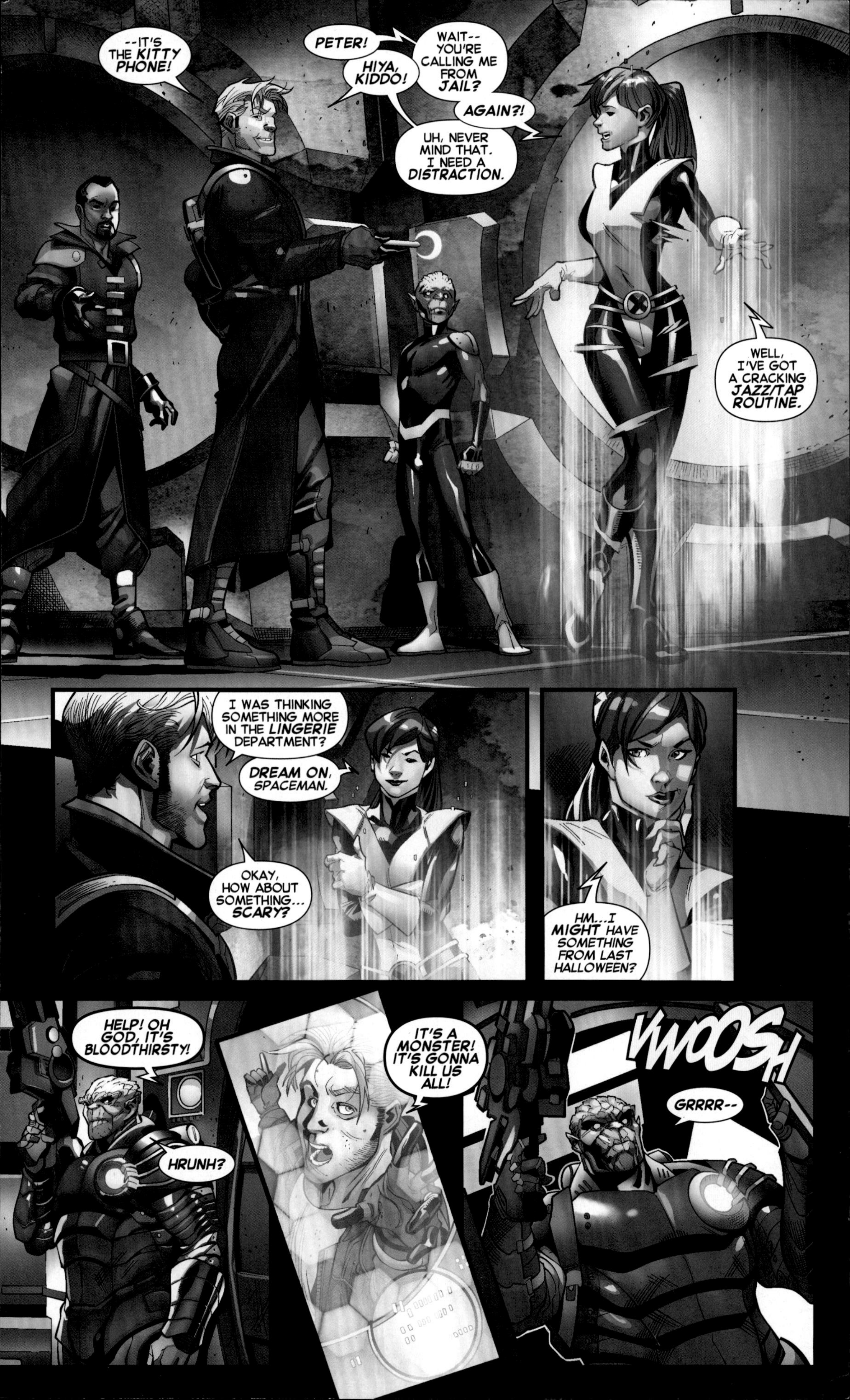
--IT'S THE KITTY PHONE!
PETER!
HIYA, KIDDO!
WAIT-- YOU'RE CALLING ME FROM JAIL?
AGAIN?!
UH, NEVER MIND THAT. I NEED A DISTRACTION.
WELL, I'VE GOT A CRACKING JAZZ/TAP ROUTINE.
I WAS THINKING SOMETHING MORE IN THE LINGERIE DEPARTMENT?
DREAM ON, SPACEMAN.
OKAY, HOW ABOUT SOMETHING... SCARY?
HM...I MIGHT HAVE SOMETHING FROM LAST HALLOWEEN?
HELP! OH GOD, IT'S BLOODTHIRSTY!
HRUNH?
IT'S A MONSTER! IT'S GONNA KILL US ALL!
VWOOSH
GRRRR--

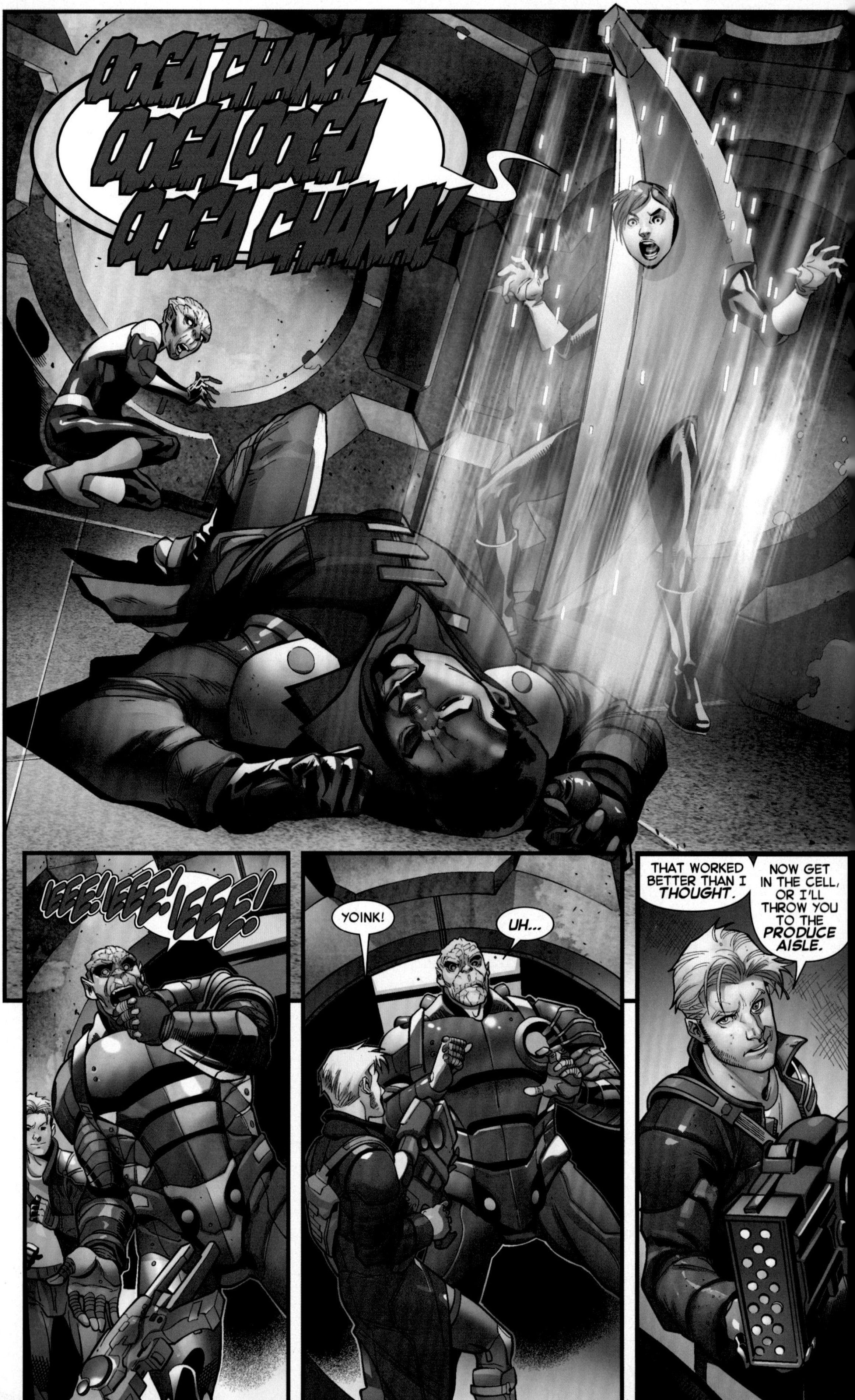
OOGA CHAKA! OOGA OOGA OOGA CHAKA!
IEEE! IEEE! IEEE!
YOINK!
UH...
THAT WORKED BETTER THAN I THOUGHT.
NOW GET IN THE CELL, OR I'LL THROW YOU TO THE PRODUCE AISLE.

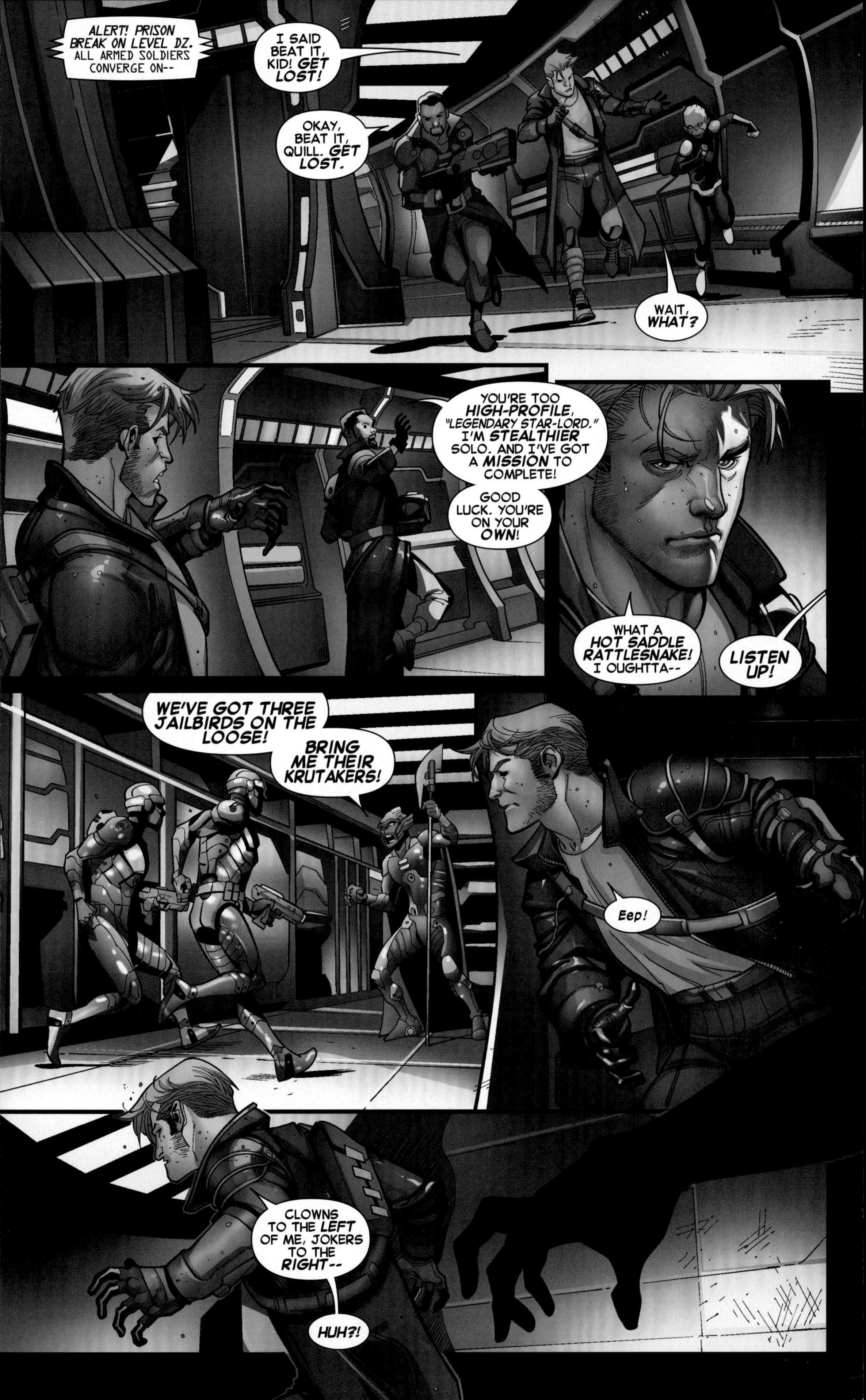
ALERT! PRISON BREAK ON LEVEL DZ. ALL ARMED SOLDIERS CONVERGE ON--
I SAID BEAT IT, KID! GET LOST!
OKAY, BEAT IT, QUILL. GET LOST.
WAIT, WHAT?
YOU'RE TOO HIGH-PROFILE, "LEGENDARY STAR-LORD." I'M STEALTHIER SOLO. AND I'VE GOT A MISSION TO COMPLETE!
GOOD LUCK. YOU'RE ON YOUR OWN!
WHAT A HOT SADDLE RATTLESNAKE! I OUGHTTA--
LISTEN UP!
WE'VE GOT THREE JAILBIRDS ON THE LOOSE!
BRING ME THEIR KRUTAKERS!
Eep!
CLOWNS TO THE LEFT OF ME, JOKERS TO THE RIGHT--
HUH?!

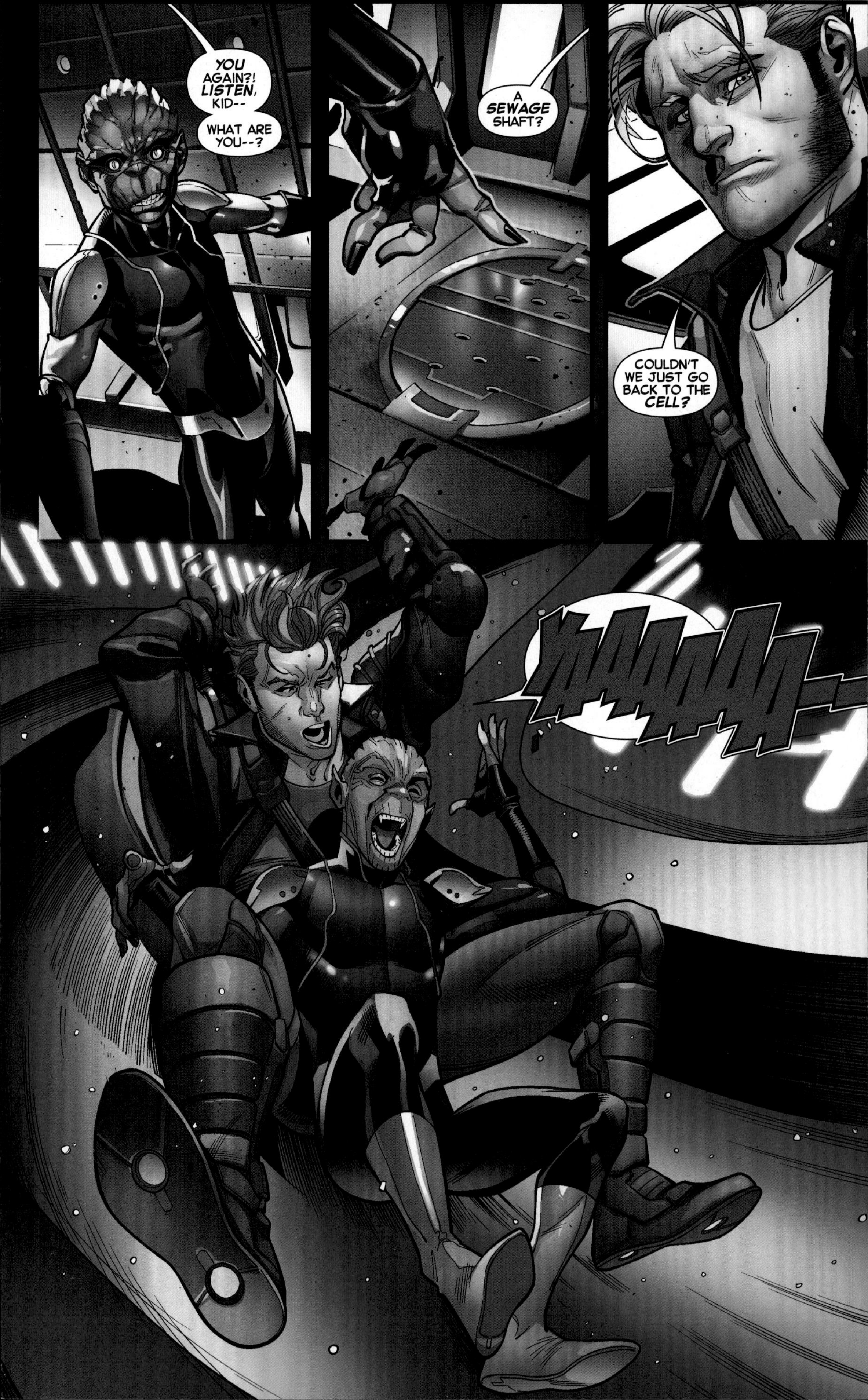
YOU AGAIN?! LISTEN, KID--
WHAT ARE YOU--?
A SEWAGE SHAFT?
COULDN'T WE JUST GO BACK TO THE CELL?
WAAAAAA--

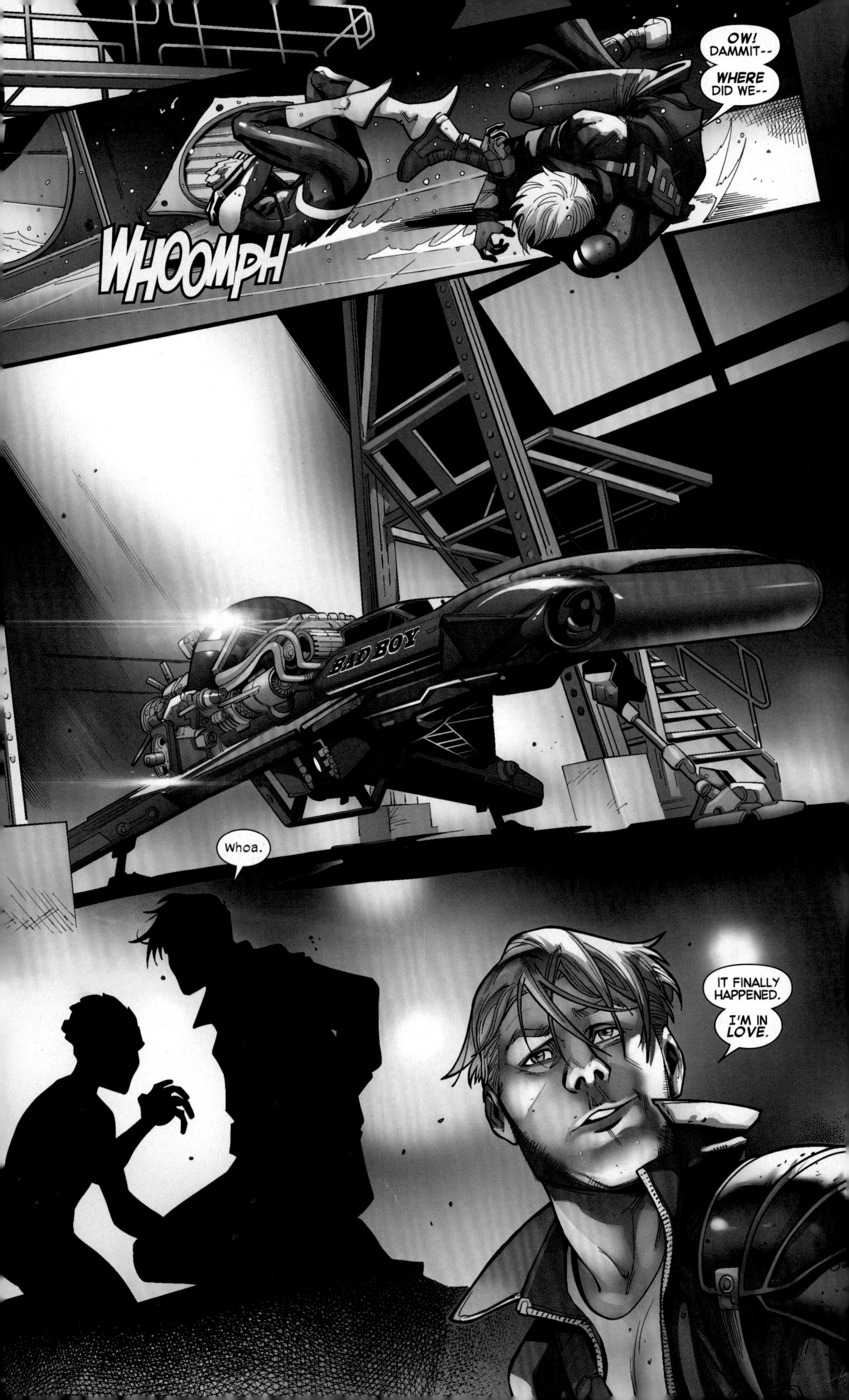
OW! DAMMIT--
WHERE DID WE--
WHOOMPH
BAD BOY
Whoa.
IT FINALLY HAPPENED.
I'M IN LOVE.

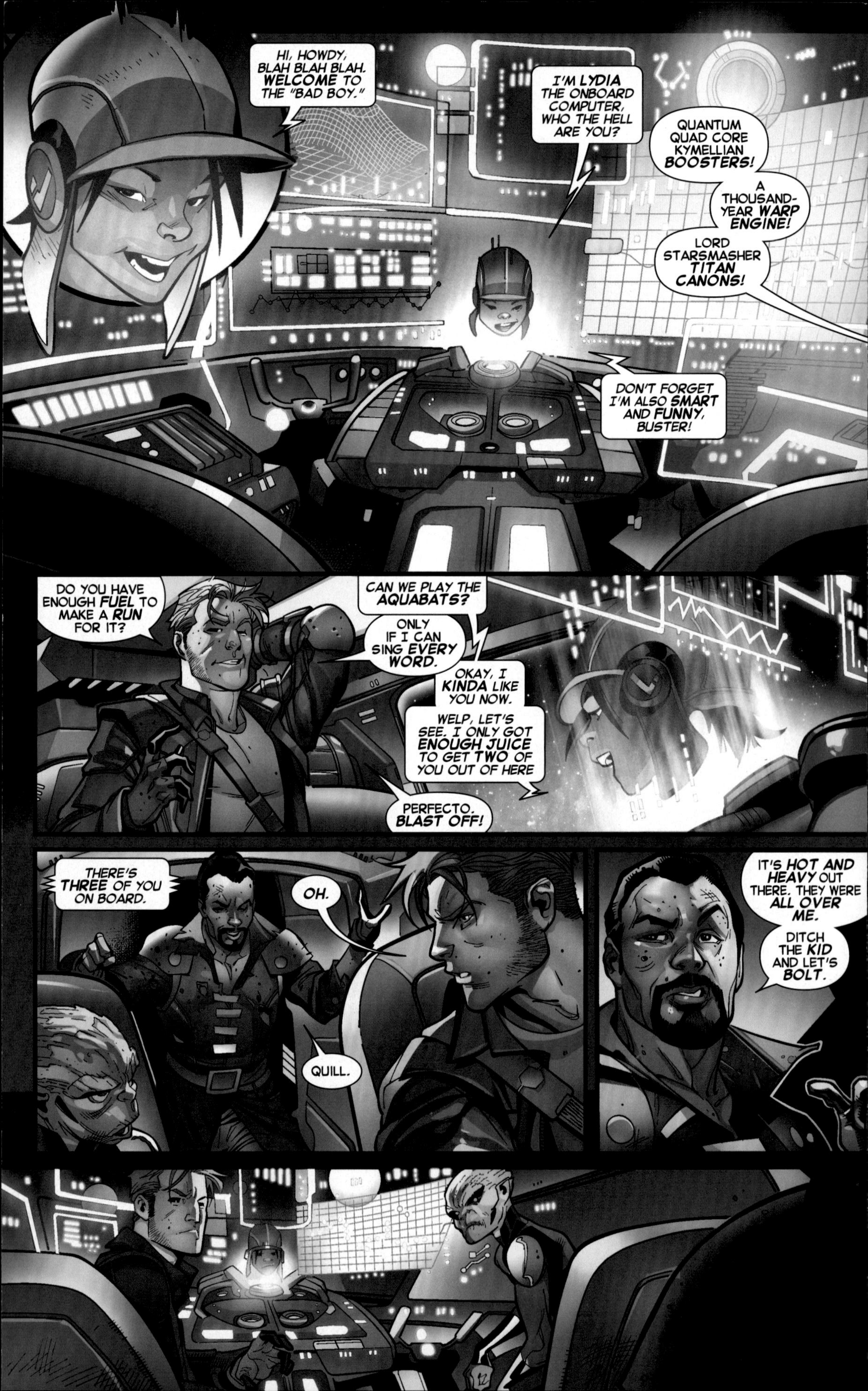
HI, HOWDY, BLAH BLAH BLAH. WELCOME TO THE "BAD BOY."
I'M LYDIA THE ONBOARD COMPUTER, WHO THE HELL ARE YOU?
QUANTUM QUAD CORE KYMELLIAN BOOSTERS!
A THOUSAND-YEAR WARP ENGINE!
LORD STARSMASHER TITAN CANONS!
DON'T FORGET I'M ALSO SMART AND FUNNY, BUSTER!
DO YOU HAVE ENOUGH FUEL TO MAKE A RUN FOR IT?
CAN WE PLAY THE AQUABATS?
ONLY IF I CAN SING EVERY WORD.
OKAY, I KINDA LIKE YOU NOW.
WELP, LET'S SEE. I ONLY GOT ENOUGH JUICE TO GET TWO OF YOU OUT OF HERE
PERFECTO. BLAST OFF!
THERE'S THREE OF YOU ON BOARD.
OH.
QUILL.
IT'S HOT AND HEAVY OUT THERE. THEY WERE ALL OVER ME.
DITCH THE KID AND LET'S BOLT.

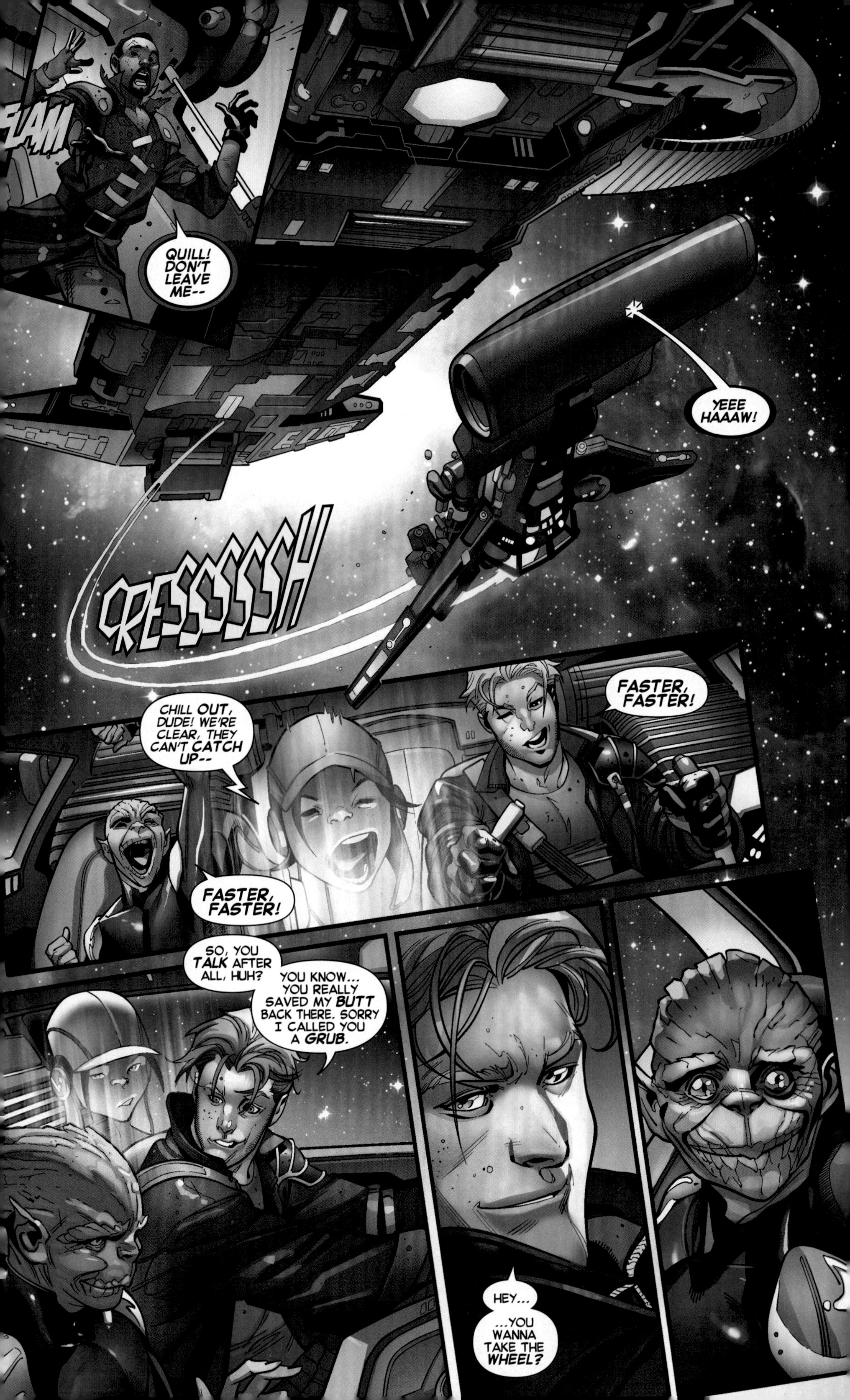

FLAM
QUILL! DON'T LEAVE ME--
YEEE HAAAW!
CRESSSSSH
FASTER, FASTER!
CHILL OUT, DUDE! WE'RE CLEAR, THEY CAN'T CATCH UP--
FASTER, FASTER!
SO, YOU TALK AFTER ALL, HUH?
YOU KNOW... YOU REALLY SAVED MY BUTT BACK THERE. SORRY I CALLED YOU A GRUB.
HEY...
...YOU WANNA TAKE THE WHEEL?

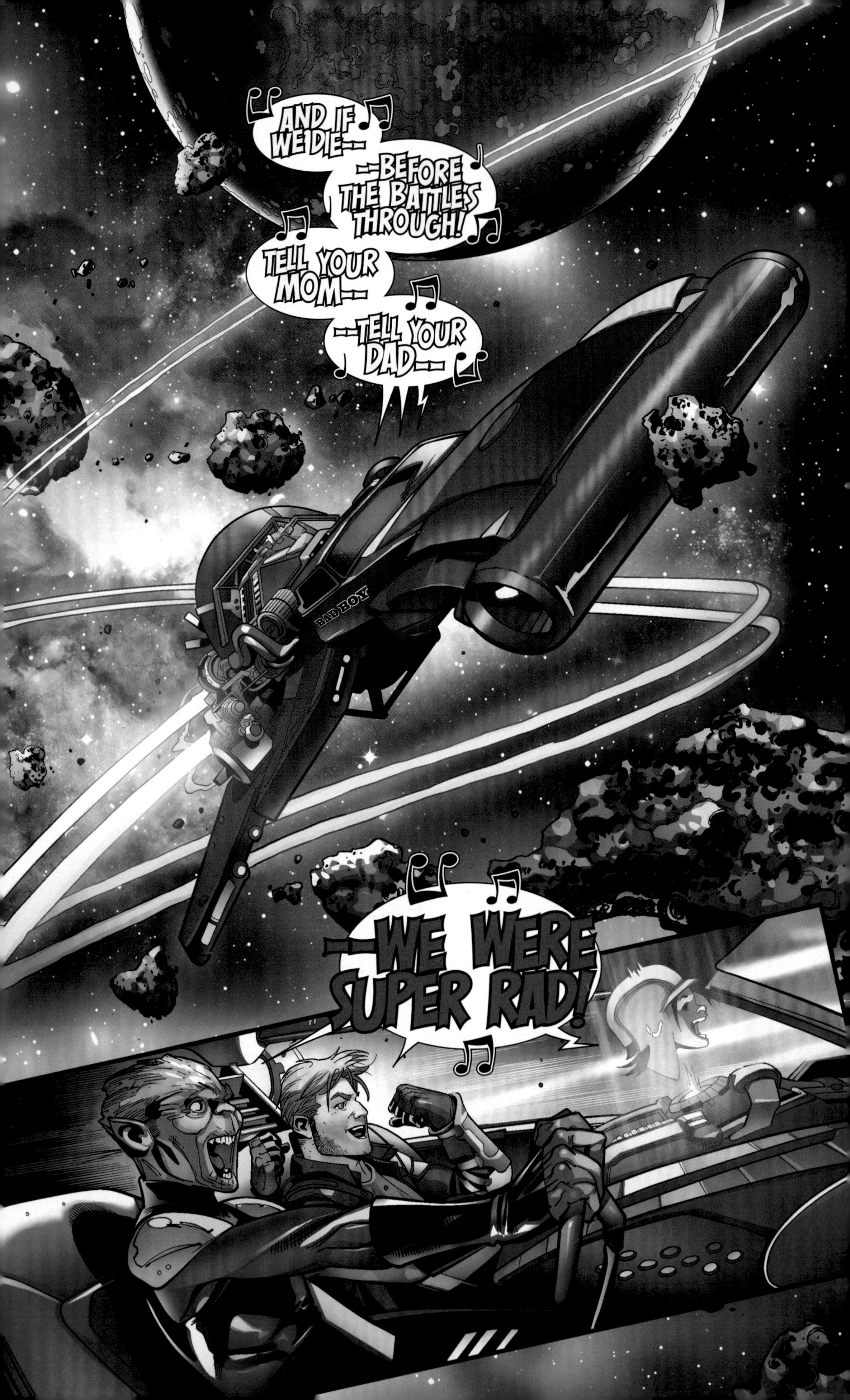
AND IF WE DIE--
--BEFORE THE BATTLE'S THROUGH!
TELL YOUR MOM--
--TELL YOUR DAD--
BAD BOY
--WE WERE SUPER RAD!

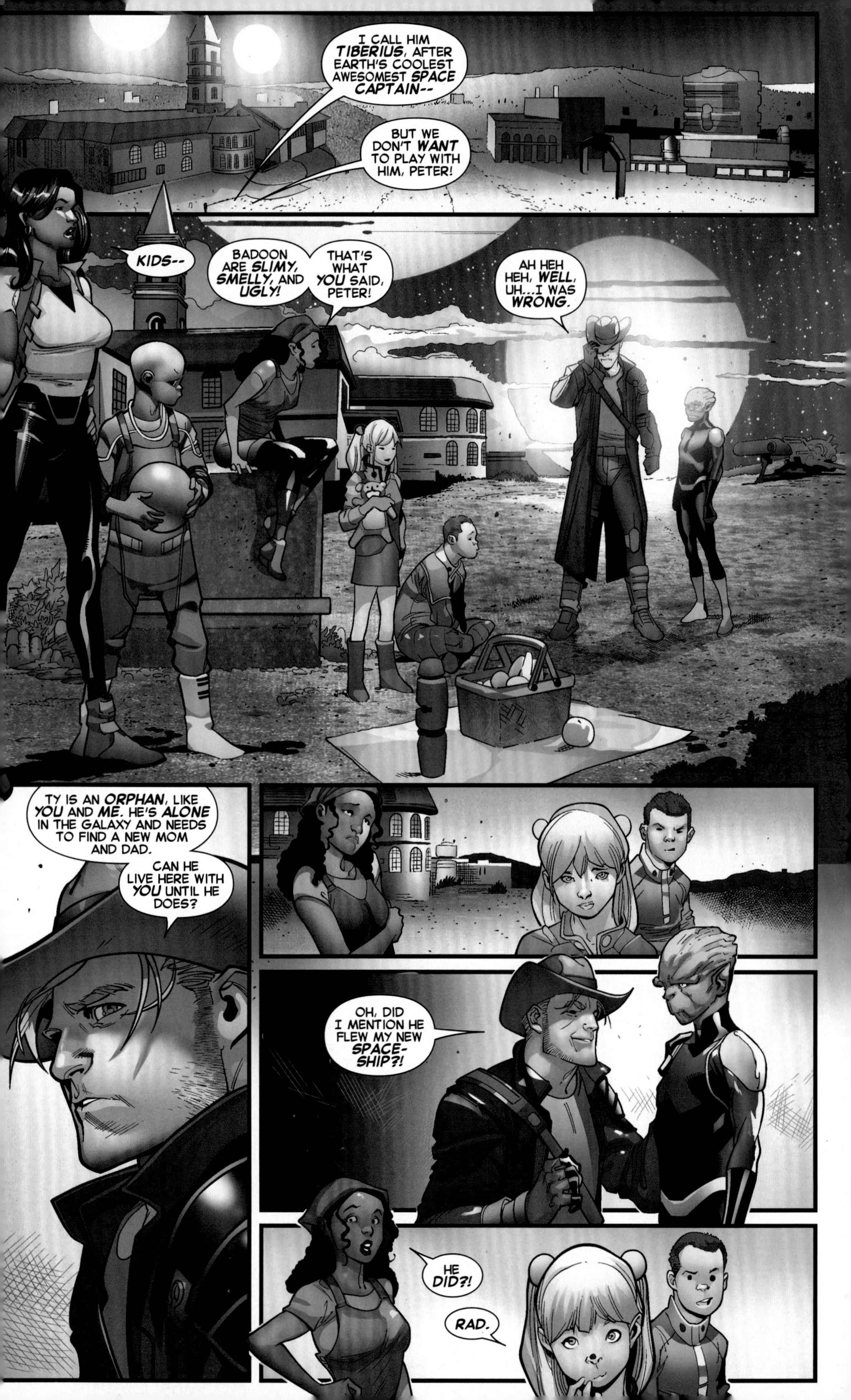

I CALL HIM TIBERIUS, AFTER EARTH'S COOLEST AWESOMEST SPACE CAPTAIN--
BUT WE DON'T WANT TO PLAY WITH HIM, PETER!
KIDS--
BADOON ARE SLIMY, SMELLY, AND UGLY!
THAT'S WHAT YOU SAID, PETER!
AH HEH HEH, WELL, UH...I WAS WRONG.
TY IS AN ORPHAN, LIKE YOU AND ME. HE'S ALONE IN THE GALAXY AND NEEDS TO FIND A NEW MOM AND DAD.
CAN HE LIVE HERE WITH YOU UNTIL HE DOES?
OH, DID I MENTION HE FLEW MY NEW SPACE-SHIP?!
HE DID?!
RAD.

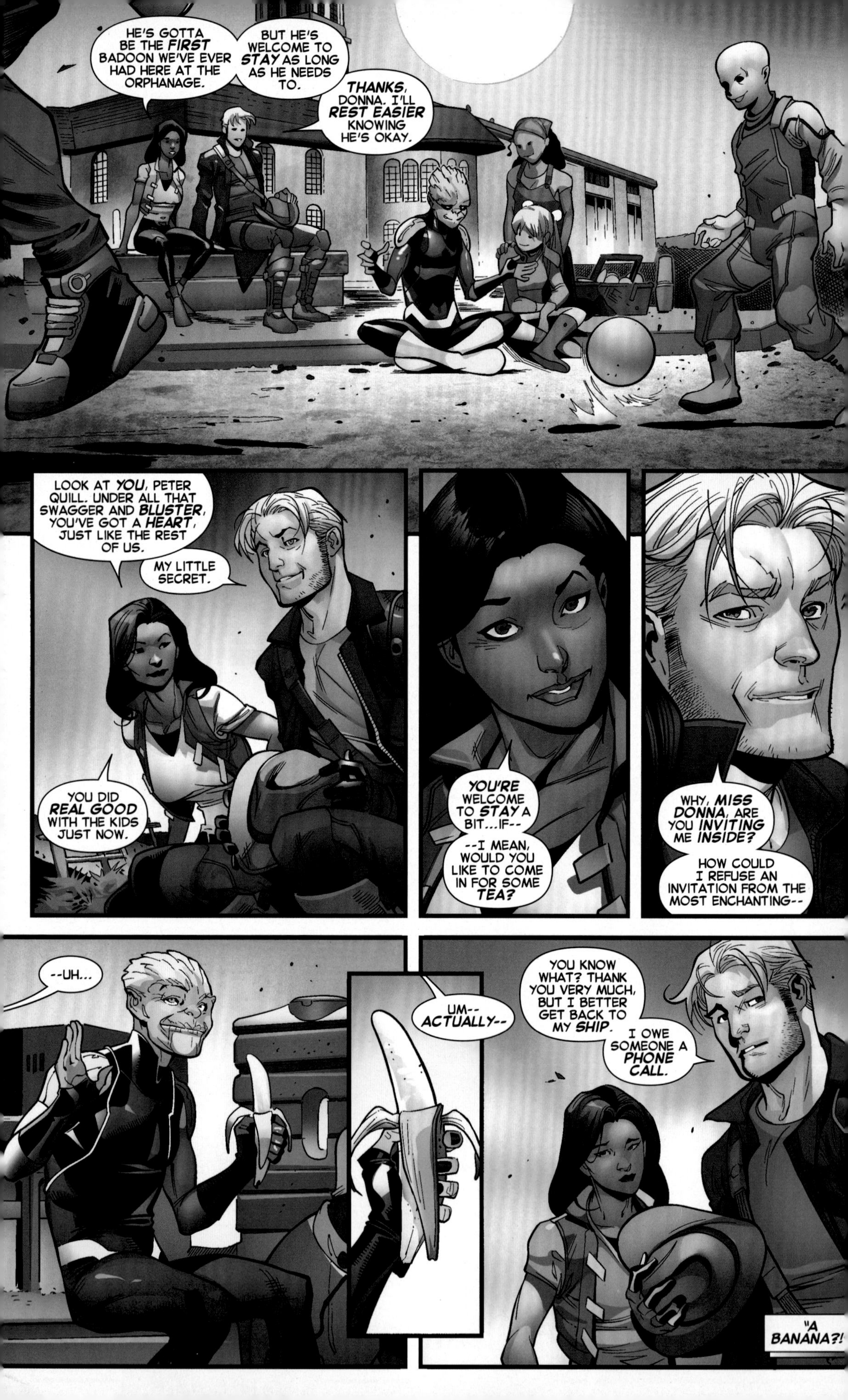

HE'S GOTTA BE THE FIRST BADOON WE'VE EVER HAD HERE AT THE ORPHANAGE.
BUT HE'S WELCOME TO STAY AS LONG AS HE NEEDS TO.
THANKS, DONNA. I'LL REST EASIER KNOWING HE'S OKAY.
LOOK AT YOU, PETER QUILL. UNDER ALL THAT SWAGGER AND BLUSTER, YOU'VE GOT A HEART, JUST LIKE THE REST OF US.
MY LITTLE SECRET.
YOU DID REAL GOOD WITH THE KIDS JUST NOW.
YOU'RE WELCOME TO STAY A BIT...IF--
--I MEAN, WOULD YOU LIKE TO COME IN FOR SOME TEA?
WHY, MISS DONNA, ARE YOU INVITING ME INSIDE?
HOW COULD I REFUSE AN INVITATION FROM THE MOST ENCHANTING--
--UH...
UM-- ACTUALLY--
YOU KNOW WHAT? THANK YOU VERY MUCH, BUT I BETTER GET BACK TO MY SHIP.
I OWE SOMEONE A PHONE CALL.
"A BANANA?!

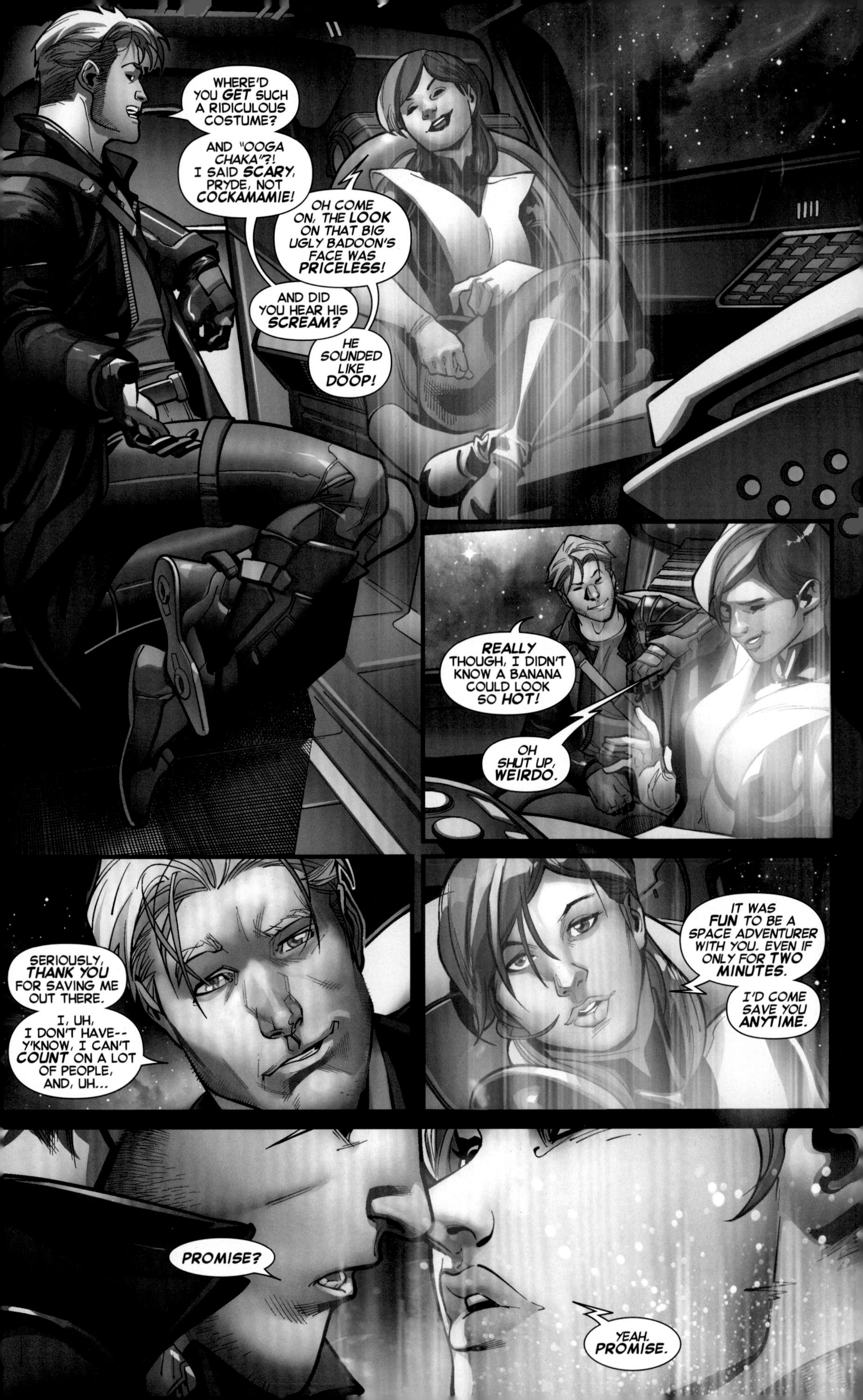
WHERE'D YOU GET SUCH A RIDICULOUS COSTUME?
AND "OOGA CHAKA"?! I SAID SCARY, PRYDE, NOT COCKAMAMIE!
OH COME ON, THE LOOK ON THAT BIG UGLY BADOON'S FACE WAS PRICELESS!
AND DID YOU HEAR HIS SCREAM?
HE SOUNDED LIKE DOOP!
REALLY THOUGH, I DIDN'T KNOW A BANANA COULD LOOK SO HOT!
OH SHUT UP, WEIRDO.
SERIOUSLY, THANK YOU FOR SAVING ME OUT THERE.
I, UH, I DON'T HAVE-- Y'KNOW, I CAN'T COUNT ON A LOT OF PEOPLE, AND, UH...
IT WAS FUN TO BE A SPACE ADVENTURER WITH YOU. EVEN IF ONLY FOR TWO MINUTES.
I'D COME SAVE YOU ANYTIME.
PROMISE?
YEAH. PROMISE.

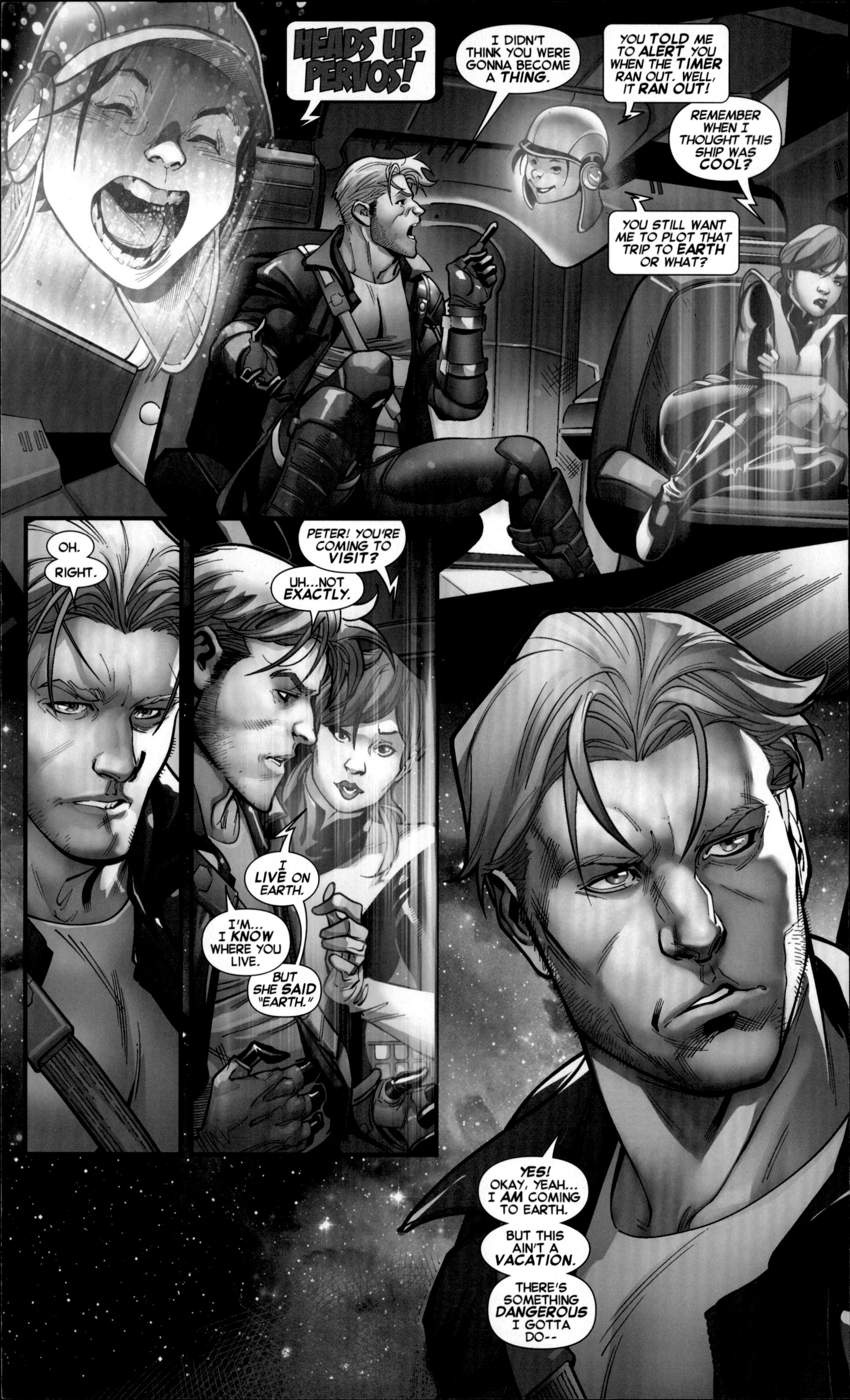
HEADS UP, PERVOS!
I DIDN'T THINK YOU WERE GONNA BECOME A THING.
YOU TOLD ME TO ALERT YOU WHEN THE TIMER RAN OUT. WELL, IT RAN OUT!
REMEMBER WHEN I THOUGHT THIS SHIP WAS COOL?
YOU STILL WANT ME TO PLOT THAT TRIP TO EARTH OR WHAT?
OH.
RIGHT.
PETER! YOU'RE COMING TO VISIT?
UH...NOT EXACTLY.
I LIVE ON EARTH.
I'M... I KNOW WHERE YOU LIVE.
BUT SHE SAID "EARTH."
YES! OKAY, YEAH... I AM COMING TO EARTH.
BUT THIS AIN'T A VACATION.
THERE'S SOMETHING DANGEROUS I GOTTA DO--

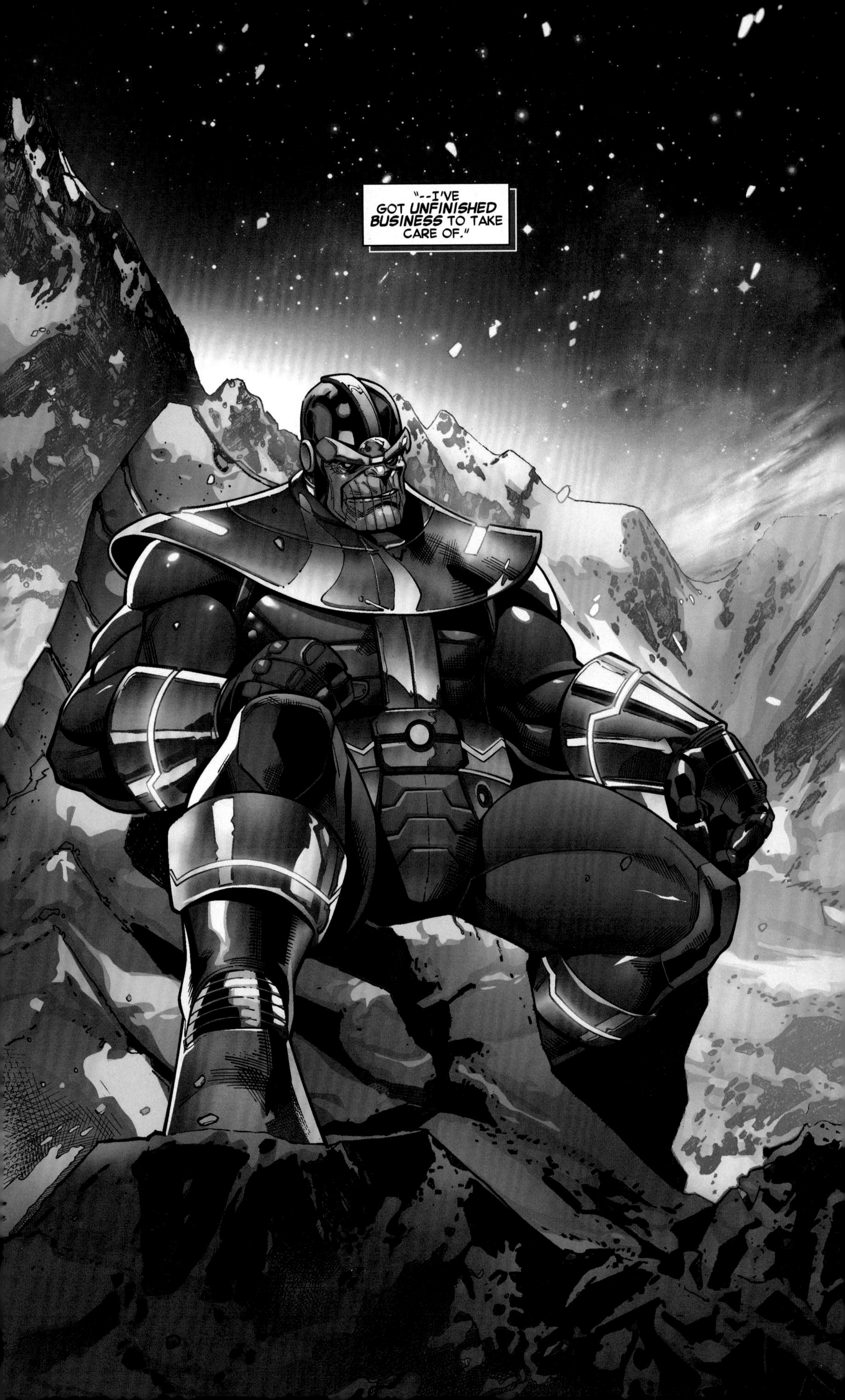
"--I'VE GOT UNFINISHED BUSINESS TO TAKE CARE OF."

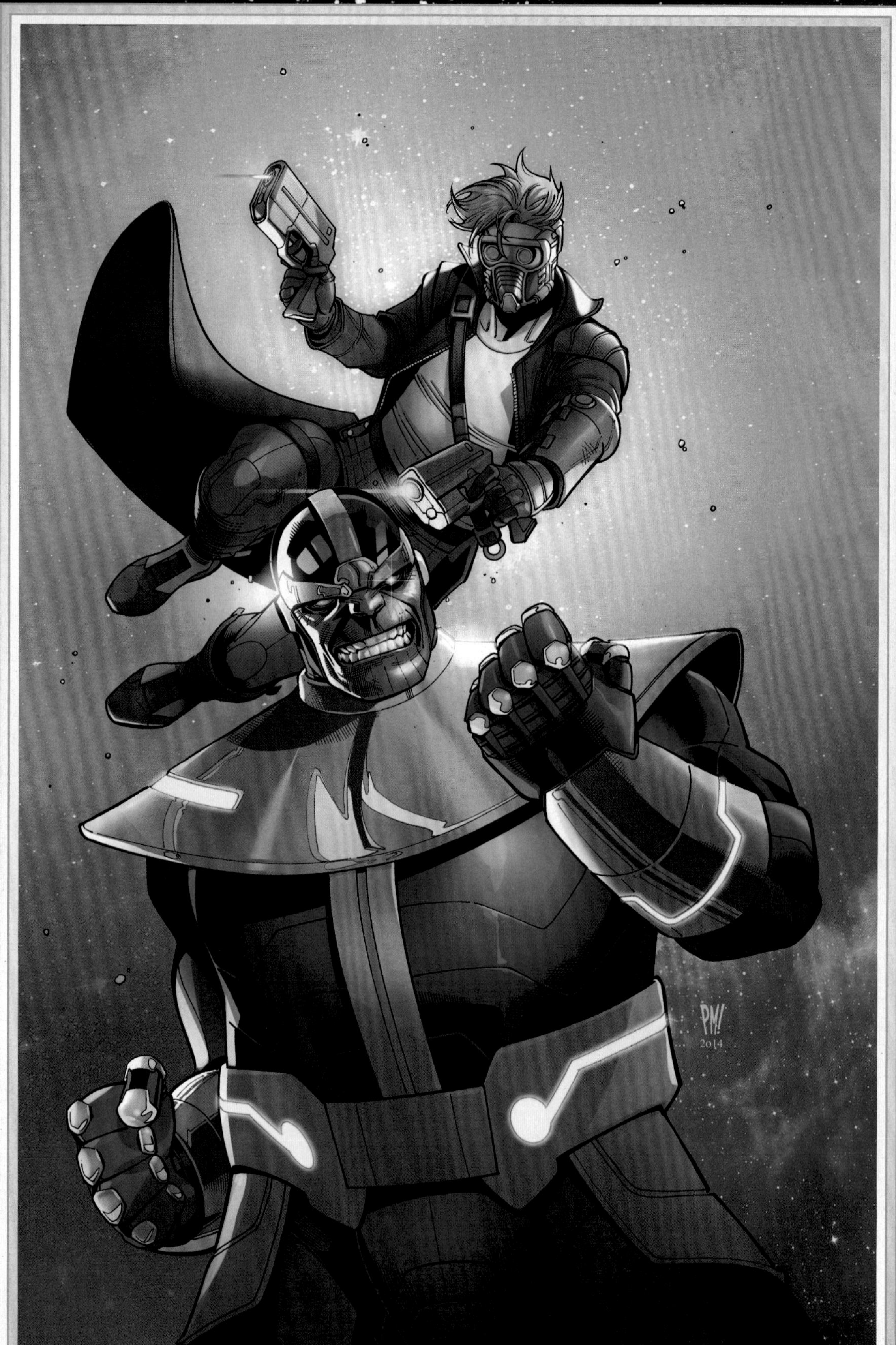
PM!
2014

FOUR

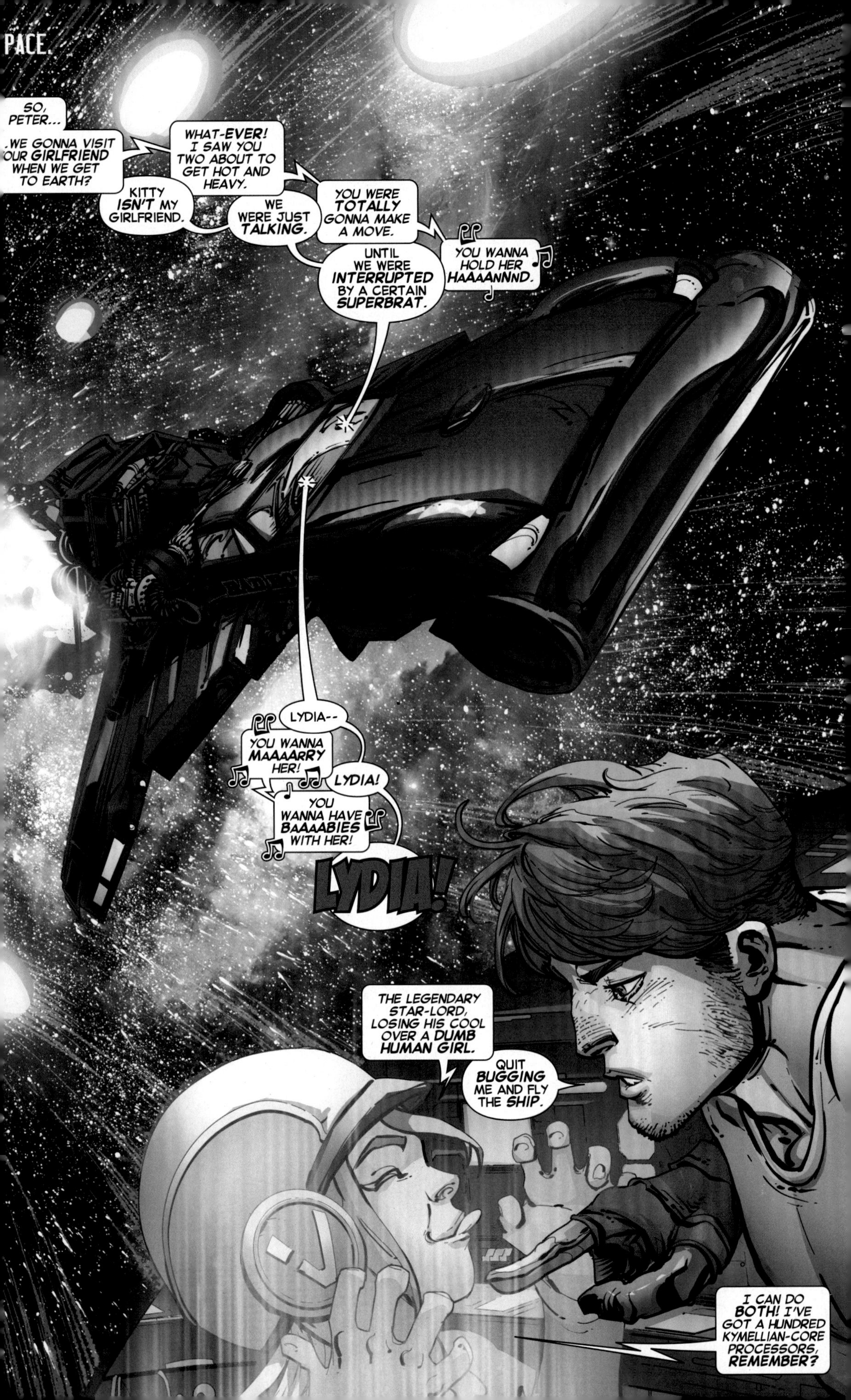
PACE.
SO, PETER...
...WE GONNA VISIT YOUR GIRLFRIEND WHEN WE GET TO EARTH?
KITTY ISN'T MY GIRLFRIEND.
WHAT-EVER! I SAW YOU TWO ABOUT TO GET HOT AND HEAVY.
WE WERE JUST TALKING.
YOU WERE TOTALLY GONNA MAKE A MOVE.
UNTIL WE WERE INTERRUPTED BY A CERTAIN SUPERBRAT.
YOU WANNA HOLD HER HAAAANNND.
LYDIA--
YOU WANNA MAAAARRY HER!
LYDIA!
YOU WANNA HAVE BAAAABIES WITH HER!
LYDIA!
THE LEGENDARY STAR-LORD, LOSING HIS COOL OVER A DUMB HUMAN GIRL.
QUIT BUGGING ME AND FLY THE SHIP.
I CAN DO BOTH! I'VE GOT A HUNDRED KYMELLIAN-CORE PROCESSORS, REMEMBER?

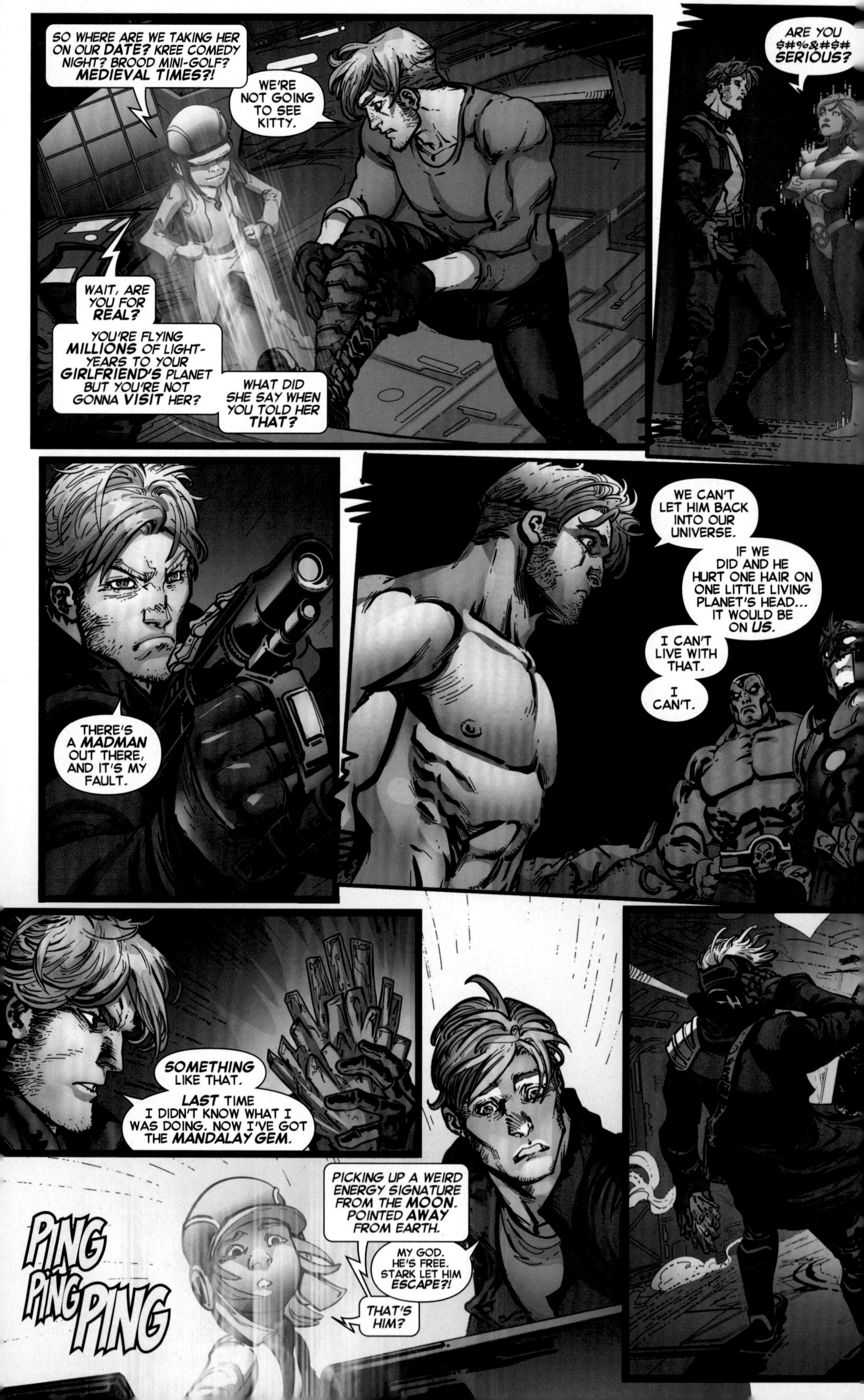

SO WHERE ARE WE TAKING HER ON OUR DATE? KREE COMEDY NIGHT? BROOD MINI-GOLF? MEDIEVAL TIMES?!
WE'RE NOT GOING TO SEE KITTY.
WAIT, ARE YOU FOR REAL?
YOU'RE FLYING MILLIONS OF LIGHT-YEARS TO YOUR GIRLFRIEND'S PLANET BUT YOU'RE NOT GONNA VISIT HER?
WHAT DID SHE SAY WHEN YOU TOLD HER THAT?
ARE YOU $#%&#$# SERIOUS?
THERE'S A MADMAN OUT THERE, AND IT'S MY FAULT.
WE CAN'T LET HIM BACK INTO OUR UNIVERSE.
IF WE DID AND HE HURT ONE HAIR ON ONE LITTLE LIVING PLANET'S HEAD... IT WOULD BE ON US.
I CAN'T LIVE WITH THAT.
I CAN'T.
SOMETHING LIKE THAT.
LAST TIME I DIDN'T KNOW WHAT I WAS DOING. NOW I'VE GOT THE MANDALAY GEM.
PING PING PING
PICKING UP A WEIRD ENERGY SIGNATURE FROM THE MOON. POINTED AWAY FROM EARTH.
MY GOD. HE'S FREE. STARK LET HIM ESCAPE?!
THAT'S HIM?

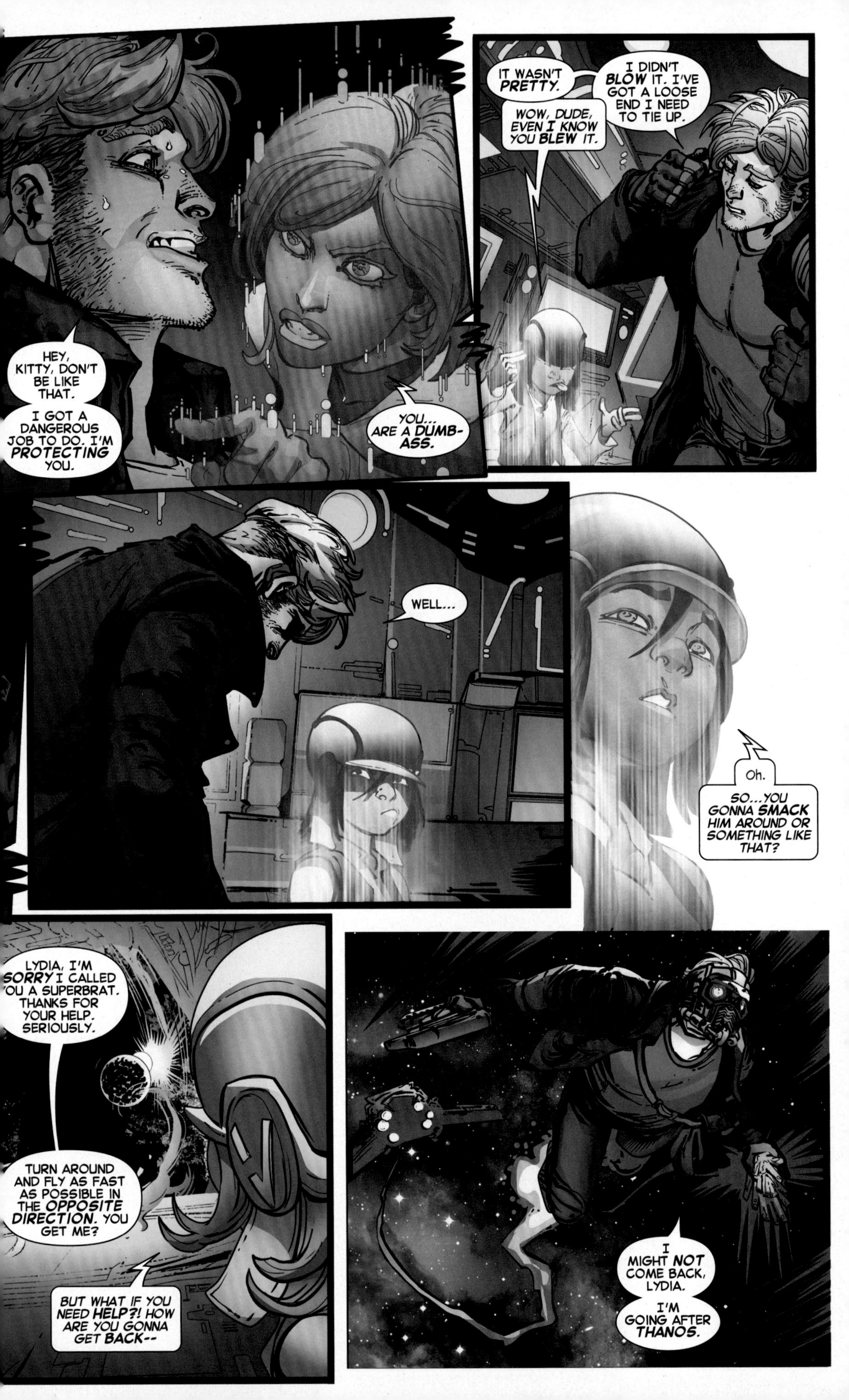
HEY, KITTY, DON'T BE LIKE THAT.
I GOT A DANGEROUS JOB TO DO. I'M PROTECTING YOU.
YOU... ARE A DUMB-ASS.
IT WASN'T PRETTY.
WOW, DUDE, EVEN I KNOW YOU BLEW IT.
I DIDN'T BLOW IT. I'VE GOT A LOOSE END I NEED TO TIE UP.
WELL...
Oh.
SO...YOU GONNA SMACK HIM AROUND OR SOMETHING LIKE THAT?
LYDIA, I'M SORRY I CALLED YOU A SUPERBRAT. THANKS FOR YOUR HELP. SERIOUSLY.
TURN AROUND AND FLY AS FAST AS POSSIBLE IN THE OPPOSITE DIRECTION. YOU GET ME?
BUT WHAT IF YOU NEED HELP?! HOW ARE YOU GONNA GET BACK--
I MIGHT NOT COME BACK, LYDIA.
I'M GOING AFTER THANOS.

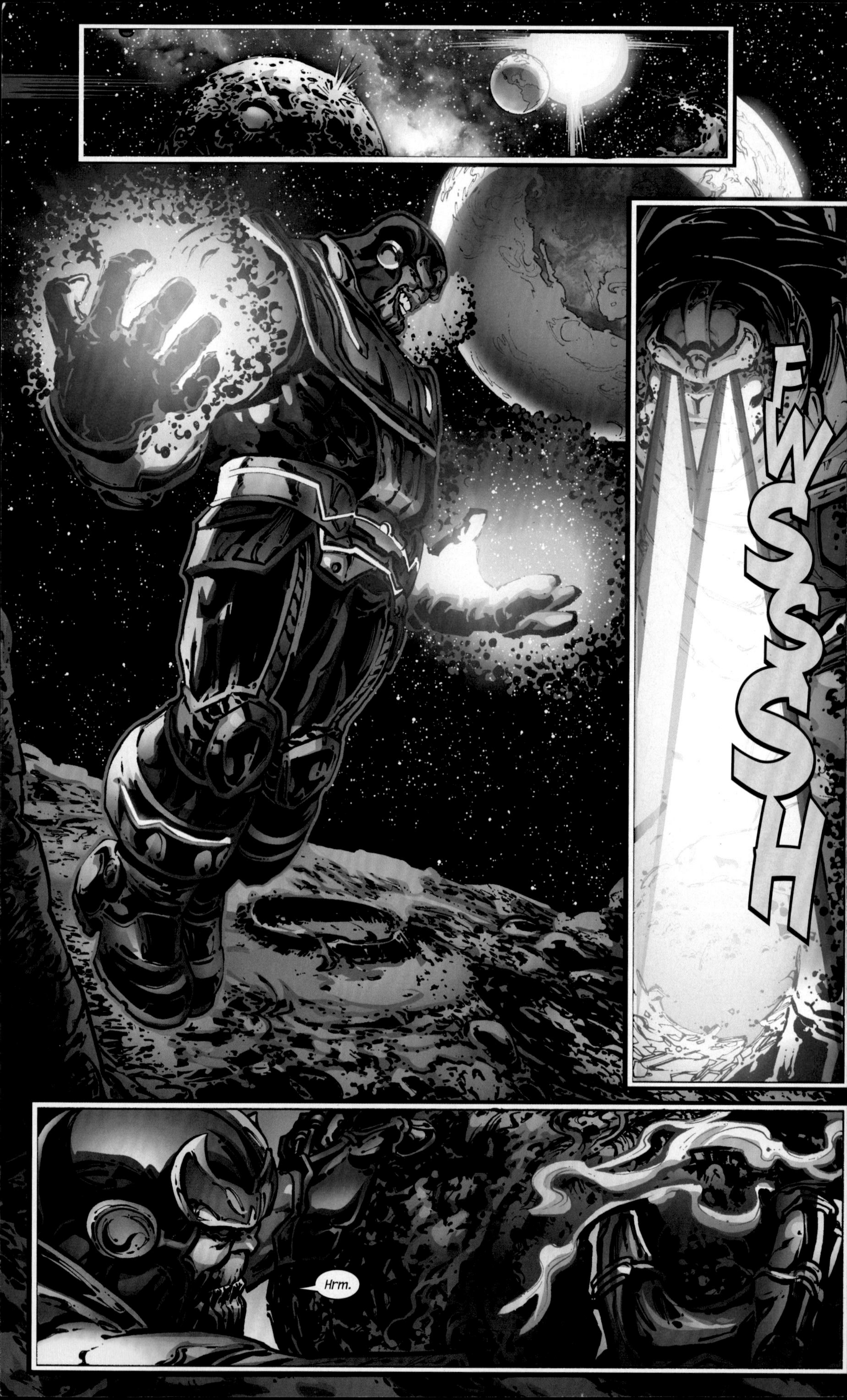
FWSSSH
Hrm.

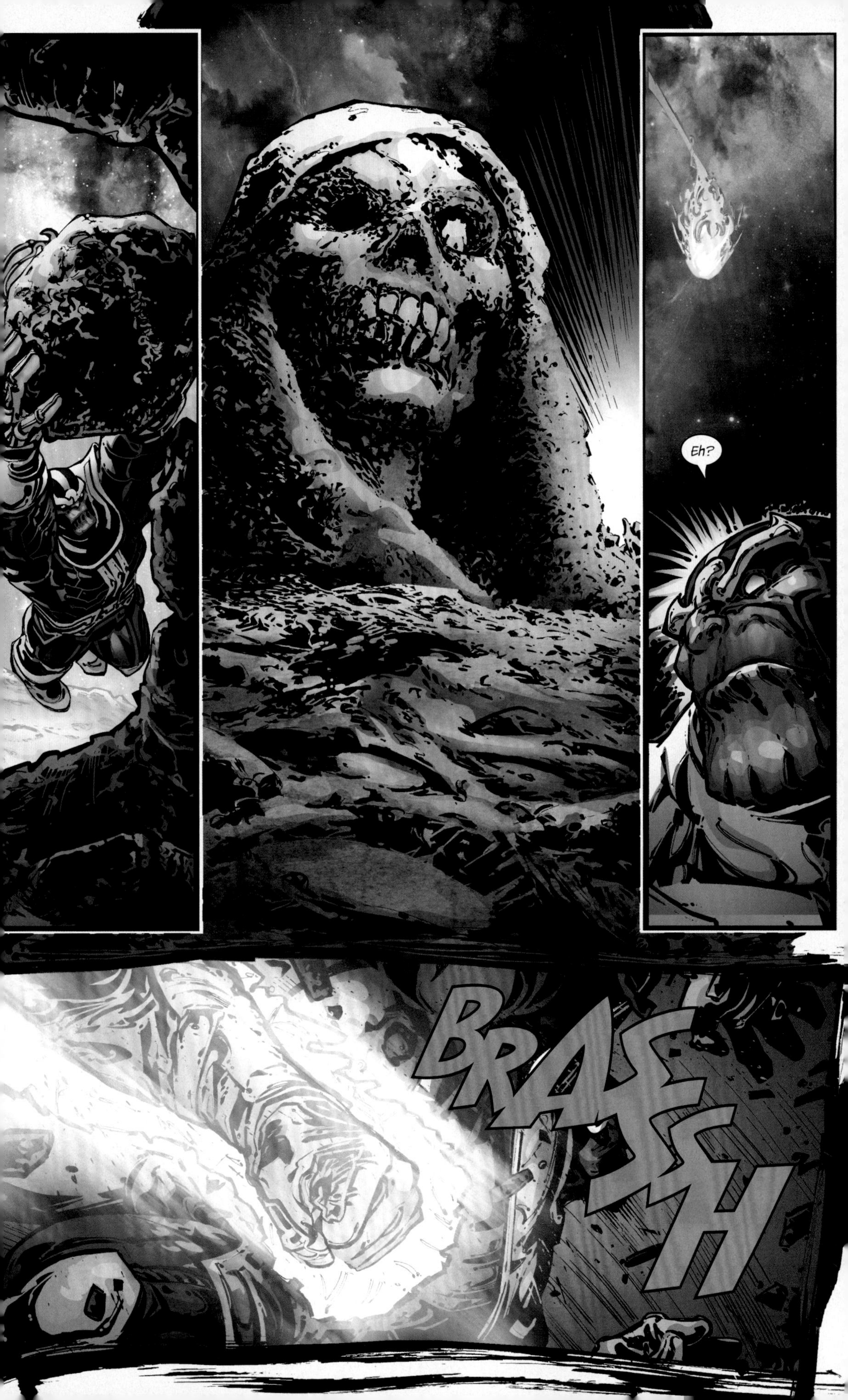
Eh?
BRASSH

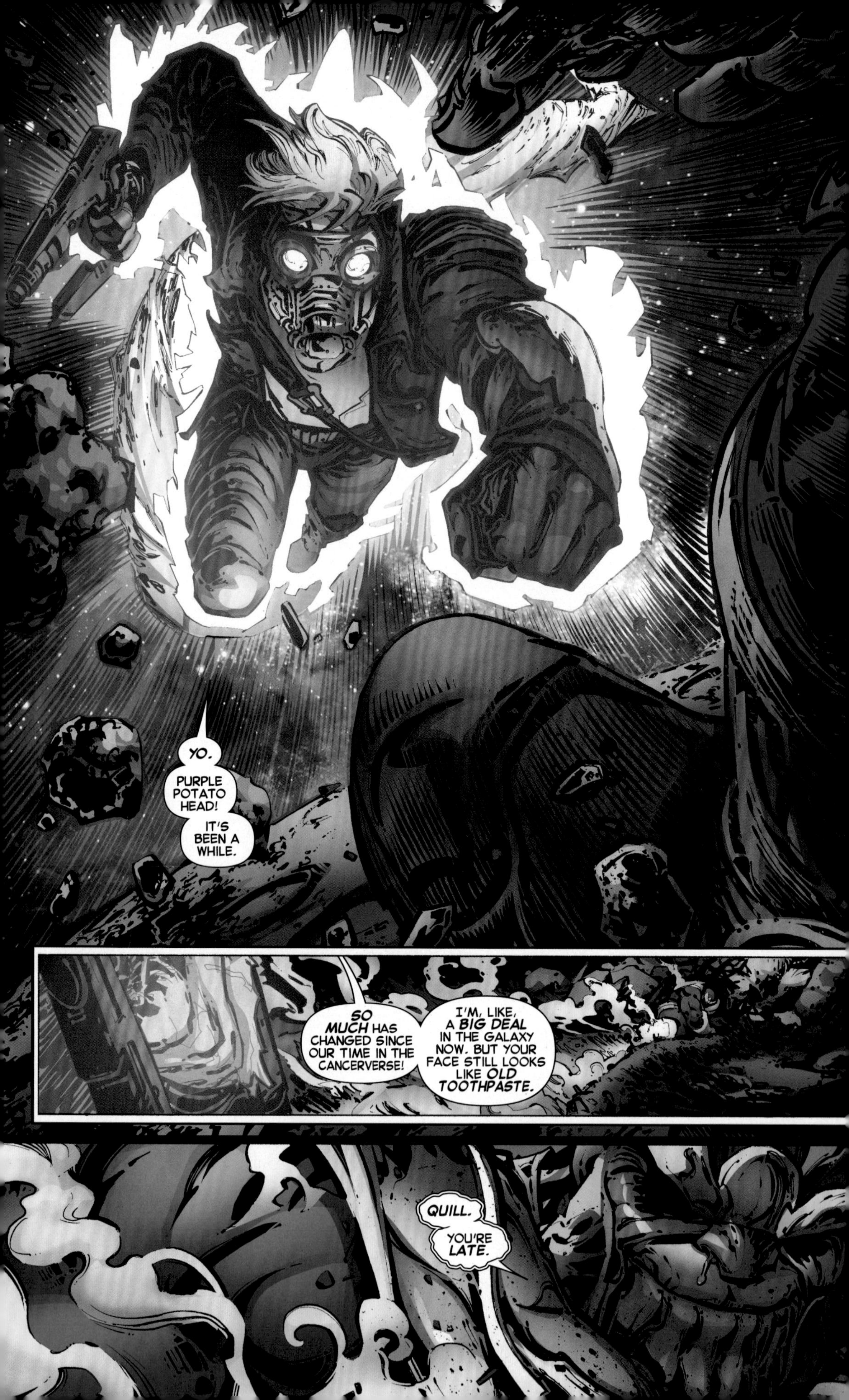
YO.
PURPLE POTATO HEAD!
IT'S BEEN A WHILE.
SO MUCH HAS CHANGED SINCE OUR TIME IN THE CANCERVERSE!
I'M, LIKE, A BIG DEAL IN THE GALAXY NOW. BUT YOUR FACE STILL LOOKS LIKE OLD TOOTHPASTE.
QUILL.
YOU'RE LATE.

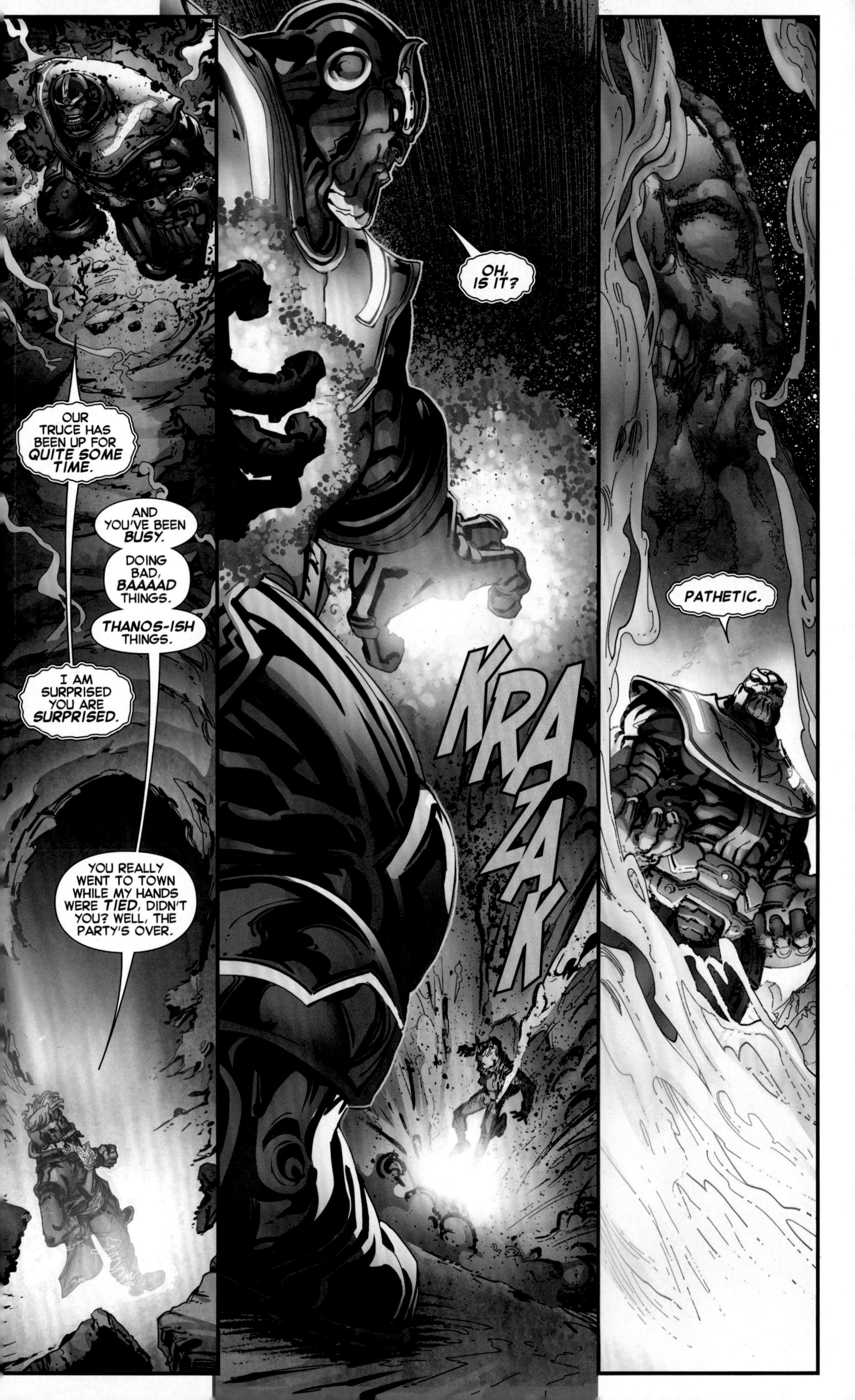
OUR TRUCE HAS BEEN UP FOR QUITE SOME TIME.
AND YOU'VE BEEN BUSY.
DOING BAD, BAAAAD THINGS.
THANOS-ISH THINGS.
I AM SURPRISED YOU ARE SURPRISED.
YOU REALLY WENT TO TOWN WHILE MY HANDS WERE TIED, DIDN'T YOU? WELL, THE PARTY'S OVER.
OH, IS IT?
KRAZAK
PATHETIC.

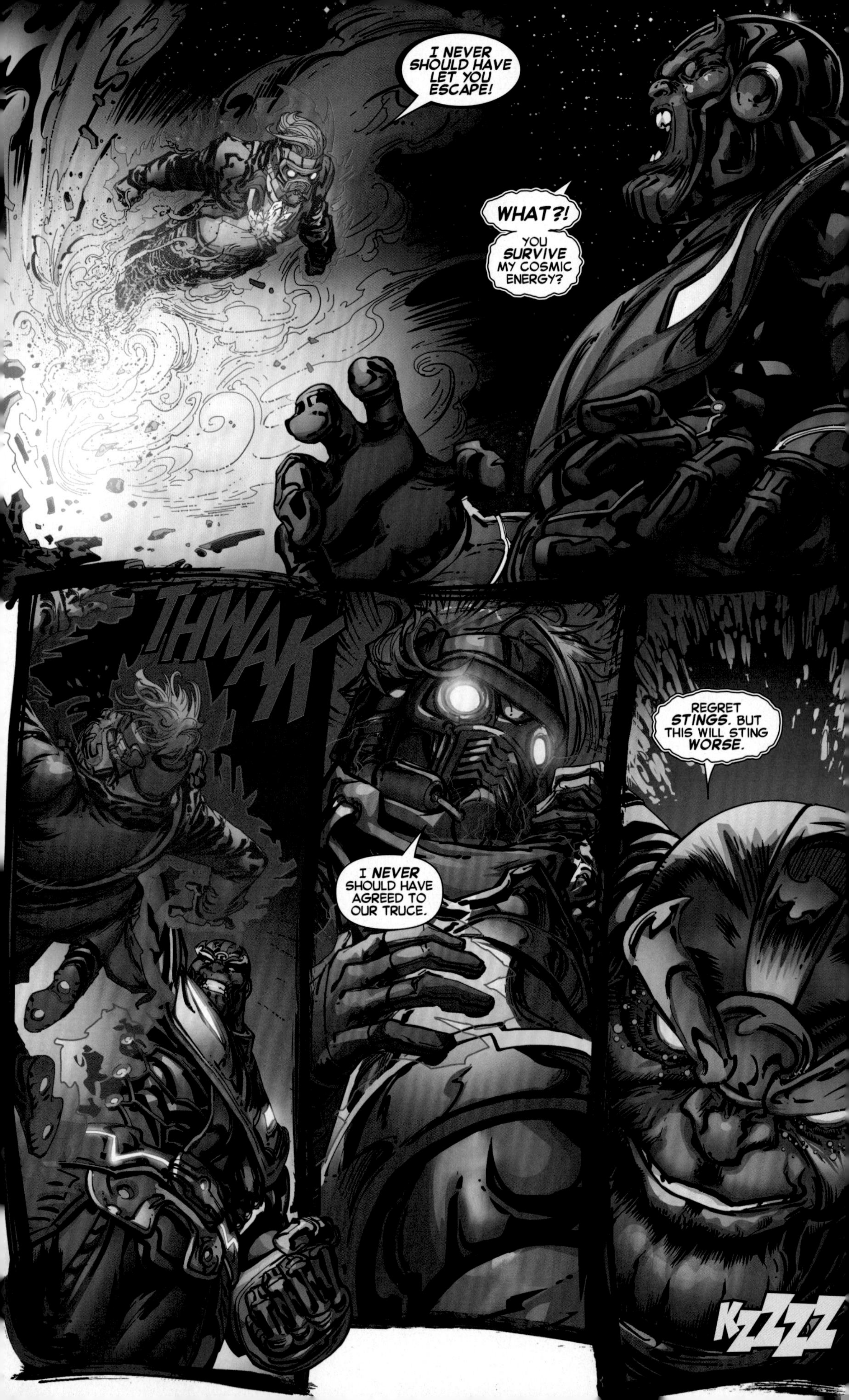
I NEVER SHOULD HAVE LET YOU ESCAPE!
WHAT?!
YOU SURVIVE MY COSMIC ENERGY?
THWAK
I NEVER SHOULD HAVE AGREED TO OUR TRUCE.
REGRET STINGS. BUT THIS WILL STING WORSE.
KZZZZ

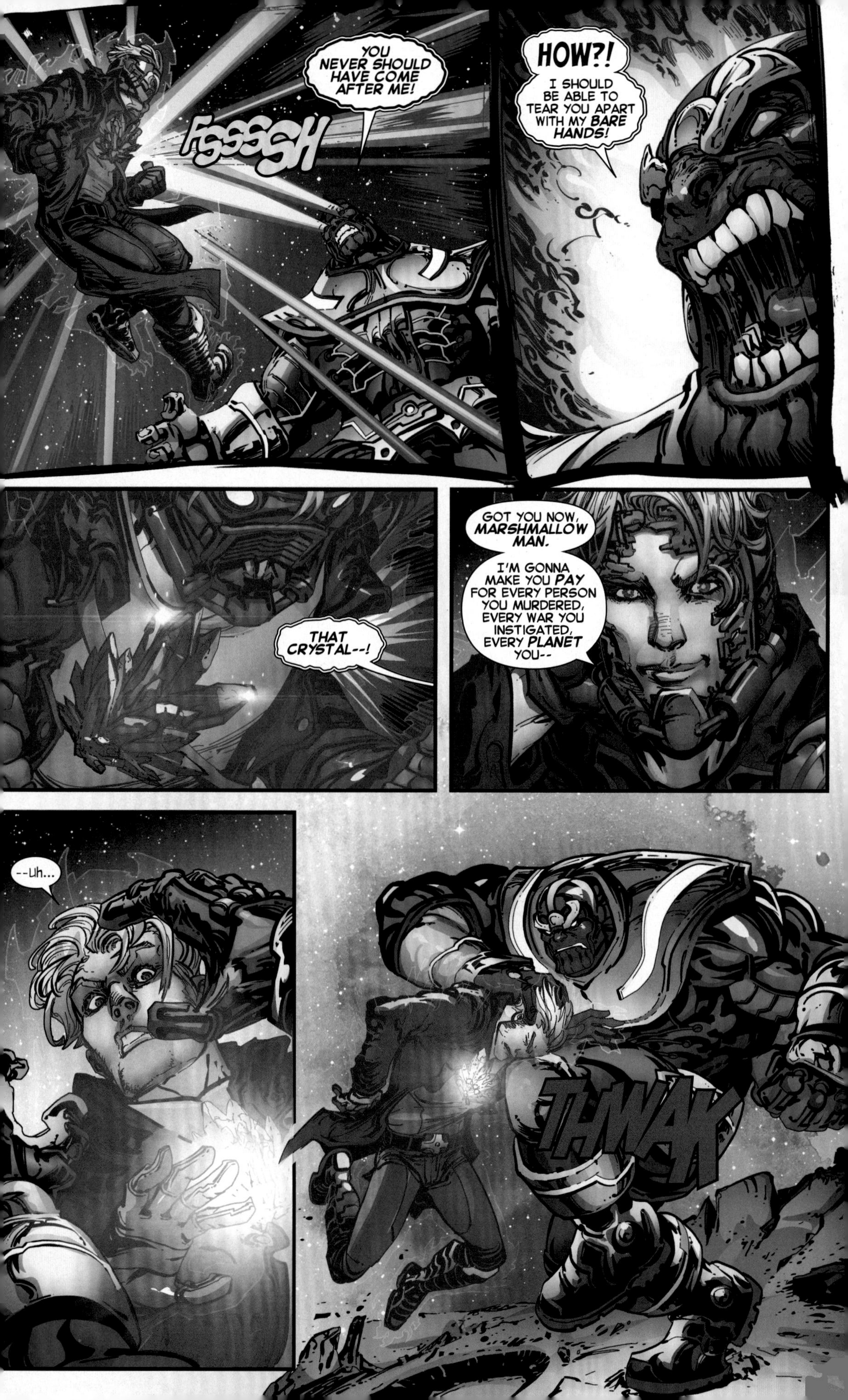
FSSSSH
YOU NEVER SHOULD HAVE COME AFTER ME!
HOW?!
I SHOULD BE ABLE TO TEAR YOU APART WITH MY BARE HANDS!
THAT CRYSTAL--!
GOT YOU NOW, MARSHMALLOW MAN.
I'M GONNA MAKE YOU PAY FOR EVERY PERSON YOU MURDERED, EVERY WAR YOU INSTIGATED, EVERY PLANET YOU--
--UH...
THWAK

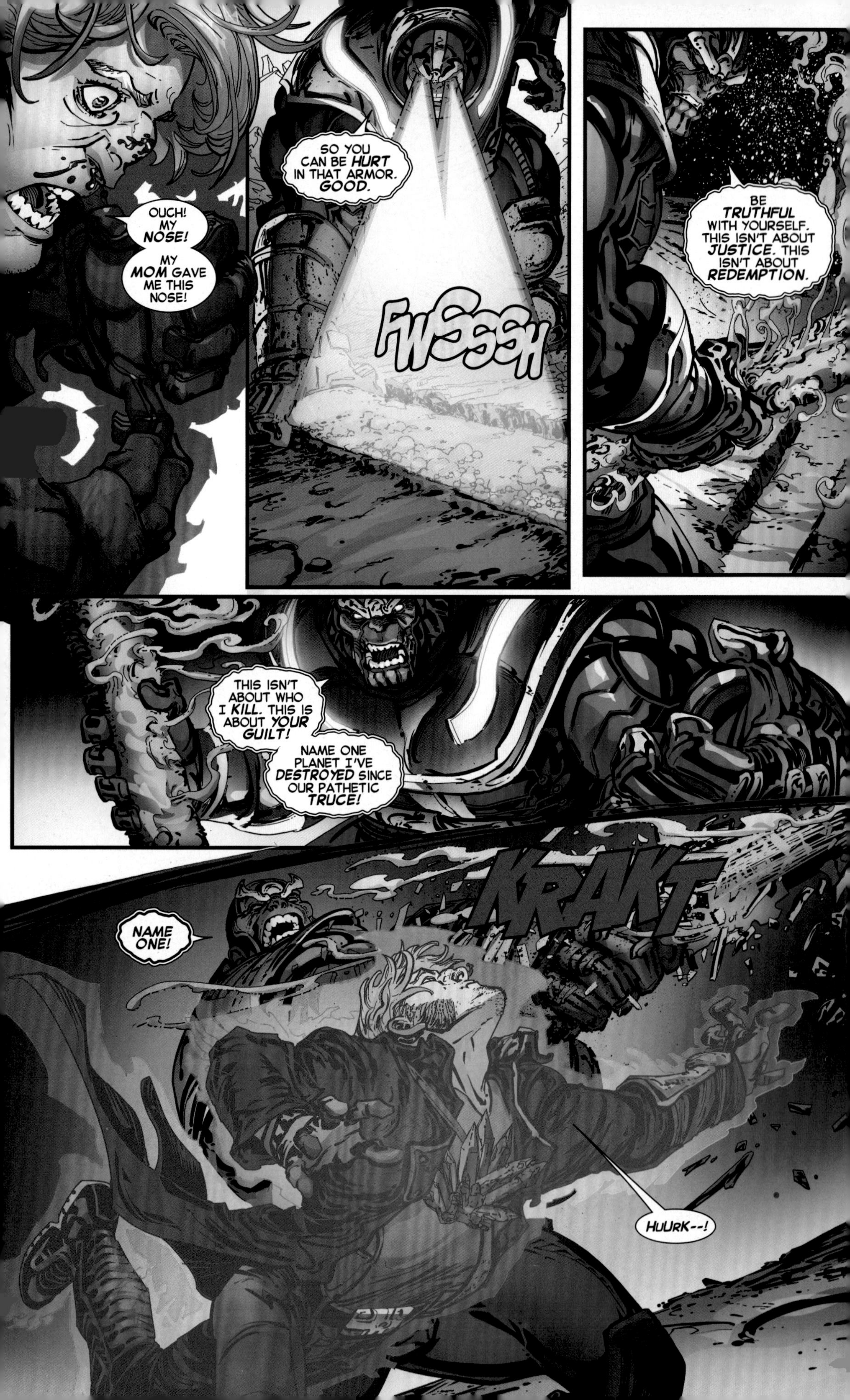

OUCH! MY NOSE!
MY MOM GAVE ME THIS NOSE!
SO YOU CAN BE HURT IN THAT ARMOR. GOOD.
FWSSSH
BE TRUTHFUL WITH YOURSELF. THIS ISN'T ABOUT JUSTICE. THIS ISN'T ABOUT REDEMPTION.
THIS ISN'T ABOUT WHO I KILL. THIS IS ABOUT YOUR GUILT!
NAME ONE PLANET I'VE DESTROYED SINCE OUR PATHETIC TRUCE!
KRAKT
NAME ONE!
HUURK--!

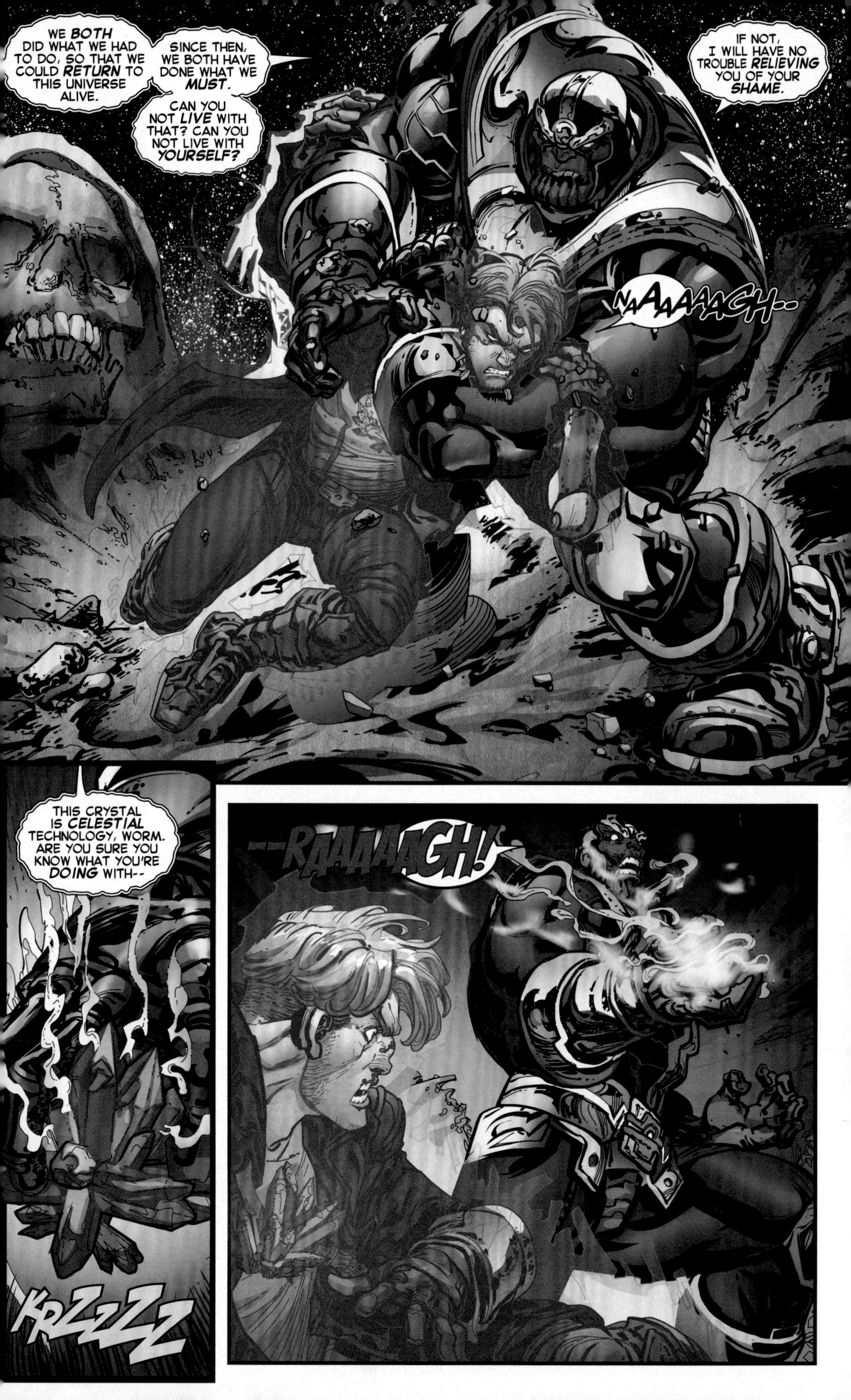
WE BOTH DID WHAT WE HAD TO DO, SO THAT WE COULD RETURN TO THIS UNIVERSE ALIVE.
SINCE THEN, WE BOTH HAVE DONE WHAT WE MUST.
CAN YOU NOT LIVE WITH THAT? CAN YOU NOT LIVE WITH YOURSELF?
IF NOT, I WILL HAVE NO TROUBLE RELIEVING YOU OF YOUR SHAME.
NAAAAAAGH--
THIS CRYSTAL IS CELESTIAL TECHNOLOGY, WORM. ARE YOU SURE YOU KNOW WHAT YOU'RE DOING WITH--
KRZZZZ
--RAAAAAGH!

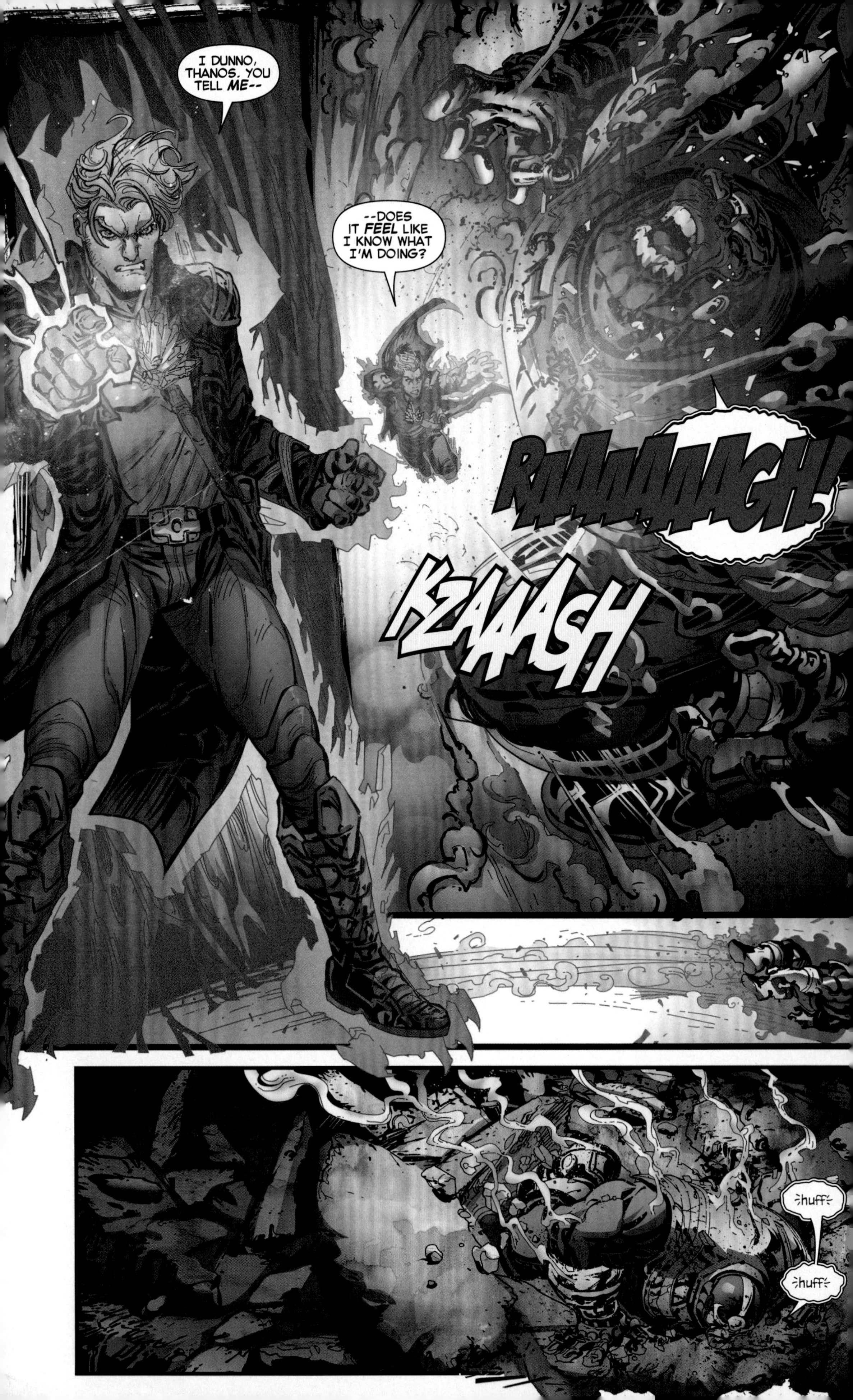
I DUNNO, THANOS. YOU TELL ME--
--DOES IT FEEL LIKE I KNOW WHAT I'M DOING?
RAAAAAAGH!
KZAAASH
huff
huff

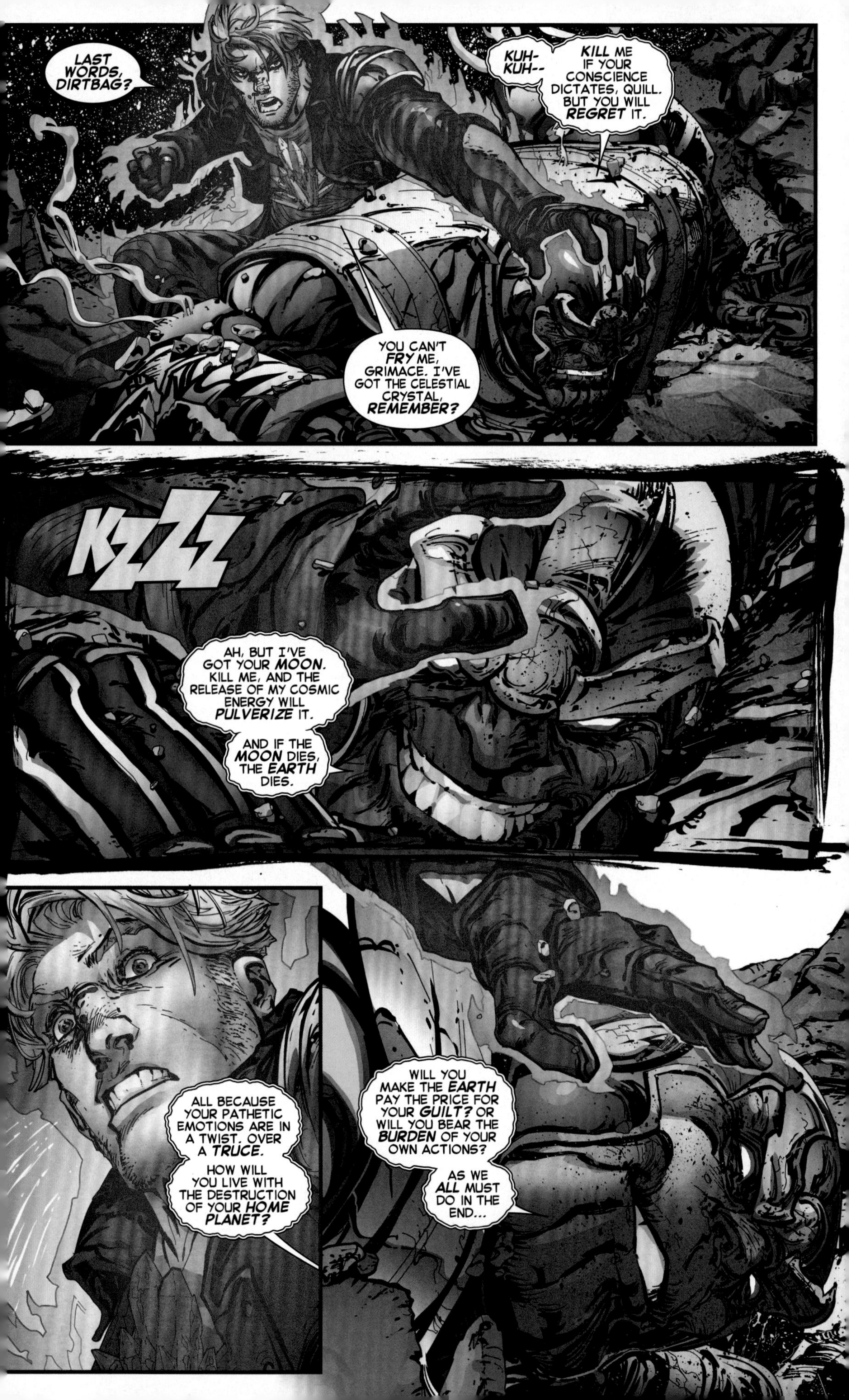
LAST WORDS, DIRTBAG?
KUH-KUH--
KILL ME IF YOUR CONSCIENCE DICTATES, QUILL. BUT YOU WILL REGRET IT.
YOU CAN'T FRY ME, GRIMACE. I'VE GOT THE CELESTIAL CRYSTAL, REMEMBER?
KZZZZ
AH, BUT I'VE GOT YOUR MOON. KILL ME, AND THE RELEASE OF MY COSMIC ENERGY WILL PULVERIZE IT.
AND IF THE MOON DIES, THE EARTH DIES.
ALL BECAUSE YOUR PATHETIC EMOTIONS ARE IN A TWIST. OVER A TRUCE.
HOW WILL YOU LIVE WITH THE DESTRUCTION OF YOUR HOME PLANET?
WILL YOU MAKE THE EARTH PAY THE PRICE FOR YOUR GUILT? OR WILL YOU BEAR THE BURDEN OF YOUR OWN ACTIONS?
AS WE ALL MUST DO IN THE END...

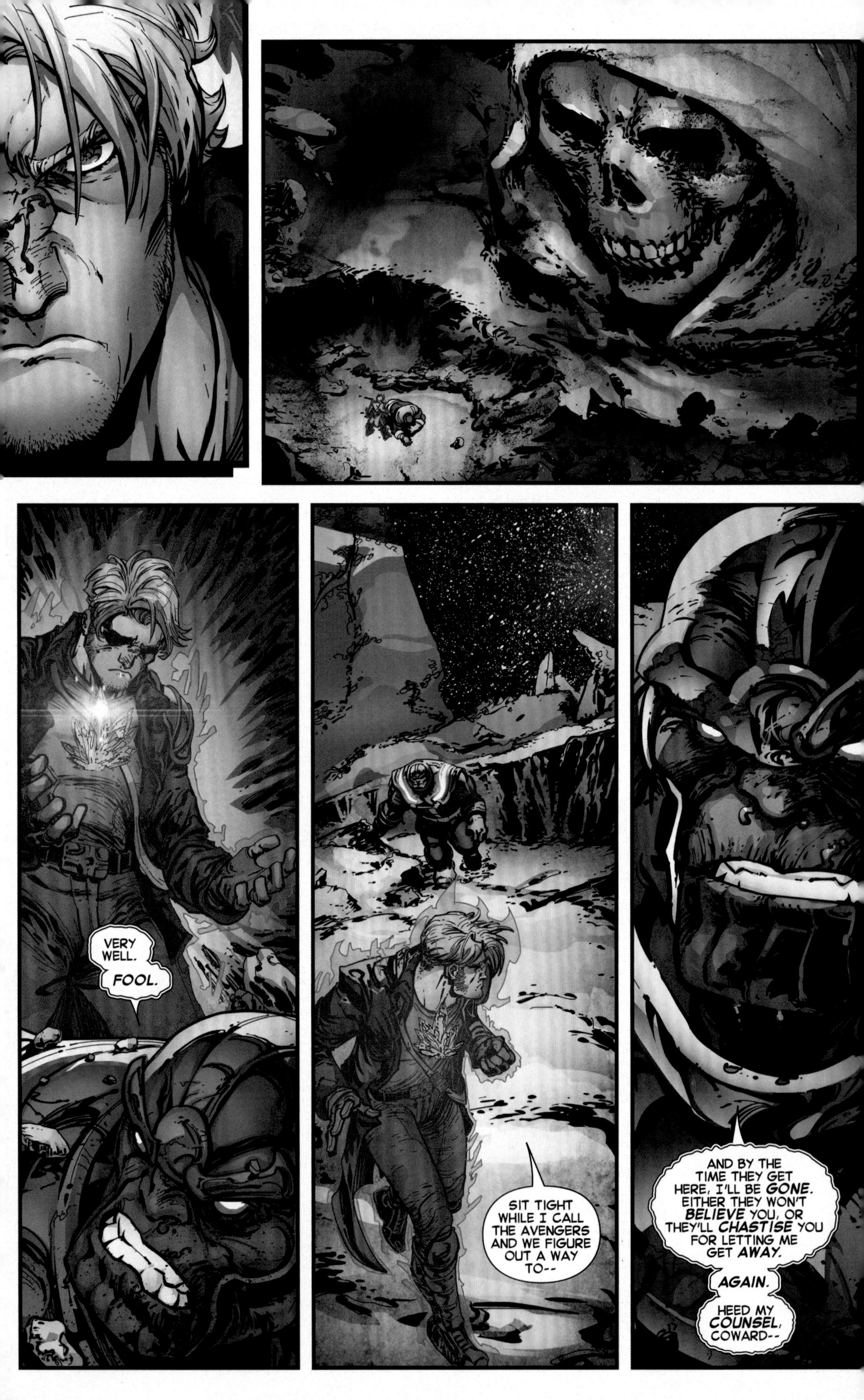
VERY WELL.
FOOL.
SIT TIGHT WHILE I CALL THE AVENGERS AND WE FIGURE OUT A WAY TO--
AND BY THE TIME THEY GET HERE, I'LL BE GONE. EITHER THEY WON'T BELIEVE YOU, OR THEY'LL CHASTISE YOU FOR LETTING ME GET AWAY.
AGAIN.
HEED MY COUNSEL, COWARD--

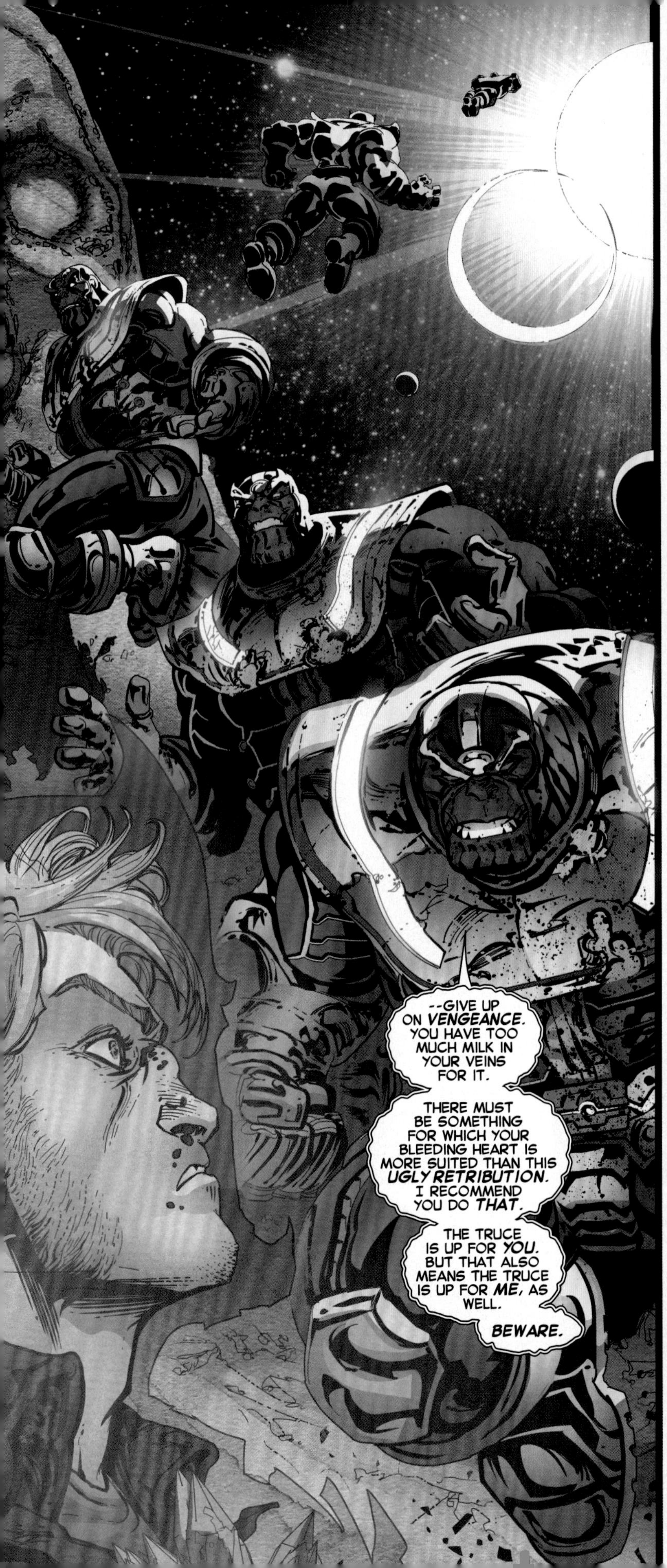
--GIVE UP ON VENGEANCE. YOU HAVE TOO MUCH MILK IN YOUR VEINS FOR IT.
THERE MUST BE SOMETHING FOR WHICH YOUR BLEEDING HEART IS MORE SUITED THAN THIS UGLY RETRIBUTION. I RECOMMEND YOU DO THAT.
THE TRUCE IS UP FOR YOU. BUT THAT ALSO MEANS THE TRUCE IS UP FOR ME, AS WELL.
BEWARE.

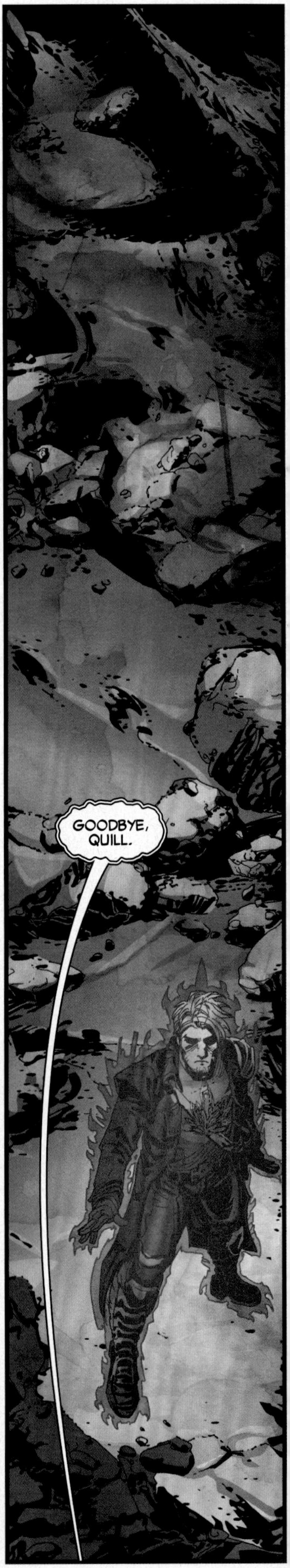
GOODBYE, QUILL.

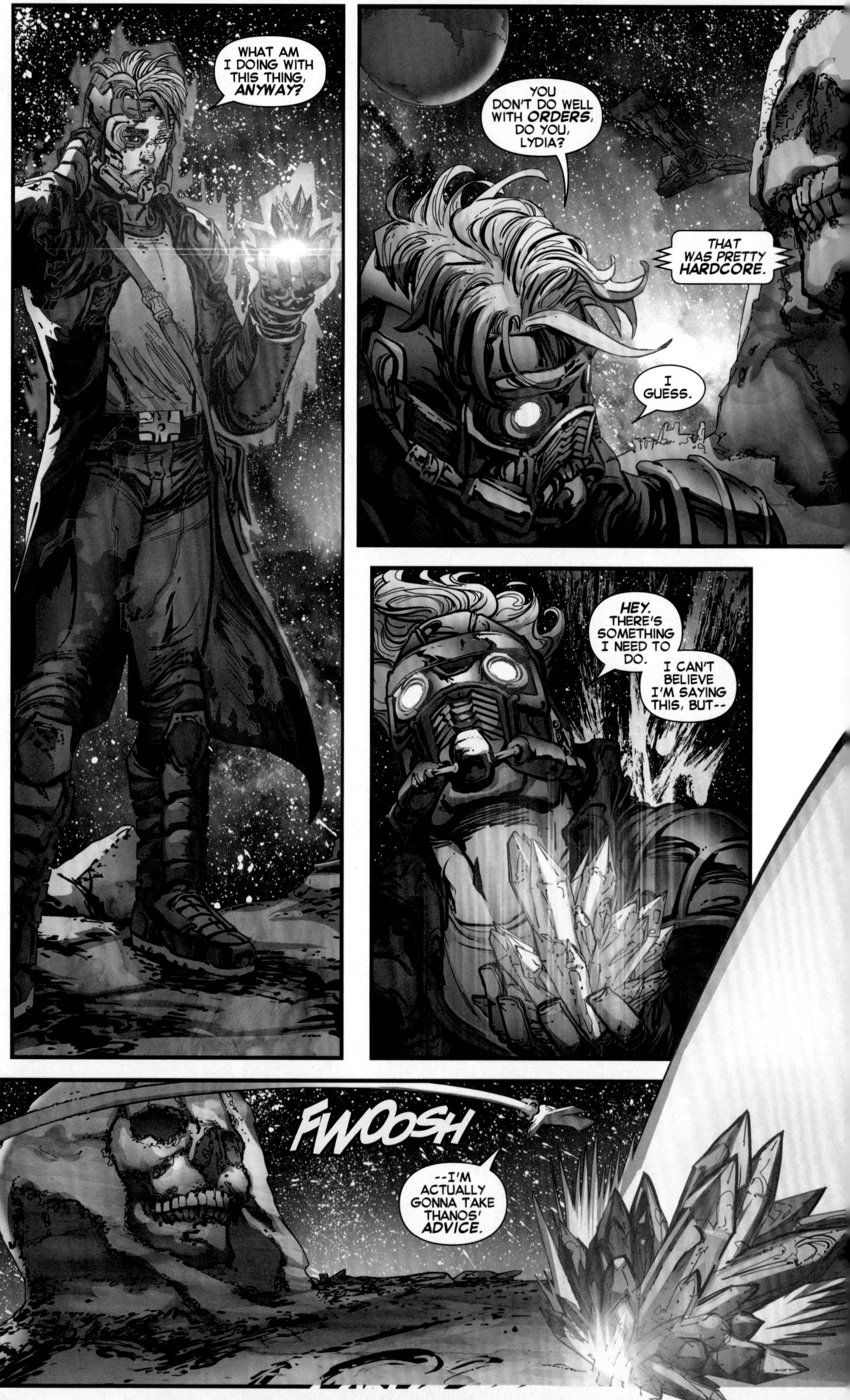
WHAT AM I DOING WITH THIS THING, ANYWAY?
YOU DON'T DO WELL WITH ORDERS, DO YOU, LYDIA?
THAT WAS PRETTY HARDCORE.
I GUESS.
HEY. THERE'S SOMETHING I NEED TO DO.
I CAN'T BELIEVE I'M SAYING THIS, BUT--
FWOOSH
--I'M ACTUALLY GONNA TAKE THANOS' ADVICE.

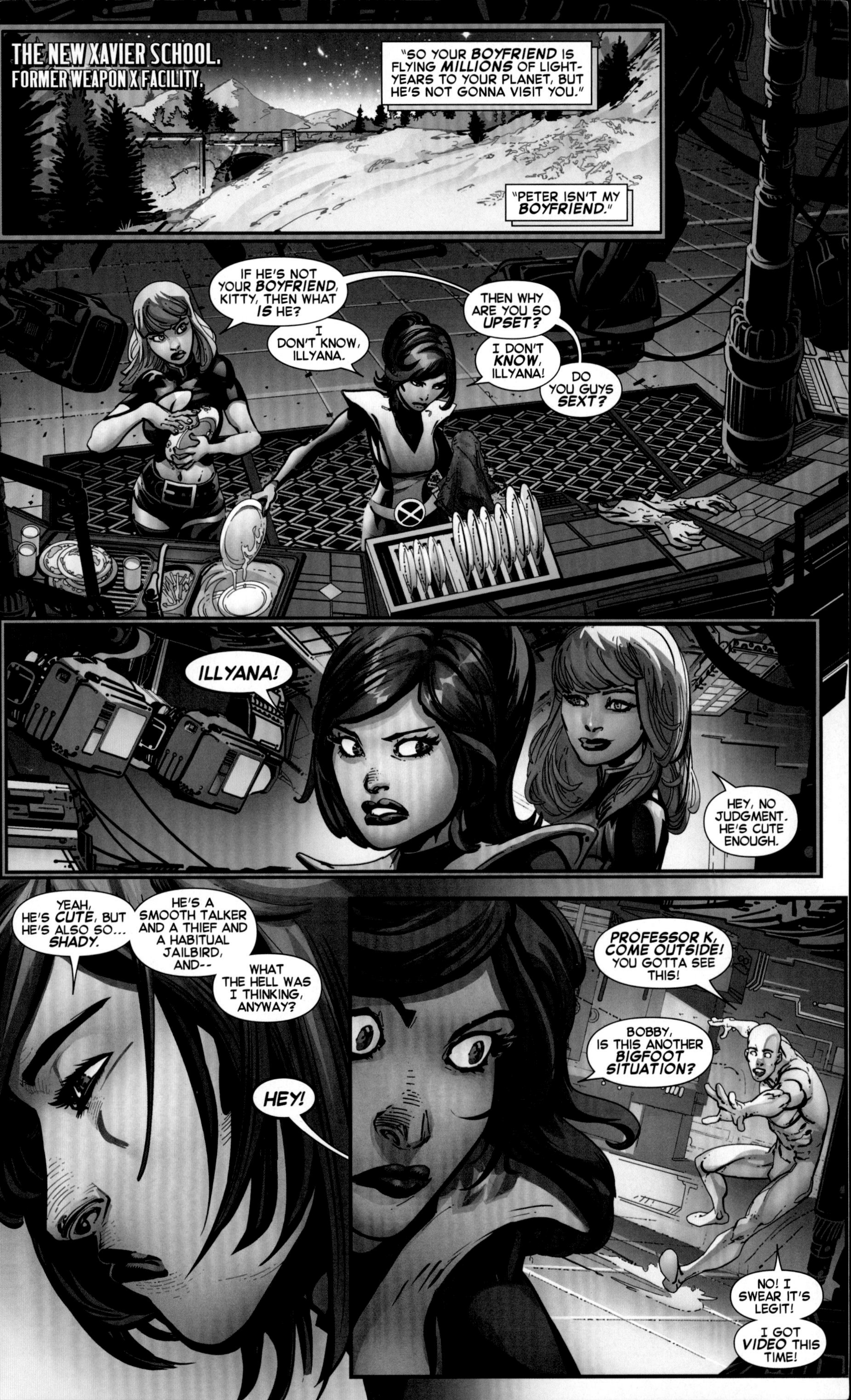
THE NEW XAVIER SCHOOL. FORMER WEAPON X FACILITY.
"SO YOUR BOYFRIEND IS FLYING MILLIONS OF LIGHT-YEARS TO YOUR PLANET, BUT HE'S NOT GONNA VISIT YOU."
"PETER ISN'T MY BOYFRIEND."
IF HE'S NOT YOUR BOYFRIEND, KITTY, THEN WHAT IS HE?
I DON'T KNOW, ILLYANA.
THEN WHY ARE YOU SO UPSET?
I DON'T KNOW, ILLYANA!
DO YOU GUYS SEXT?
ILLYANA!
HEY, NO JUDGMENT. HE'S CUTE ENOUGH.
YEAH, HE'S CUTE, BUT HE'S ALSO SO... SHADY.
HE'S A SMOOTH TALKER AND A THIEF AND A HABITUAL JAILBIRD, AND--
WHAT THE HELL WAS I THINKING, ANYWAY?
HEY!
PROFESSOR K, COME OUTSIDE! YOU GOTTA SEE THIS!
BOBBY, IS THIS ANOTHER BIGFOOT SITUATION?
NO! I SWEAR IT'S LEGIT!
I GOT VIDEO THIS TIME!

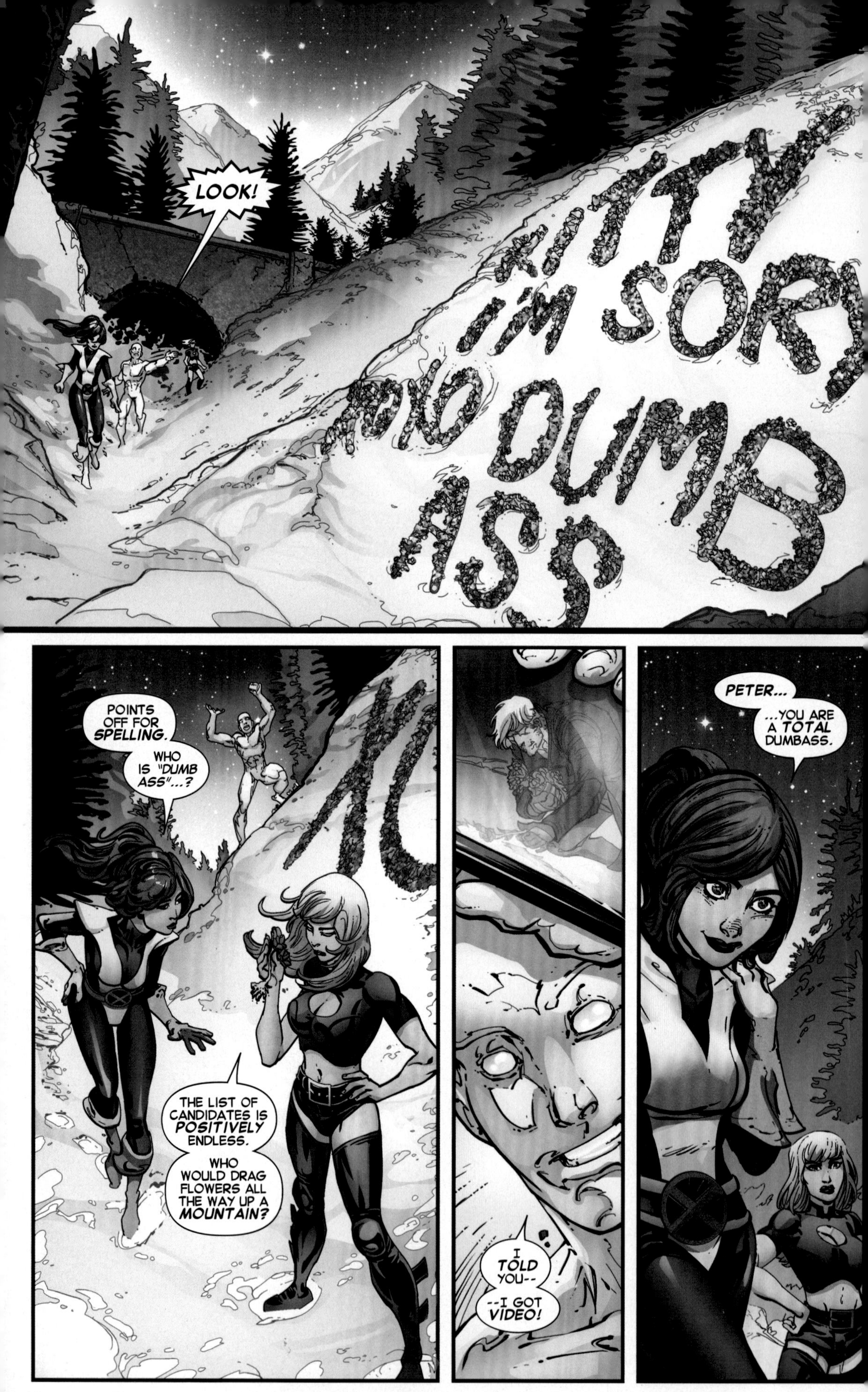

LOOK!
KITTY
I'M SOR
XOXO DUMB ASS
POINTS OFF FOR SPELLING.
WHO IS "DUMB ASS"...?
THE LIST OF CANDIDATES IS POSITIVELY ENDLESS.
WHO WOULD DRAG FLOWERS ALL THE WAY UP A MOUNTAIN?
I TOLD YOU--
--I GOT VIDEO!
PETER...
...YOU ARE A TOTAL DUMBASS.

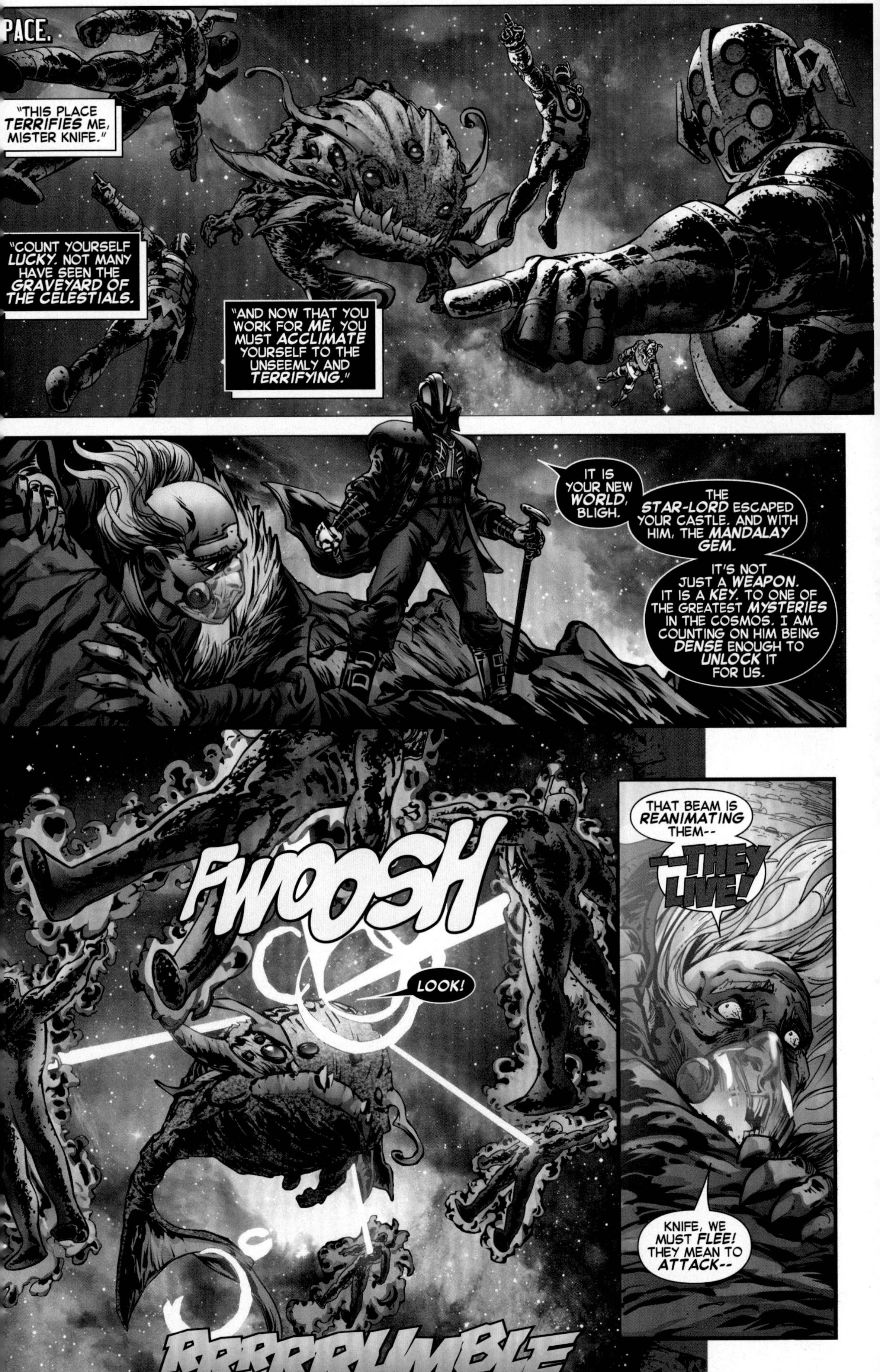
PACE.
"THIS PLACE TERRIFIES ME, MISTER KNIFE."
"COUNT YOURSELF LUCKY. NOT MANY HAVE SEEN THE GRAVEYARD OF THE CELESTIALS.
"AND NOW THAT YOU WORK FOR ME, YOU MUST ACCLIMATE YOURSELF TO THE UNSEEMLY AND TERRIFYING."
IT IS YOUR NEW WORLD, BLIGH.
THE STAR-LORD ESCAPED YOUR CASTLE, AND WITH HIM, THE MANDALAY GEM.
IT'S NOT JUST A WEAPON. IT IS A KEY. TO ONE OF THE GREATEST MYSTERIES IN THE COSMOS. I AM COUNTING ON HIM BEING DENSE ENOUGH TO UNLOCK IT FOR US.
FWOOSH
LOOK!
THAT BEAM IS REANIMATING THEM--
--THEY LIVE!
KNIFE, WE MUST FLEE! THEY MEAN TO ATTACK--
RRRRRUMBLE

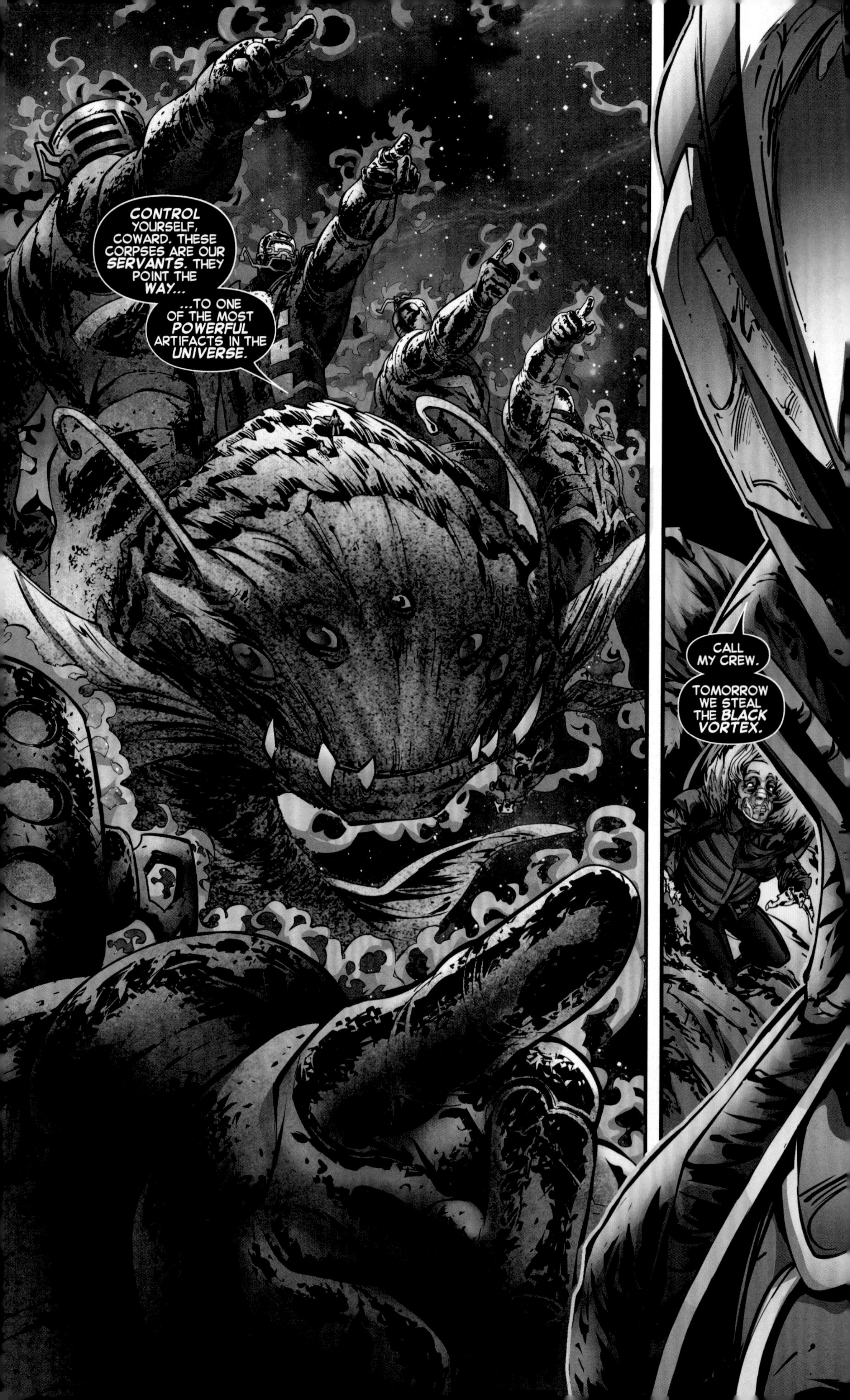
CONTROL YOURSELF, COWARD. THESE CORPSES ARE OUR SERVANTS. THEY POINT THE WAY...
...TO ONE OF THE MOST POWERFUL ARTIFACTS IN THE UNIVERSE.
CALL MY CREW.
TOMORROW WE STEAL THE BLACK VORTEX.

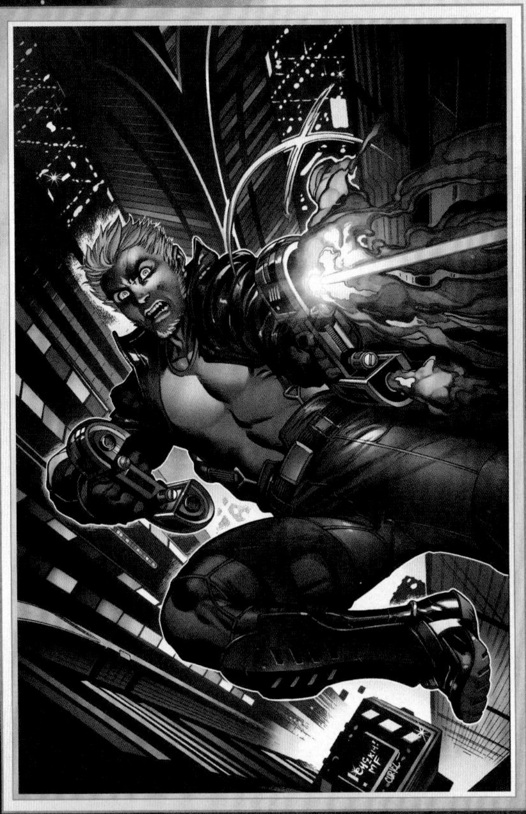

#2 VARIANT BY
ED McGUINNESS & DAVID CURIEL

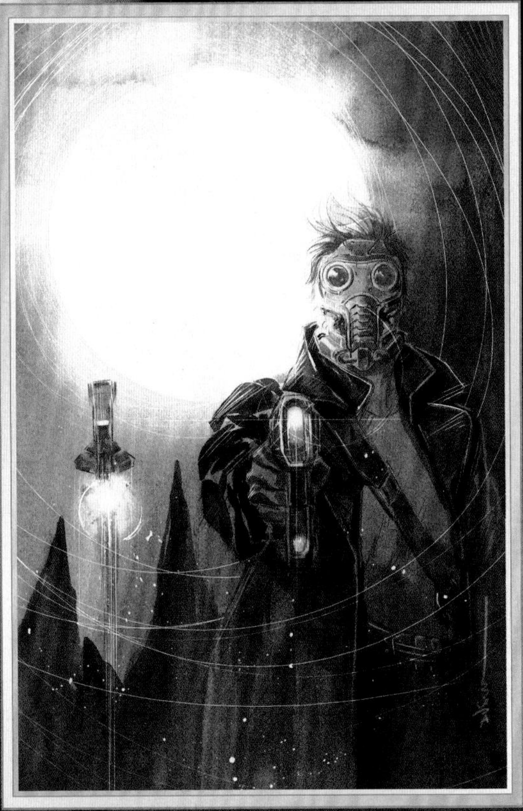

#3 VARIANT BY
DUSTIN NGUYEN

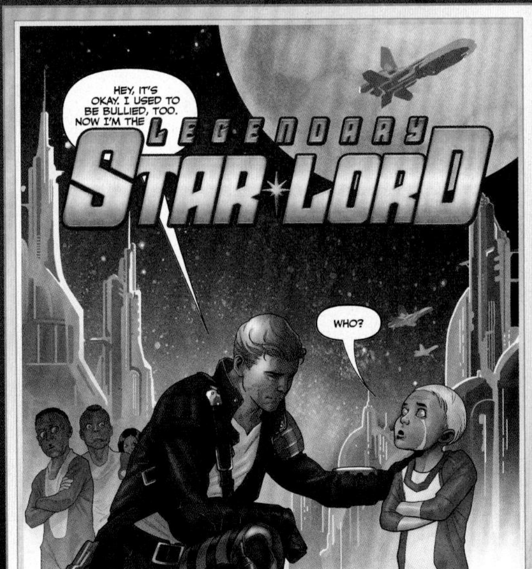

HEY, IT'S OKAY. I USED TO BE BULLIED, TOO. NOW I'M THE
LEGENDARY
STAR-LORD
WHO?

#4 STOMP OUT BULLYING VARIANT BY
PAUL RENAUD

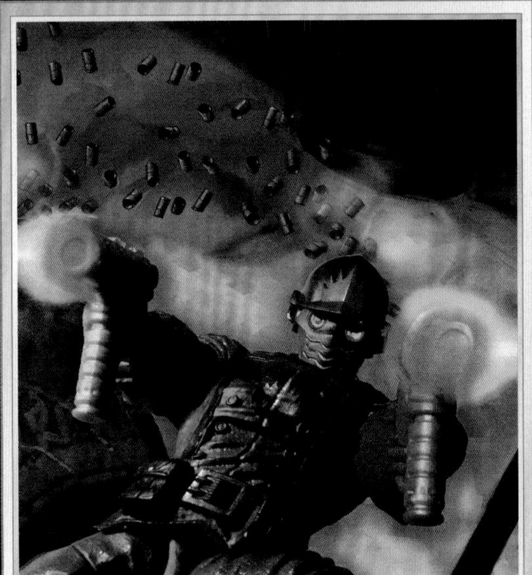

#4 HASBRO VARIANT

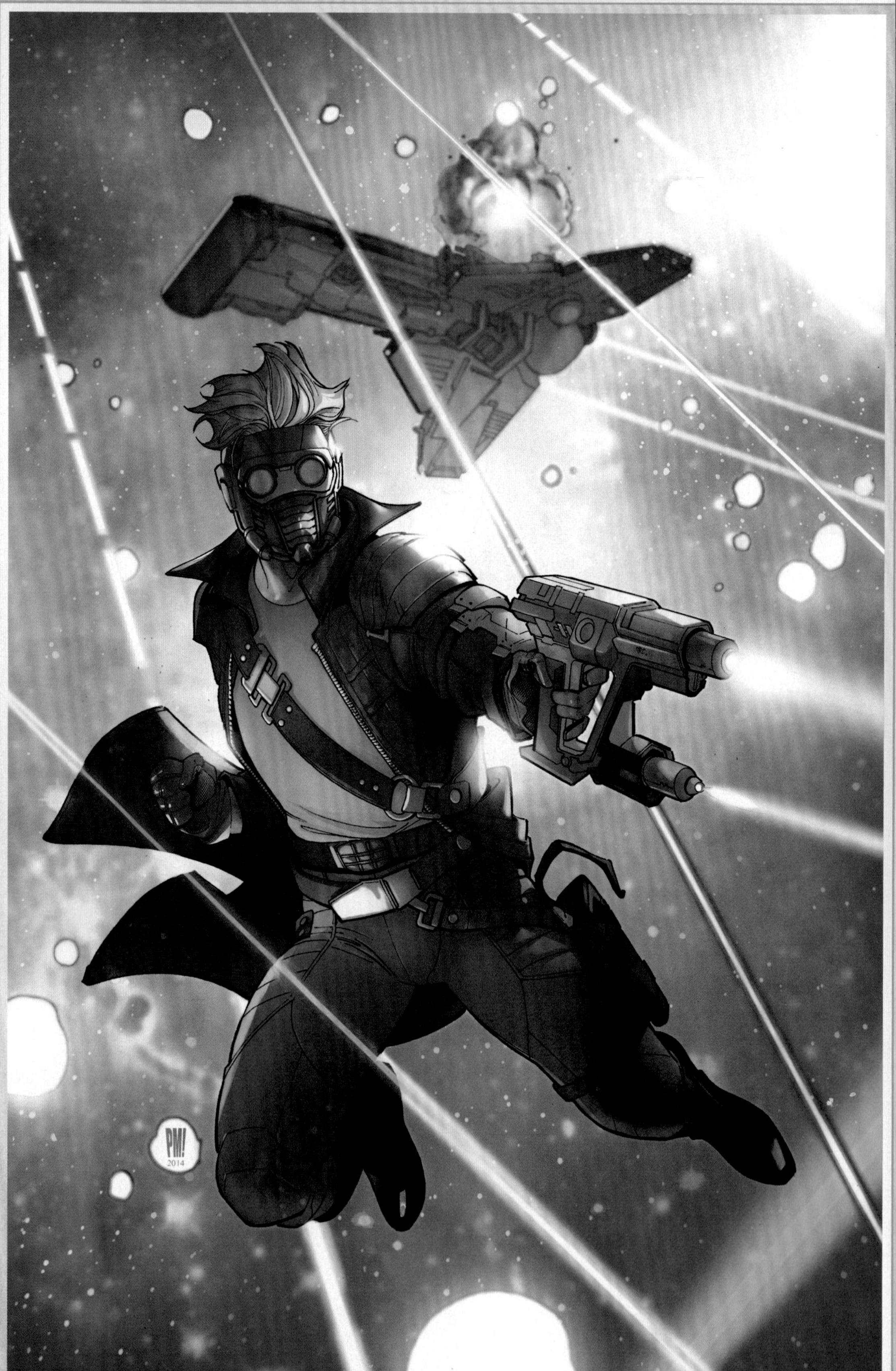
PM!
2014

FIVE

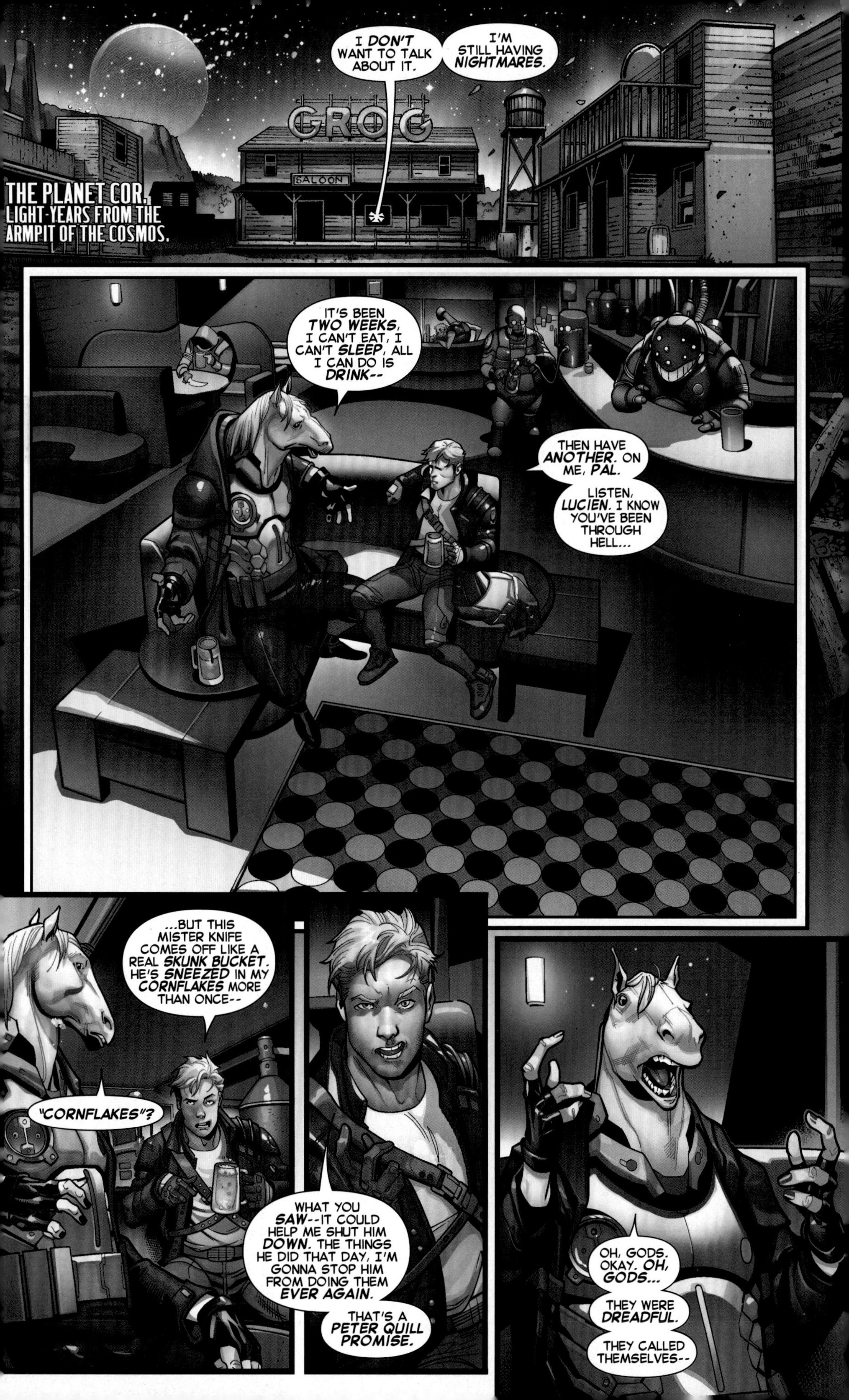

THE PLANET COR. LIGHT-YEARS FROM THE ARMPIT OF THE COSMOS.
GROG
SALOON
I DON'T WANT TO TALK ABOUT IT.
I'M STILL HAVING NIGHTMARES.
IT'S BEEN TWO WEEKS, I CAN'T EAT, I CAN'T SLEEP, ALL I CAN DO IS DRINK--
THEN HAVE ANOTHER. ON ME, PAL.
LISTEN, LUCIEN. I KNOW YOU'VE BEEN THROUGH HELL...
...BUT THIS MISTER KNIFE COMES OFF LIKE A REAL SKUNK BUCKET. HE'S SNEEZED IN MY CORNFLAKES MORE THAN ONCE--
"CORNFLAKES"?
WHAT YOU SAW--IT COULD HELP ME SHUT HIM DOWN. THE THINGS HE DID THAT DAY, I'M GONNA STOP HIM FROM DOING THEM EVER AGAIN.
THAT'S A PETER QUILL PROMISE.
OH, GODS. OKAY. OH, GODS...
THEY WERE DREADFUL.
THEY CALLED THEMSELVES--

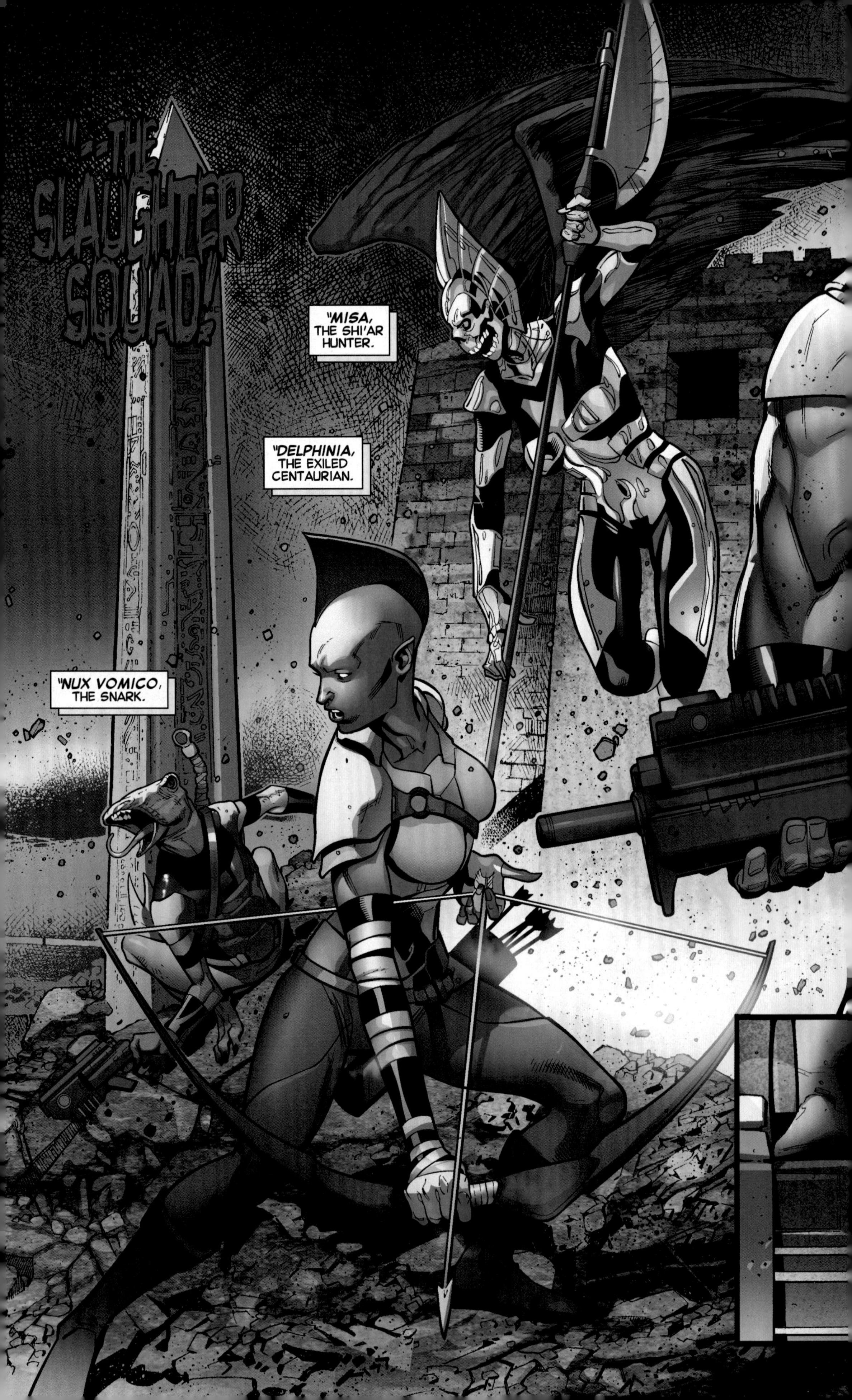
"--THE SLAUGHTER SQUAD!
"MISA, THE SHI'AR HUNTER.
"DELPHINIA, THE EXILED CENTAURIAN.
"NUX VOMICO, THE SNARK.

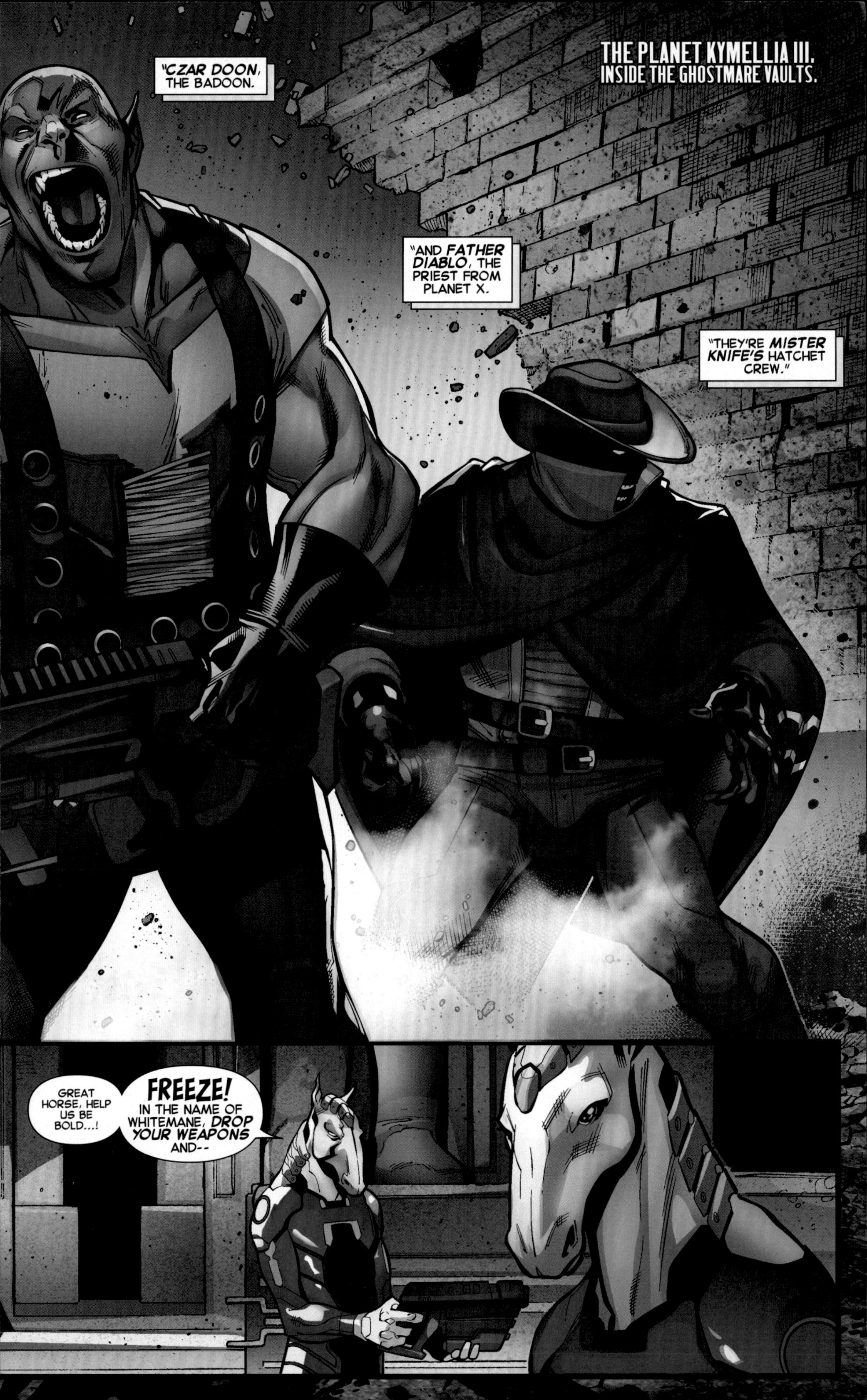

THE PLANET KYMELLIA III.
INSIDE THE GHOSTMARE VAULTS.
"CZAR DOON, THE BADOON.
"AND FATHER DIABLO, THE PRIEST FROM PLANET X.
"THEY'RE MISTER KNIFE'S HATCHET CREW."
GREAT HORSE, HELP US BE BOLD...!
FREEZE! IN THE NAME OF WHITEMANE, DROP YOUR WEAPONS AND--

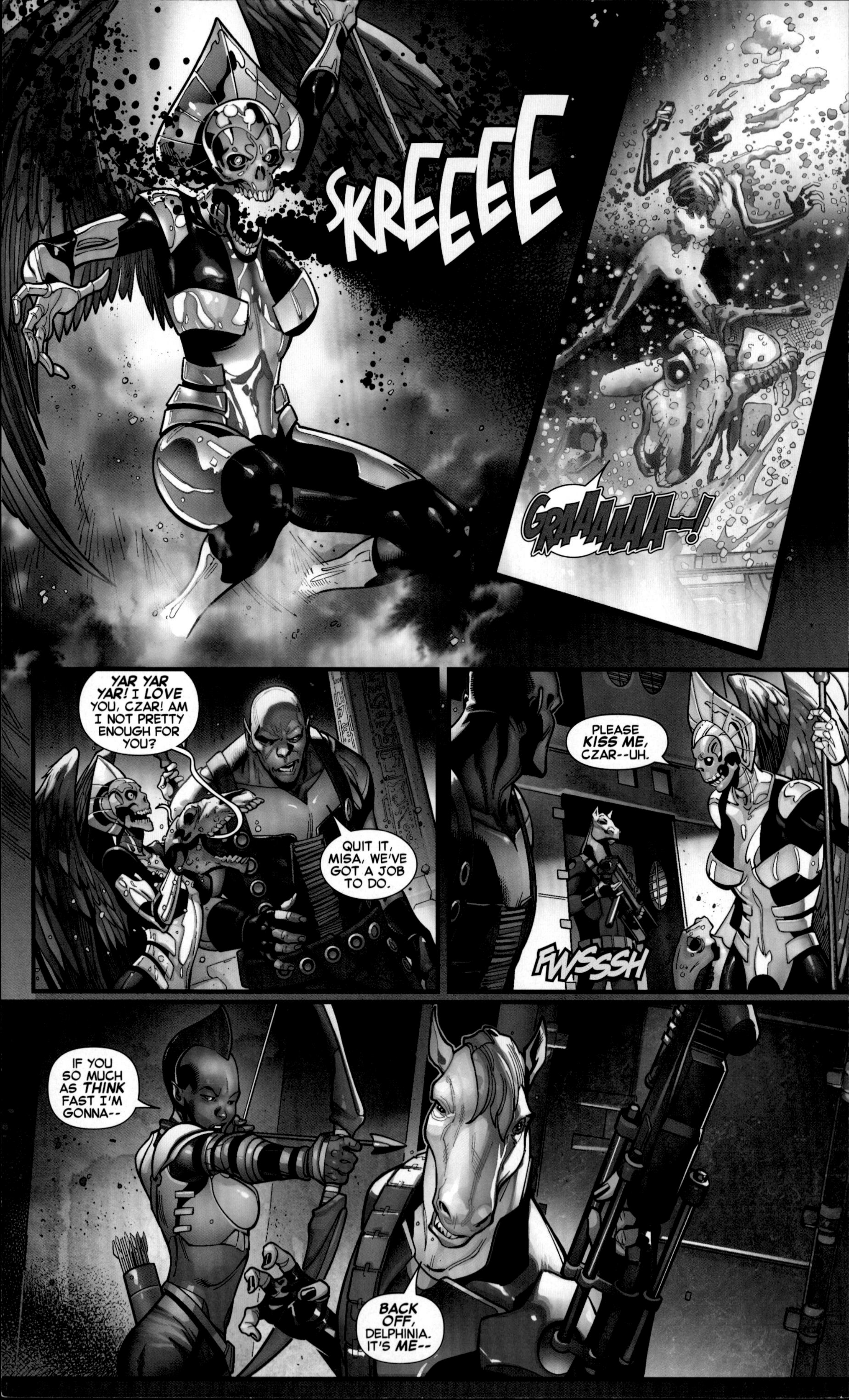
SKREEEE
GRAAAAAA--!
YAR YAR YAR! I LOVE YOU, CZAR! AM I NOT PRETTY ENOUGH FOR YOU?
QUIT IT, MISA, WE'VE GOT A JOB TO DO.
PLEASE KISS ME, CZAR--UH.
FWSSSH
IF YOU SO MUCH AS THINK FAST I'M GONNA--
BACK OFF, DELPHINIA. IT'S ME--

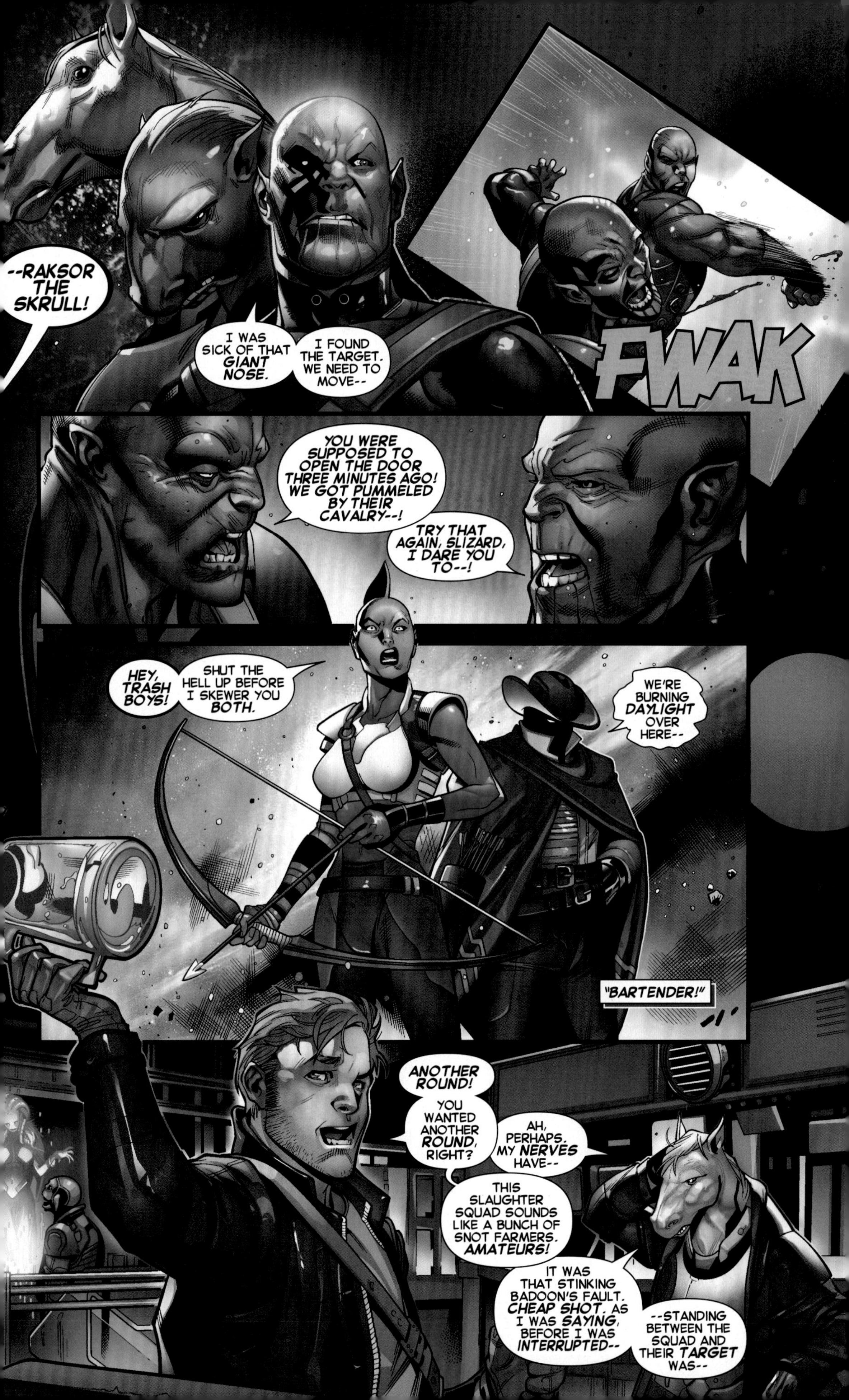
--RAKSOR THE SKRULL!
I WAS SICK OF THAT GIANT NOSE.
I FOUND THE TARGET. WE NEED TO MOVE--
FWAK
YOU WERE SUPPOSED TO OPEN THE DOOR THREE MINUTES AGO! WE GOT PUMMELED BY THEIR CAVALRY--!
TRY THAT AGAIN, SLIZARD, I DARE YOU TO--!
HEY, TRASH BOYS!
SHUT THE HELL UP BEFORE I SKEWER YOU BOTH.
WE'RE BURNING DAYLIGHT OVER HERE--
"BARTENDER!"
ANOTHER ROUND!
YOU WANTED ANOTHER ROUND, RIGHT?
AH, PERHAPS. MY NERVES HAVE--
THIS SLAUGHTER SQUAD SOUNDS LIKE A BUNCH OF SNOT FARMERS. AMATEURS!
IT WAS THAT STINKING BADOON'S FAULT. CHEAP SHOT. AS I WAS SAYING, BEFORE I WAS INTERRUPTED--
--STANDING BETWEEN THE SQUAD AND THEIR TARGET WAS--

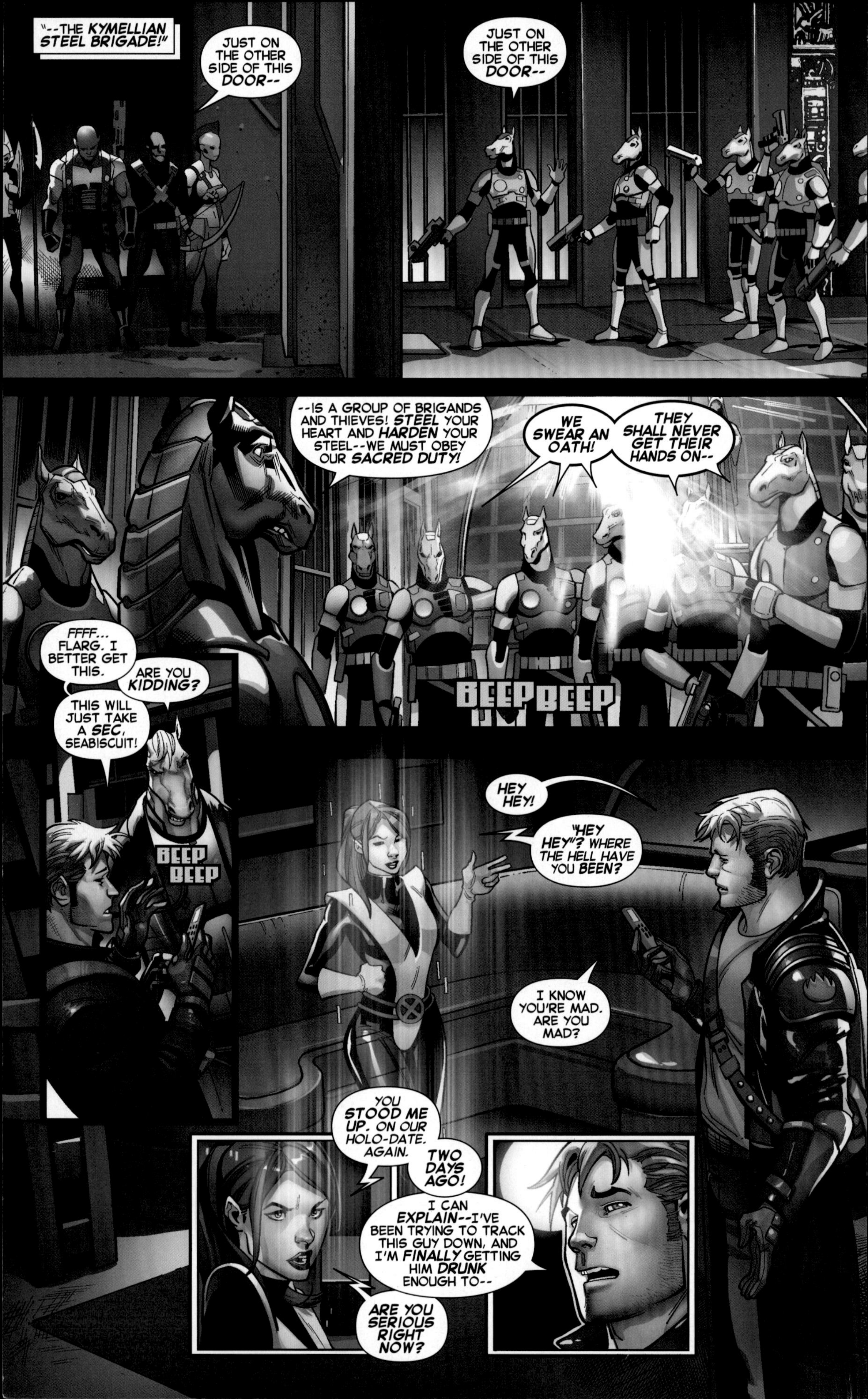
"--THE KYMELLIAN STEEL BRIGADE!"
JUST ON THE OTHER SIDE OF THIS DOOR--
JUST ON THE OTHER SIDE OF THIS DOOR--
--IS A GROUP OF BRIGANDS AND THIEVES! STEEL YOUR HEART AND HARDEN YOUR STEEL--WE MUST OBEY OUR SACRED DUTY!
WE SWEAR AN OATH!
THEY SHALL NEVER GET THEIR HANDS ON--
BEEP BEEP
FFFF... FLARG. I BETTER GET THIS.
ARE YOU KIDDING?
THIS WILL JUST TAKE A SEC, SEABISCUIT!
BEEP BEEP
HEY HEY!
"HEY HEY"? WHERE THE HELL HAVE YOU BEEN?
I KNOW YOU'RE MAD. ARE YOU MAD?
YOU STOOD ME UP. ON OUR HOLO-DATE. AGAIN.
TWO DAYS AGO!
I CAN EXPLAIN--I'VE BEEN TRYING TO TRACK THIS GUY DOWN, AND I'M FINALLY GETTING HIM DRUNK ENOUGH TO--
ARE YOU SERIOUS RIGHT NOW?

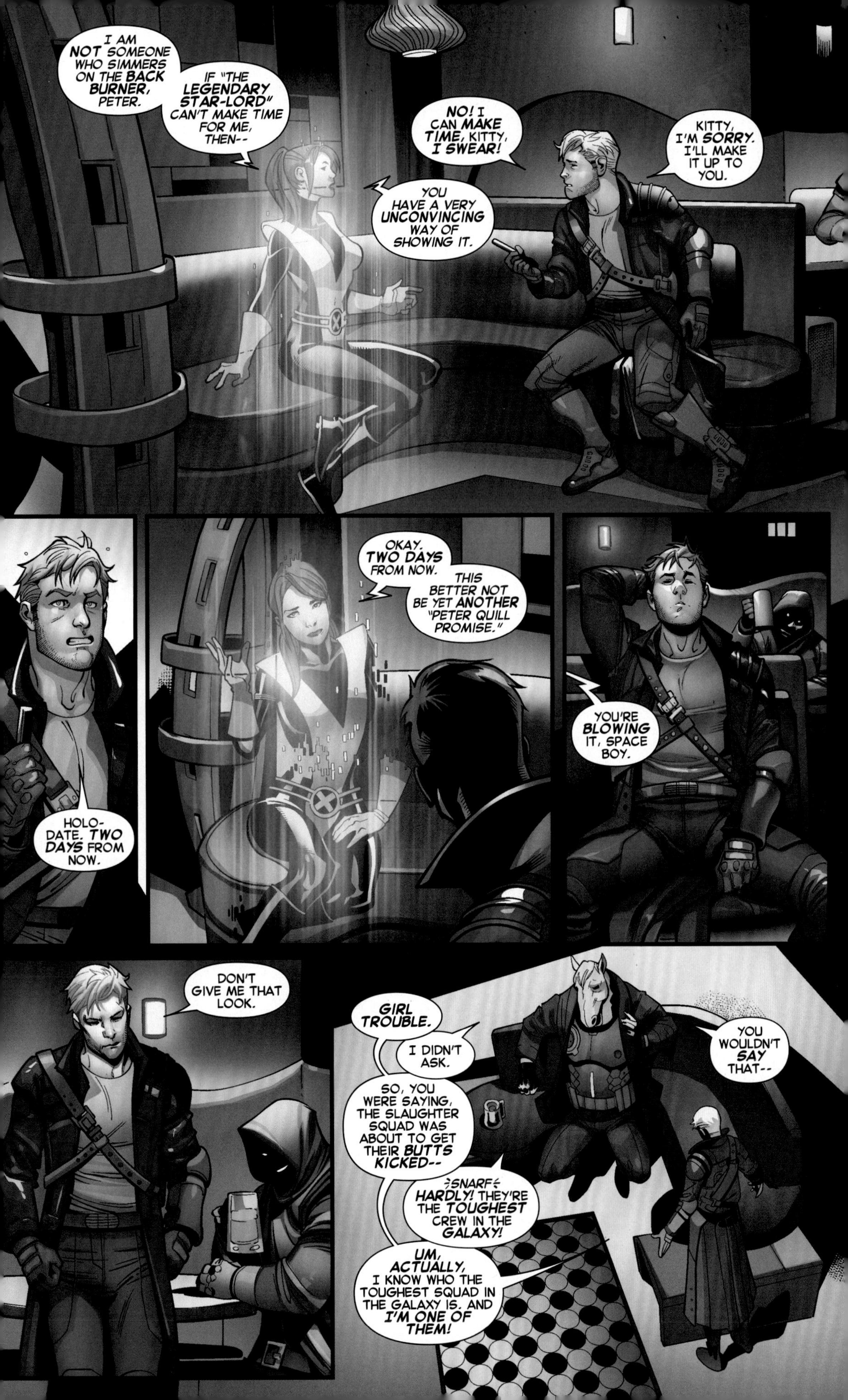
I AM NOT SOMEONE WHO SIMMERS ON THE BACK BURNER, PETER.
IF "THE LEGENDARY STAR-LORD" CAN'T MAKE TIME FOR ME, THEN--
NO! I CAN MAKE TIME, KITTY, I SWEAR!
KITTY, I'M SORRY. I'LL MAKE IT UP TO YOU.
YOU HAVE A VERY UNCONVINCING WAY OF SHOWING IT.
HOLO-DATE. TWO DAYS FROM NOW.
OKAY. TWO DAYS FROM NOW.
THIS BETTER NOT BE YET ANOTHER "PETER QUILL PROMISE."
YOU'RE BLOWING IT, SPACE BOY.
DON'T GIVE ME THAT LOOK.
GIRL TROUBLE.
I DIDN'T ASK.
YOU WOULDN'T SAY THAT--
SO, YOU WERE SAYING, THE SLAUGHTER SQUAD WAS ABOUT TO GET THEIR BUTTS KICKED--
SNARF
HARDLY! THEY'RE THE TOUGHEST CREW IN THE GALAXY!
UM, ACTUALLY, I KNOW WHO THE TOUGHEST SQUAD IN THE GALAXY IS. AND I'M ONE OF THEM!

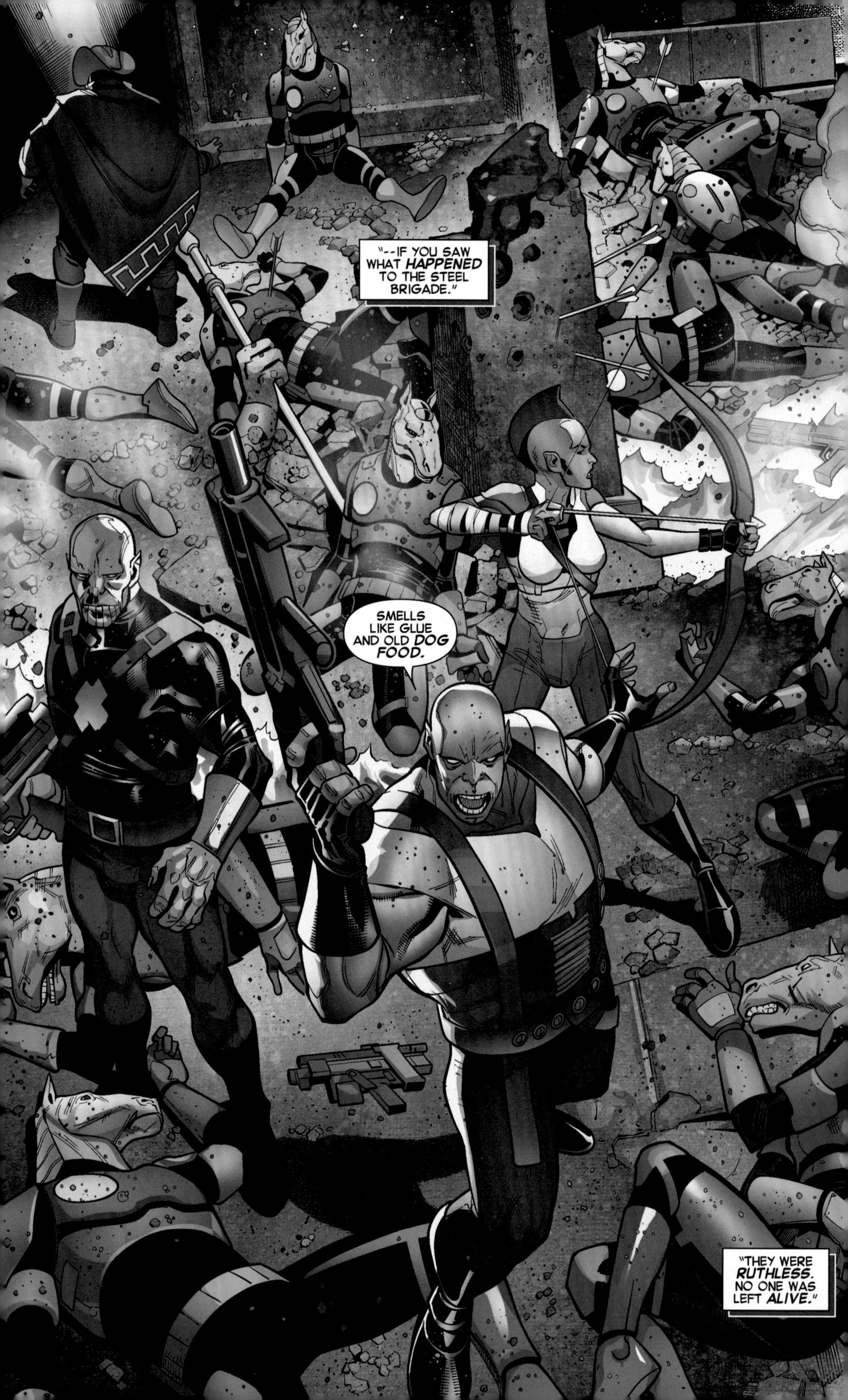
"--IF YOU SAW WHAT HAPPENED TO THE STEEL BRIGADE."
SMELLS LIKE GLUE AND OLD DOG FOOD.
"THEY WERE RUTHLESS. NO ONE WAS LEFT ALIVE."

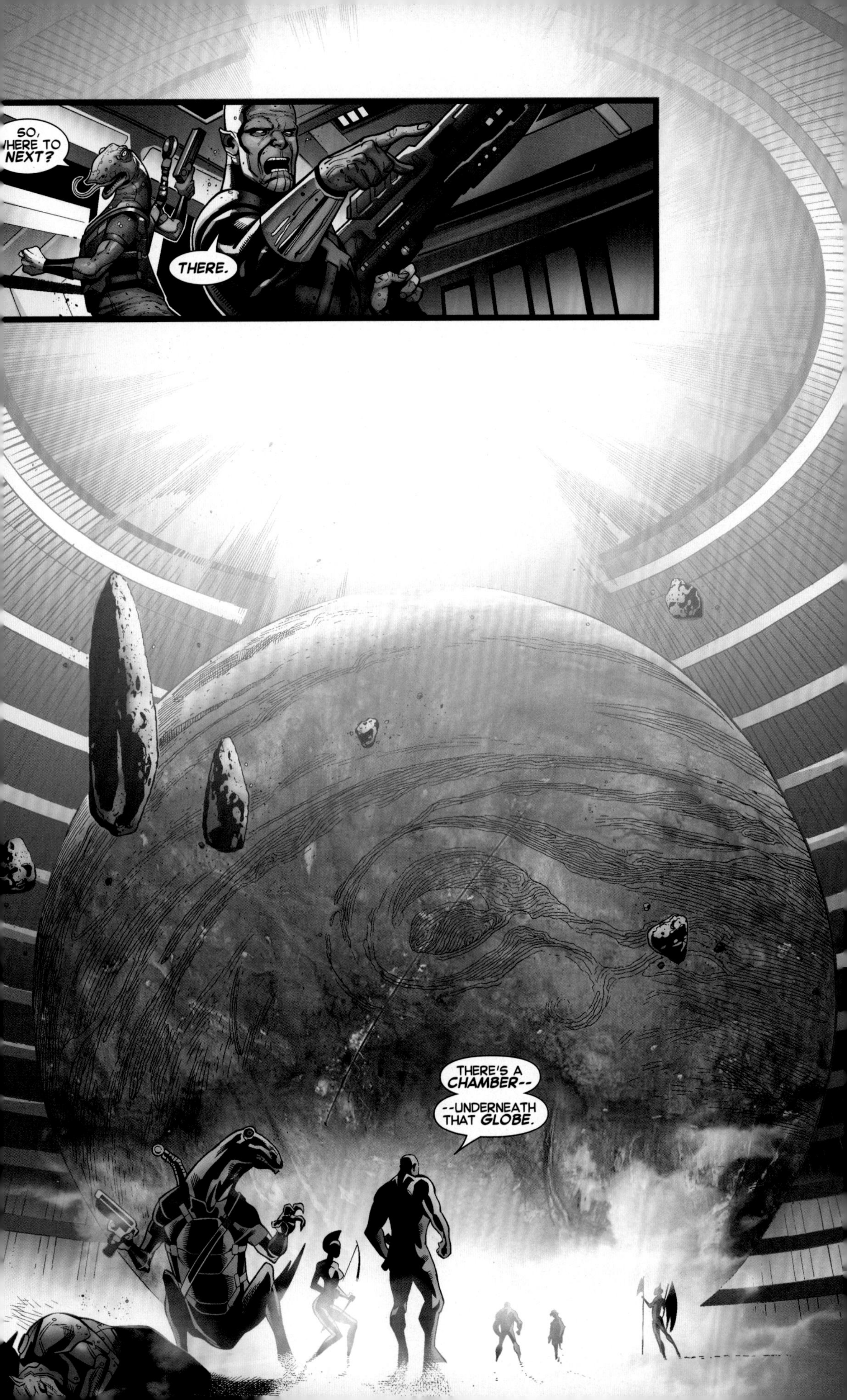
SO, WHERE TO NEXT?
THERE.
THERE'S A CHAMBER--
--UNDERNEATH THAT GLOBE.

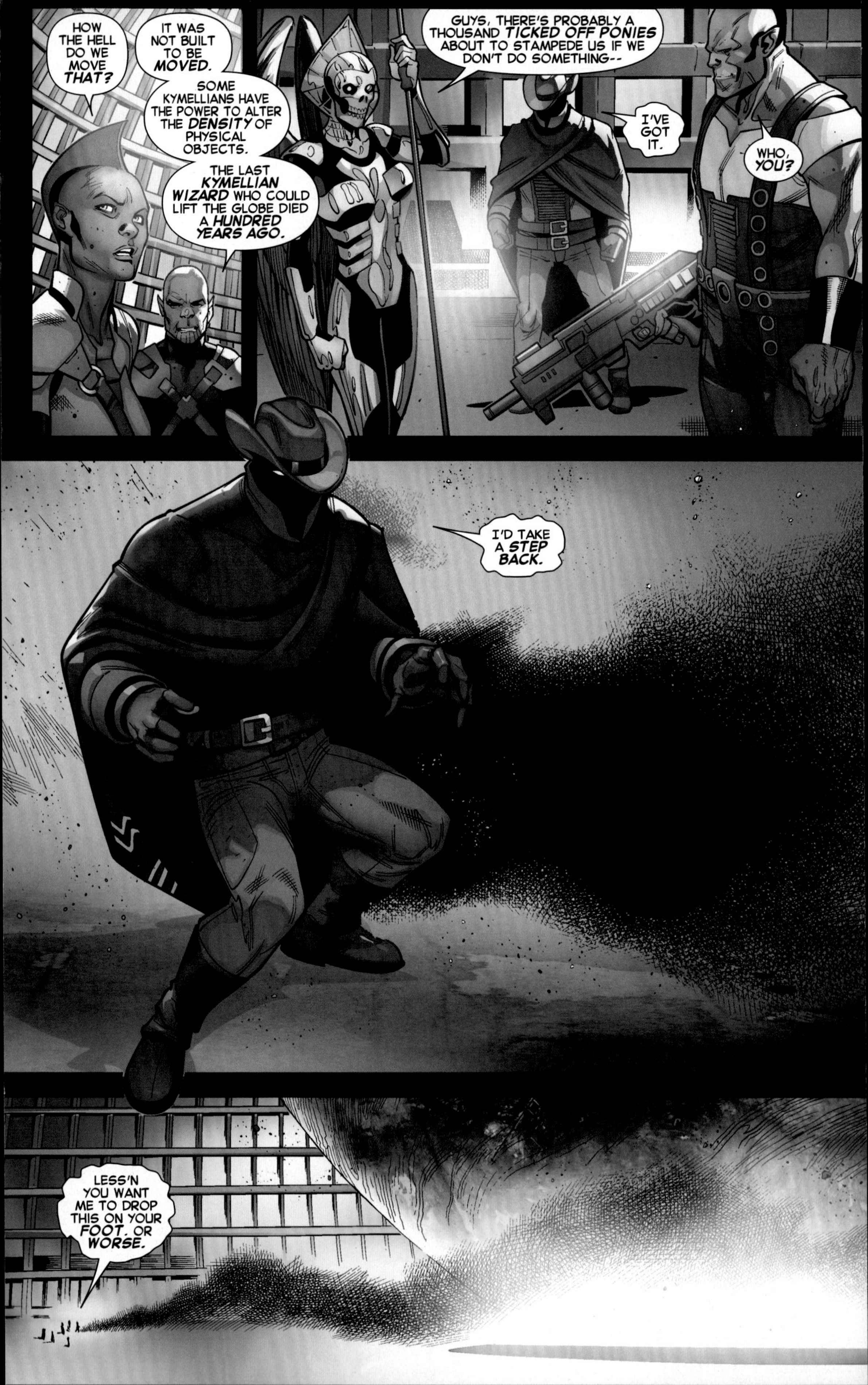
HOW THE HELL DO WE MOVE THAT?
IT WAS NOT BUILT TO BE MOVED.
SOME KYMELLIANS HAVE THE POWER TO ALTER THE DENSITY OF PHYSICAL OBJECTS.
THE LAST KYMELLIAN WIZARD WHO COULD LIFT THE GLOBE DIED A HUNDRED YEARS AGO.
GUYS, THERE'S PROBABLY A THOUSAND TICKED OFF PONIES ABOUT TO STAMPEDE US IF WE DON'T DO SOMETHING--
I'VE GOT IT.
WHO, YOU?
I'D TAKE A STEP BACK.
LESS'N YOU WANT ME TO DROP THIS ON YOUR FOOT. OR WORSE.

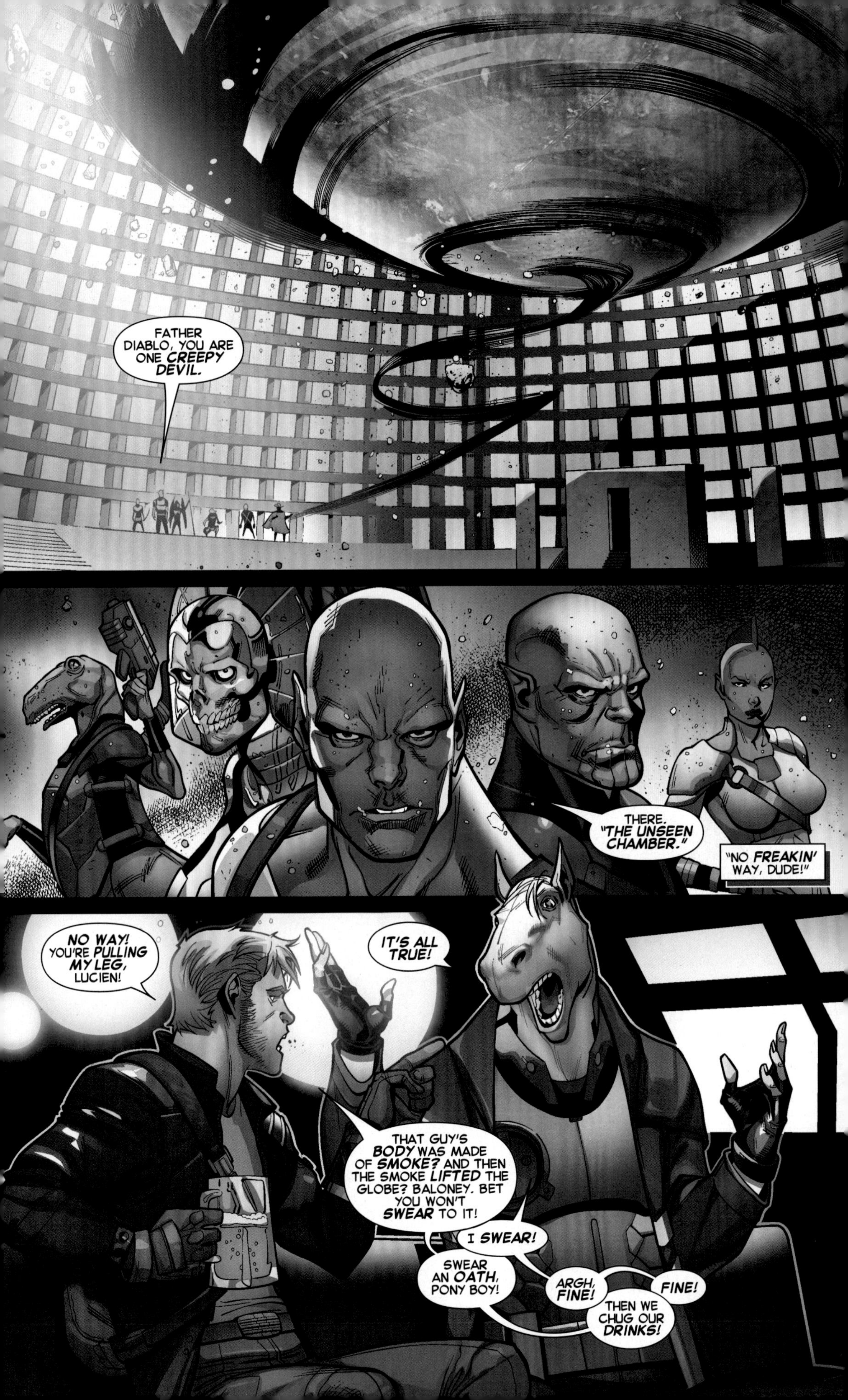
FATHER DIABLO, YOU ARE ONE CREEPY DEVIL.
THERE. "THE UNSEEN CHAMBER."
"NO FREAKIN' WAY, DUDE!"
NO WAY! YOU'RE PULLING MY LEG, LUCIEN!
IT'S ALL TRUE!
THAT GUY'S BODY WAS MADE OF SMOKE? AND THEN THE SMOKE LIFTED THE GLOBE? BALONEY. BET YOU WON'T SWEAR TO IT!
I SWEAR!
SWEAR AN OATH, PONY BOY!
ARGH, FINE!
FINE!
THEN WE CHUG OUR DRINKS!

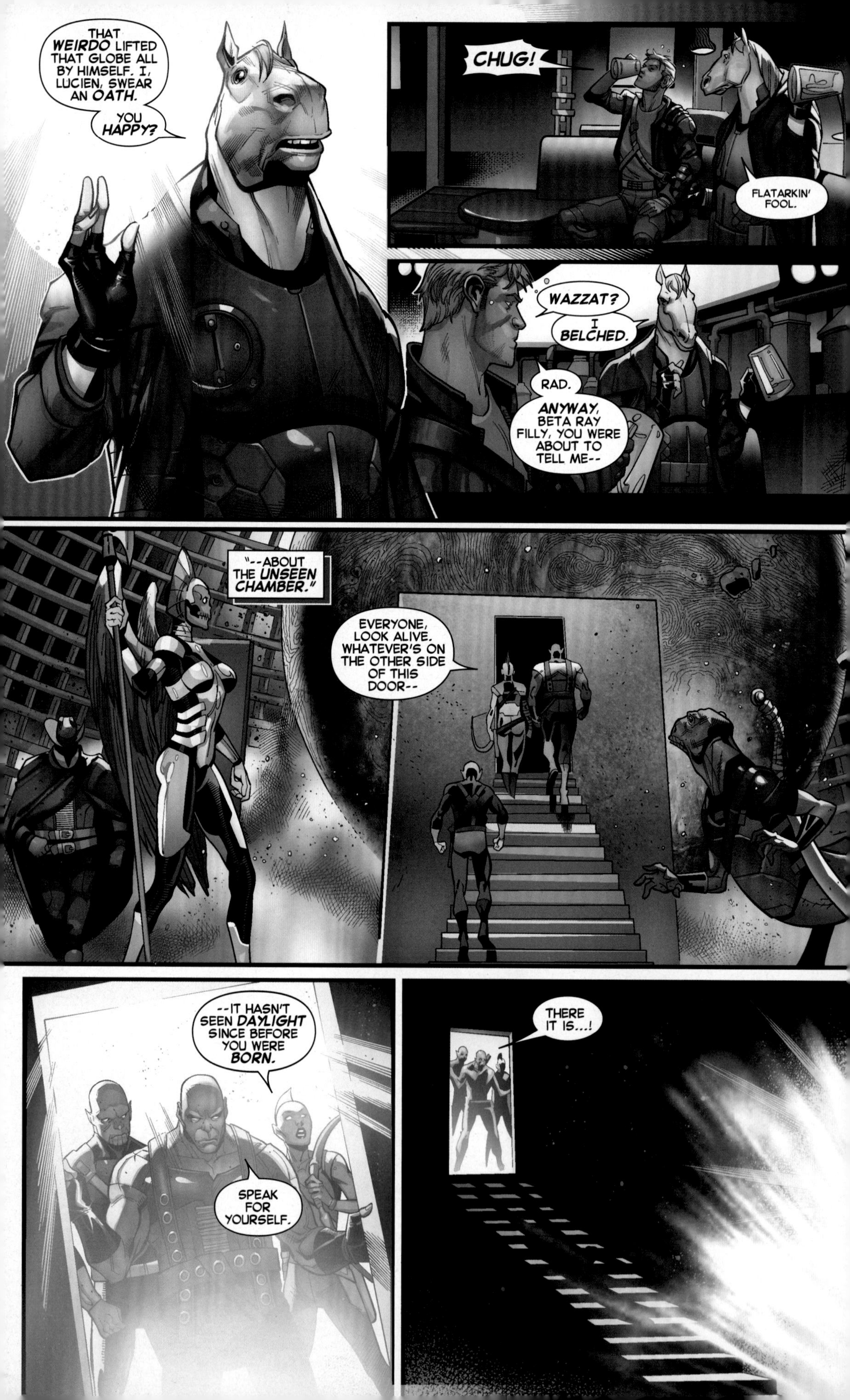
THAT WEIRDO LIFTED THAT GLOBE ALL BY HIMSELF. I, LUCIEN, SWEAR AN OATH.
YOU HAPPY?
CHUG!
FLATARKIN' FOOL.
WAZZAT?
I BELCHED.
RAD.
ANYWAY, BETA RAY FILLY, YOU WERE ABOUT TO TELL ME--
"--ABOUT THE UNSEEN CHAMBER."
EVERYONE, LOOK ALIVE. WHATEVER'S ON THE OTHER SIDE OF THIS DOOR--
--IT HASN'T SEEN DAYLIGHT SINCE BEFORE YOU WERE BORN.
SPEAK FOR YOURSELF.
THERE IT IS...!

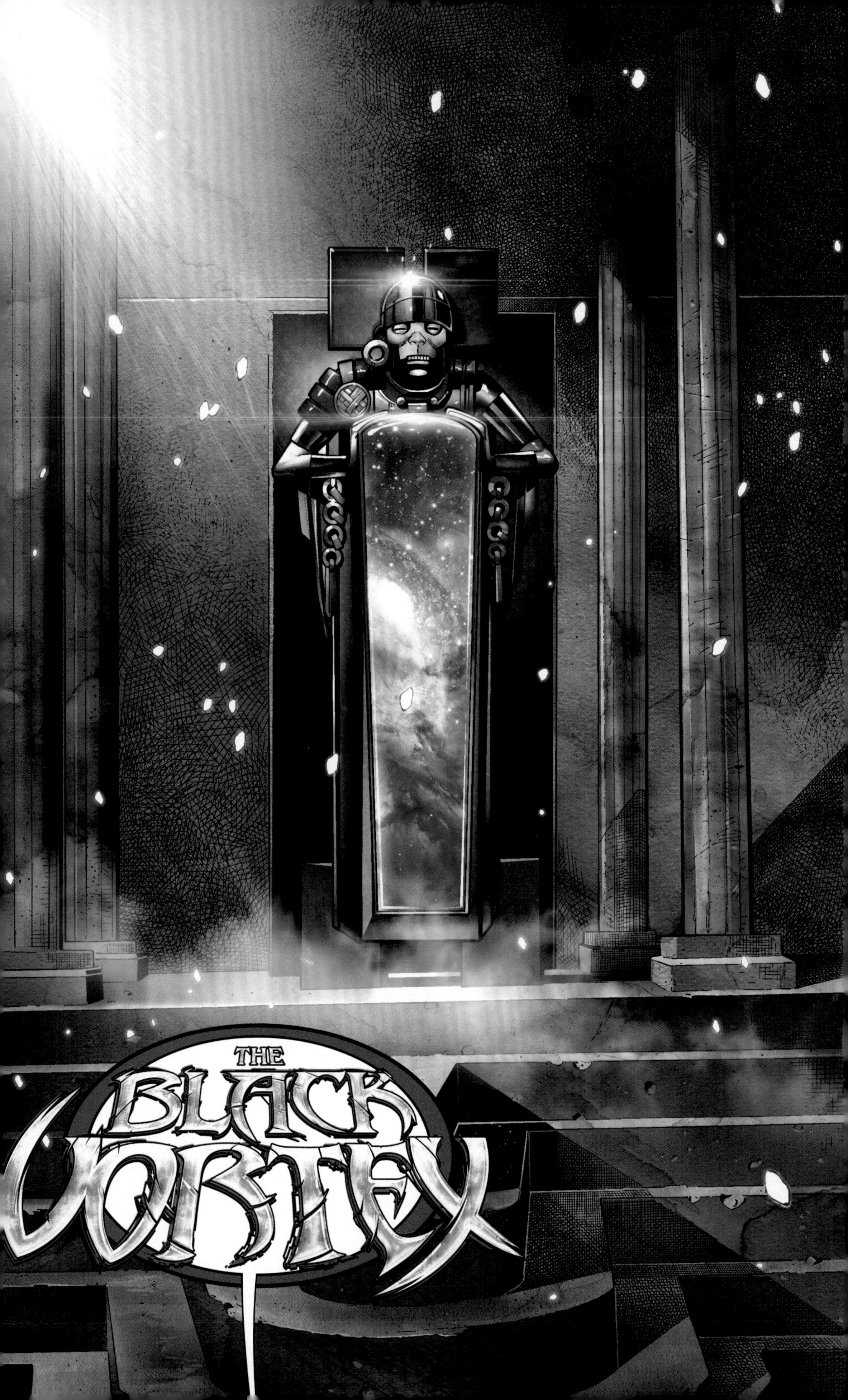
THE
BLACK
VORTEX

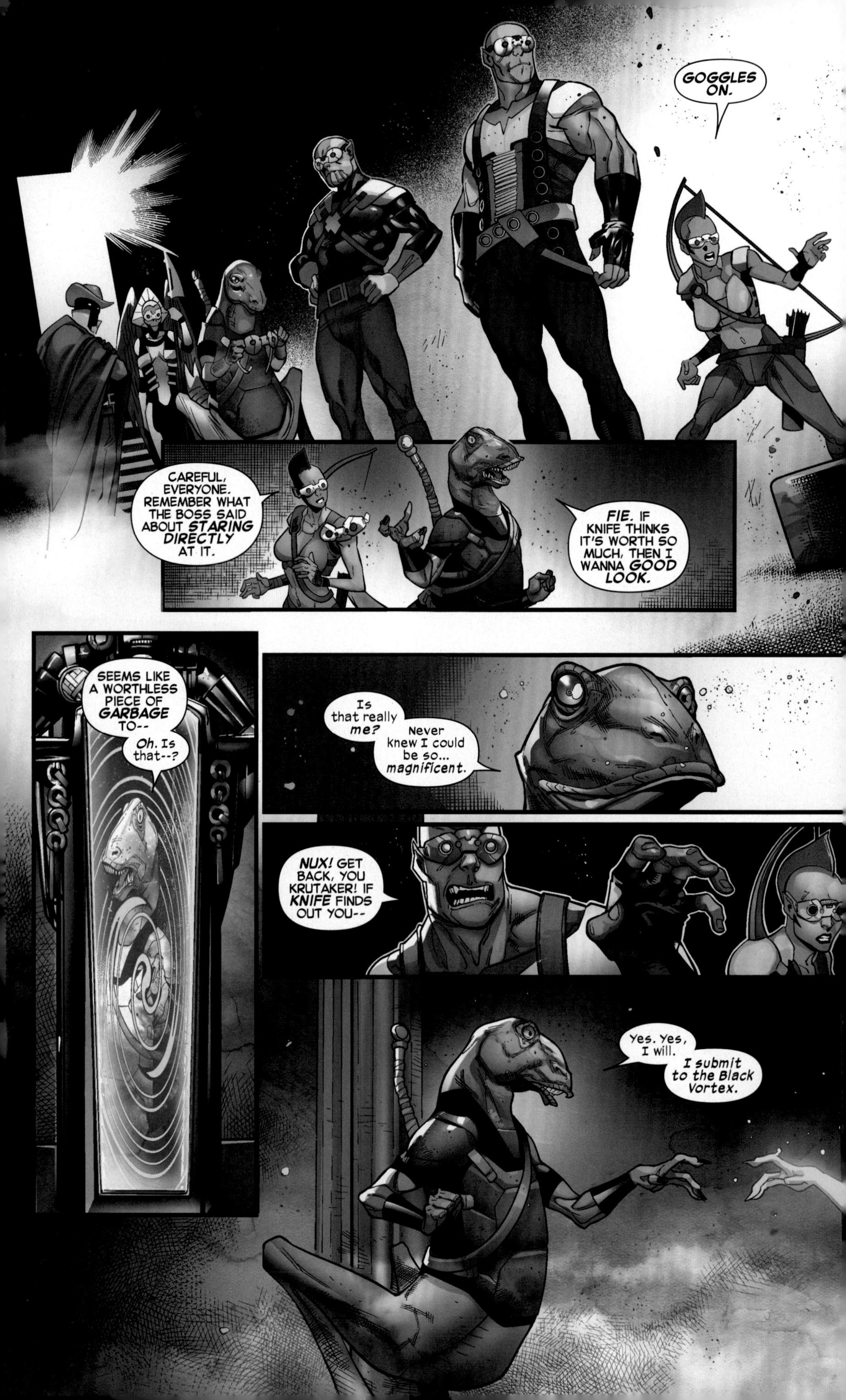
GOGGLES ON.
CAREFUL, EVERYONE. REMEMBER WHAT THE BOSS SAID ABOUT STARING DIRECTLY AT IT.
FIE. IF KNIFE THINKS IT'S WORTH SO MUCH, THEN I WANNA GOOD LOOK.
SEEMS LIKE A WORTHLESS PIECE OF GARBAGE TO--
Oh. Is that--?
Is that really me?
Never knew I could be so... magnificent.
NUX! GET BACK, YOU KRUTAKER! IF KNIFE FINDS OUT YOU--
Yes. Yes, I will.
I submit to the Black Vortex.

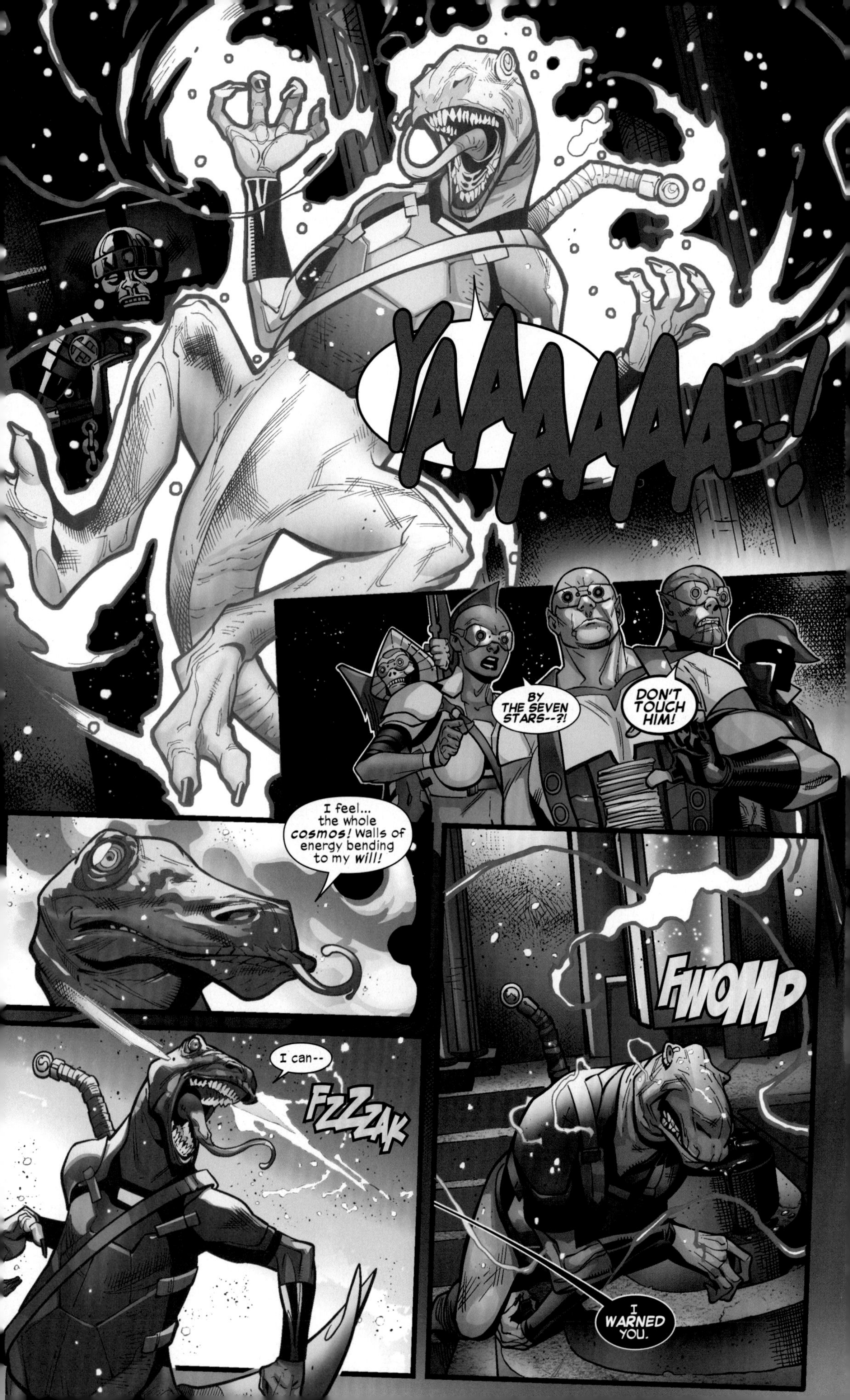
YAAAAAA--!
BY THE SEVEN STARS--?!
DON'T TOUCH HIM!
I feel... the whole *cosmos!* Walls of energy bending to my *will!*
FWOMP
I can--
FZZZAK
I WARNED YOU.

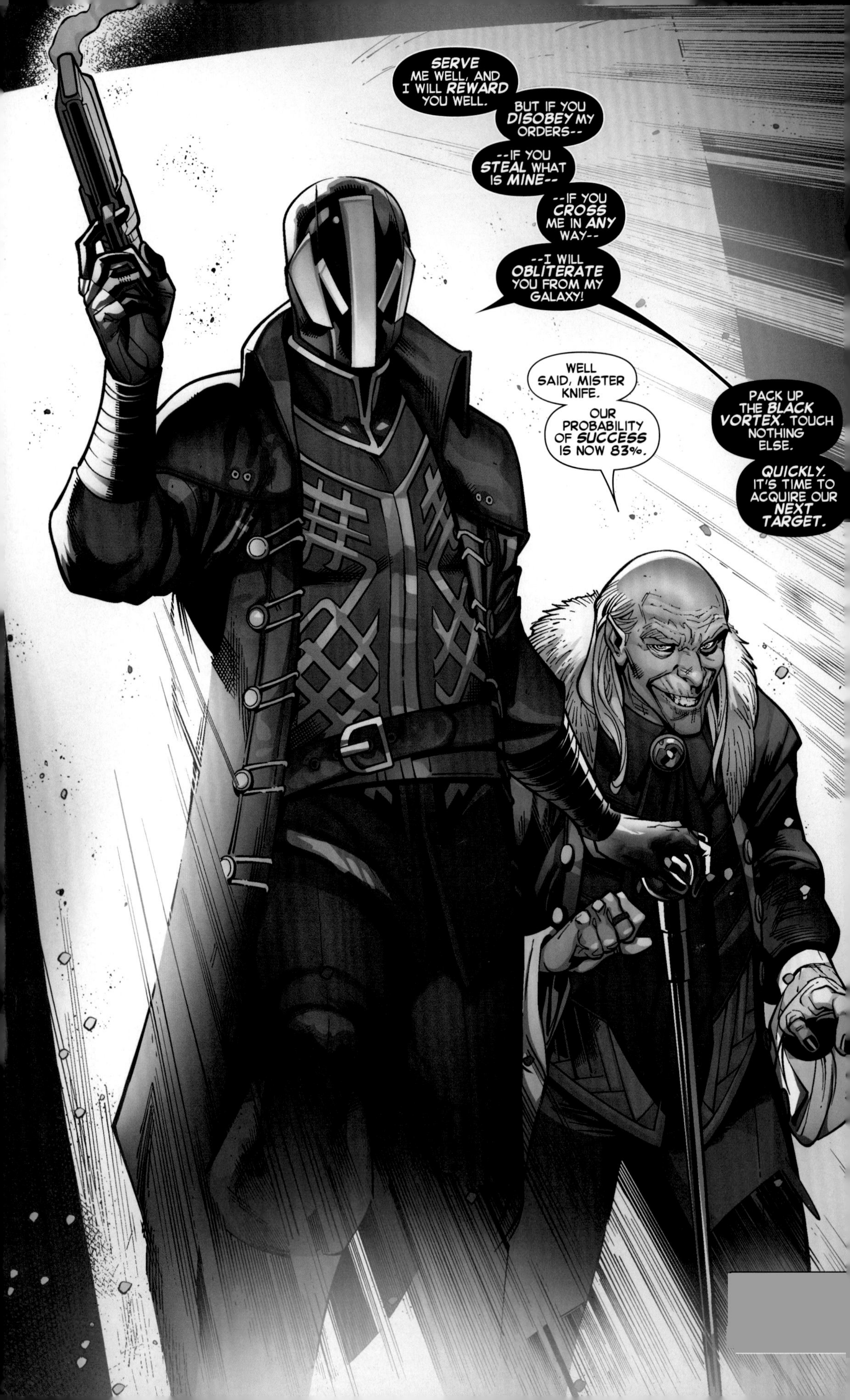
SERVE ME WELL, AND I WILL REWARD YOU WELL.
BUT IF YOU DISOBEY MY ORDERS--
--IF YOU STEAL WHAT IS MINE--
--IF YOU CROSS ME IN ANY WAY--
--I WILL OBLITERATE YOU FROM MY GALAXY!
WELL SAID, MISTER KNIFE.
OUR PROBABILITY OF SUCCESS IS NOW 83%.
PACK UP THE BLACK VORTEX. TOUCH NOTHING ELSE.
QUICKLY. IT'S TIME TO ACQUIRE OUR NEXT TARGET.

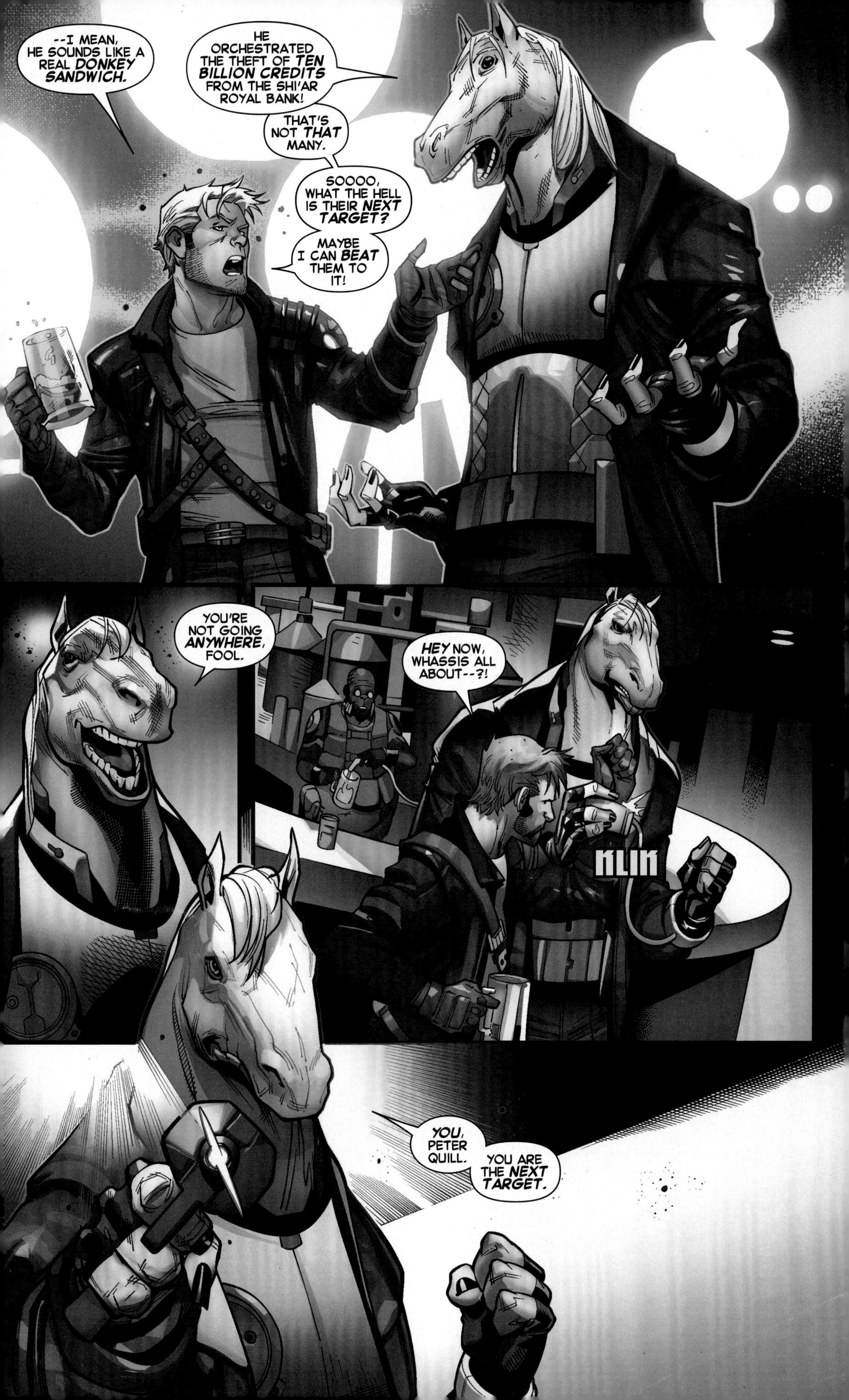

--I MEAN, HE SOUNDS LIKE A REAL DONKEY SANDWICH.
HE ORCHESTRATED THE THEFT OF TEN BILLION CREDITS FROM THE SHI'AR ROYAL BANK!
THAT'S NOT THAT MANY.
SOOOO, WHAT THE HELL IS THEIR NEXT TARGET?
MAYBE I CAN BEAT THEM TO IT!
YOU'RE NOT GOING ANYWHERE, FOOL.
HEY NOW, WHASSIS ALL ABOUT--?!
KLIK
YOU, PETER QUILL.
YOU ARE THE NEXT TARGET.

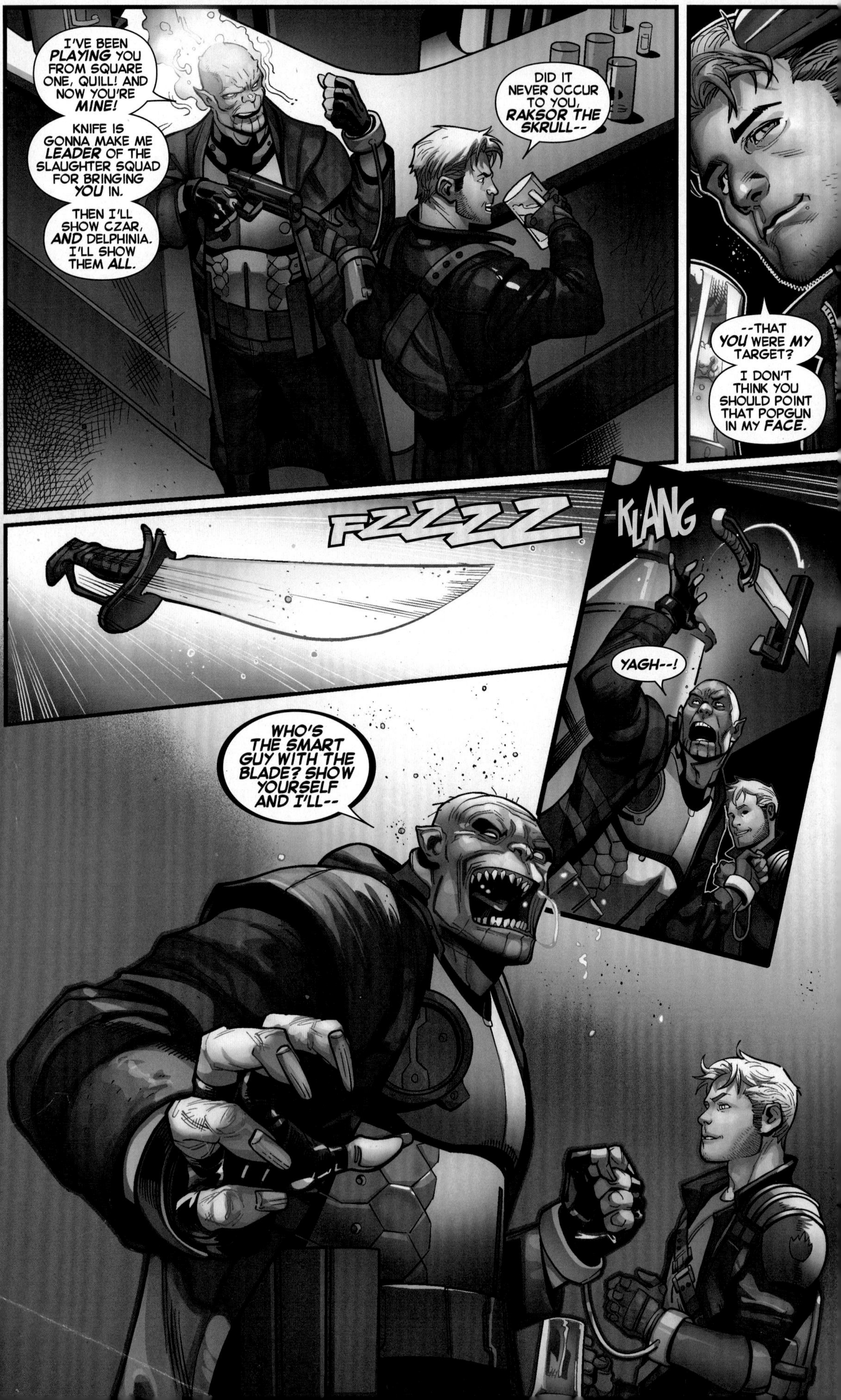
I'VE BEEN PLAYING YOU FROM SQUARE ONE, QUILL! AND NOW YOU'RE MINE!
KNIFE IS GONNA MAKE ME LEADER OF THE SLAUGHTER SQUAD FOR BRINGING YOU IN.
THEN I'LL SHOW CZAR, AND DELPHINIA. I'LL SHOW THEM ALL.
DID IT NEVER OCCUR TO YOU, RAKSOR THE SKRULL--
--THAT YOU WERE MY TARGET?
I DON'T THINK YOU SHOULD POINT THAT POPGUN IN MY FACE.
FZZZZZ
KLANG
YAGH--!
WHO'S THE SMART GUY WITH THE BLADE? SHOW YOURSELF AND I'LL--

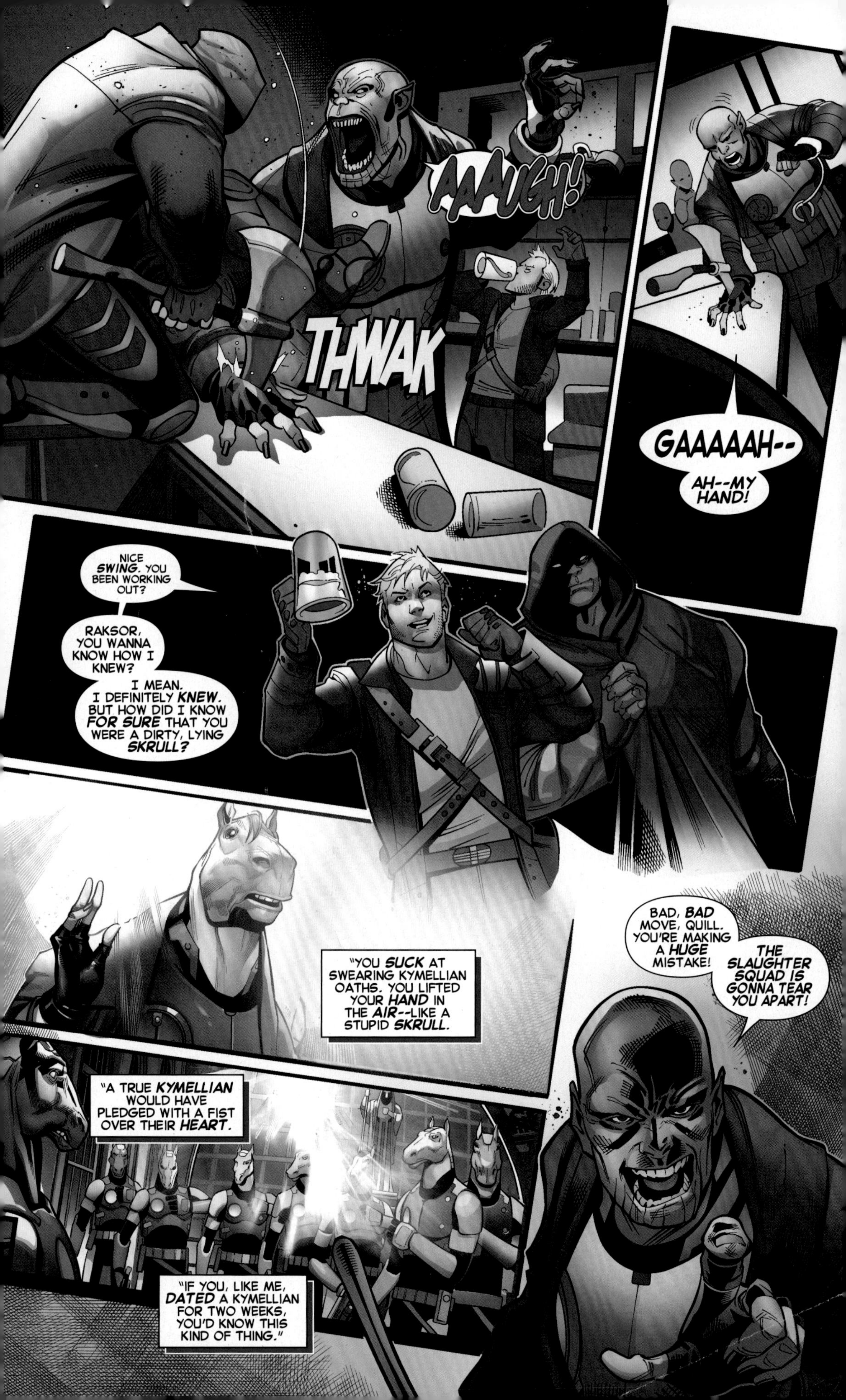
AAAUGH!
THWAK
GAAAAAH--
AH--MY HAND!
NICE SWING. YOU BEEN WORKING OUT?
RAKSOR, YOU WANNA KNOW HOW I KNEW?
I MEAN. I DEFINITELY KNEW. BUT HOW DID I KNOW FOR SURE THAT YOU WERE A DIRTY, LYING SKRULL?
"YOU SUCK AT SWEARING KYMELLIAN OATHS. YOU LIFTED YOUR HAND IN THE AIR--LIKE A STUPID SKRULL.
BAD, BAD MOVE, QUILL. YOU'RE MAKING A HUGE MISTAKE!
THE SLAUGHTER SQUAD IS GONNA TEAR YOU APART!
"A TRUE KYMELLIAN WOULD HAVE PLEDGED WITH A FIST OVER THEIR HEART.
"IF YOU, LIKE ME, DATED A KYMELLIAN FOR TWO WEEKS, YOU'D KNOW THIS KIND OF THING."

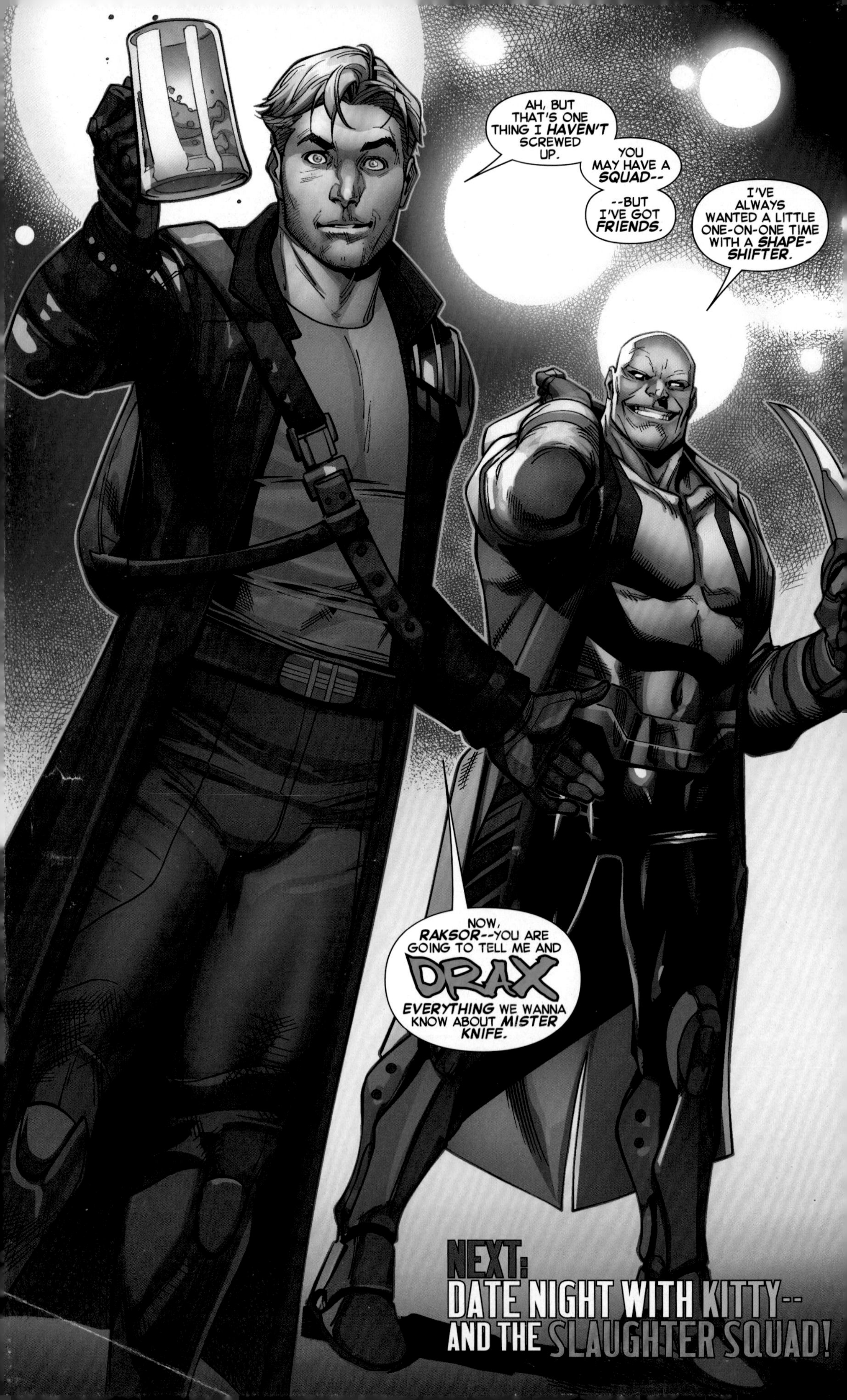
AH, BUT THAT'S ONE THING I HAVEN'T SCREWED UP.
YOU MAY HAVE A SQUAD--
--BUT I'VE GOT FRIENDS.
I'VE ALWAYS WANTED A LITTLE ONE-ON-ONE TIME WITH A SHAPE-SHIFTER.
NOW, RAKSOR--YOU ARE GOING TO TELL ME AND DRAX EVERYTHING WE WANNA KNOW ABOUT MISTER KNIFE.
NEXT:
DATE NIGHT WITH KITTY--
AND THE SLAUGHTER SQUAD!